PLACE IN RETURN BOX to remove this checkout from your record.
TO AVOID FINES return on or before date due.

DATE DUE	DATE DUE	DATE DUE
APR 09 1995	MAY 2 7 1999	
NOV 08 1995	MAR 1 1 2000	

Invisibility Blues

THE HAYMARKET SERIES

Editors: Mike Davis and Michael Sprinker

The Haymarket Series is a new publishing initiative by Verso offering original studies of politics, history and culture focused on North America. The series presents innovative but representative views from across the American left on a wide range of topics of current and continuing interest to socialists in North America and throughout the world. A century after the first May Day, the American left remains in the shadow of those martyrs whom this series honours and commemorates. The studies in the Haymarket Series testify to the living legacy of activism and political commitment for which they gave up their lives.

Invisibility Blues

From Pop to Theory

MICHELE WALLACE

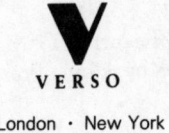

VERSO

London · New York

First published by Verso 1990
© Michele Wallace 1990
All rights reserved

Verso
UK: 6 Meard Street, London W1V 3HR
USA: 29 West 35th Street, New York, NY 10001-2291

Verso is the imprint of New Left Books

British Library Cataloguing in Publication Data

Wallace, Michele
Invisibility blues : from pop to theory. – (The Haymarket
series).
1. Culture. Black feminism, history
I. Title II. Series
306.08996073

ISBN 0-86091-301-5
ISBN 0-86091-519-0 pbk

US Library of Congress Cataloging-in-Publication Data

Wallace, Michele.
Invisibility blues : from pop to theory / Michele Wallace.
p.   cm.
ISBN 0-86091-301-5. – ISBN 0-86091-519-0 (pbk.)
1. Afro-American women. 2. Afro-American artists. 3. Wallace,
Michele. 4. United States–Popular culture–History–20th century.
5. Afro-American arts. I. Title
E185.86.W35   1990
305.48′896073–dc20

Typeset in Goudy by Leaper & Gard Ltd, Bristol
Printed in USA by Alpine Press Inc.

To my loving husband, Eugene Nesmith, without whom
my work would have been impossible

Contents

Acknowledgements

Since the essays in this book span the work of my entire career as a writer and critic of culture, it would be impossible for me accurately to acknowledge every contributing factor. Nevertheless, I would like to mention a few special people who have either read and commented on my work or provided research assistance over the years. I would like to thank Jerome Rothenberg, Sherley Anne Williams and Michael Davidson in the Department of Literature at the University of California in San Diego for giving me my start as an 'academic'. I would like to thank George Economou, R.C. Davis, Kathleen Welch, Ron Schleifer and David Gross in the Department of English at the University of Oklahoma. I would like to thank Isabel Marcus in the Law School, Carol Zemel in Art History, Michael Frisch in American Studies, Claire Kahane, Bill Warner, Neil Schmidt and William Fischer in the Department of English at the State University of New York at Buffalo, and James de Jongh, Leo Hammalian and Joshua Wilner in the Department of English at the City College of New York. I would like to extend a very special thank you to my friends and colleagues Brian Wallis, Maud Lavin, Phil Mariani, Susan McHenry, Coco Fusco, Margo Jefferson and E. Ann Kaplan.

My mother the artist Faith Ringgold has always been more than a 'mother'. She has not only provided a constant source of inspiration in my work but she has also kindly granted us permission to reprint her story quilt 'Tar Beach' (which is now in the collection of the Guggenheim Museum in New York) on the cover of the book. As for my husband, the actor Eugene Nesmith, he is quite indispensable to all my endeavors.

Also, I would like to thank Laurel Schreck, formerly at Verso, for having had the idea for the book. It has been a pleasure working with my editor Michael Sprinker and Colin Robinson, managing director of Verso.

I would also like to acknowledge the following previous appearances of the essays included in *Invisibility Blues*. Most of the revision is not really substantial and was meant to contribute to greater clarity, not to alter the main ideas. The one exception is chapter 23, 'Variations on Negation', which is substantially different from the previously published, much shorter version.

The material is here by kind permission of the following:

'Memories of a 60s Girlhood: The Harlem I Love', *The Village Voice*, New York, 6 October 1975, pp. 26–7.

'Anger in Isolation: A Black Feminist's Search for Sisterhood', *The Village Voice*, New York, 28 July 1975, pp. 6–7.

'Baby Faith', *SAGE*, Atlanta, Winter 1989, pp. 36–9; first published in *Ms* magazine, New York, July/August 1987, pp. 154–6, 216, without 'Postscript'.

'For the Women's House', *Feminist Art Journal*, New York, April 1972.

'A Women's Prison and The Movement', *Women's World*, New York, Summer 1972.

'The Dah Principle: To Be Continued', *Faith Ringgold: Twenty Years of Painting, Sculpture, Performance*, The Studio Museum of Harlem, New York 1984.

'Homelessness is Where the Heart Is', *Zeta* magazine, Boston, July/August 1988, pp. 49–53.

'Blues for Mr Spielberg', *The Village Voice*, New York, 18 March 1986, pp. 21–4, 26.

'Michael Jackson, Black Modernisms and "The Ecstasy of Communication"', *Global Television*, eds Cynthia Schneider and Brian Wallis, Wedge Press & MIT Press, Cambridge, Mass., 1989, pp. 301–18.

'Invisibility Blues' *Zeta* magazine, Boston, June 1988, pp. 17–21; and *Grey Wolf Annual 5: Multicultural Literacy*, Grey Wolf Press, Saint Paul, Minn., 1988, pp. 161–72.

'Spike Lee and Black Women', *The Nation*, New York, 4 June 1988, pp. 800–3.

'Doing the Right Thing', *Art Forum International*, New York, October 1989, pp. 20–22.

'Entertainment Tomorrow', *Zeta* magazine, Boston, October 1988, pp. 51–5.

'Invisibility Blues': '*Mississippi Burning* and *Bird*', *Art Forum International*, April 1989, pp. 11–12, here renamed '*Mississippi Burning* and *Bird*'.

'For Colored Girls, the Rainbow is Not Enough', *The Village Voice*, New York, 16 August 1976, pp. 108–9.

'Slaves of History', *The Women's Review of Books*, Wellesley, Mass., October 1986, pp. 1, 3–4.

'Ishmael Reed's Female Troubles', *The Village Voice Literary Supplement*, New York, December 1986, pp. 9–11.

'Wilma Mankiller: Profile', *Ms* magazine, New York, January 1988, pp. 68–9.

'Twenty Years Later', *Zeta* magazine, Boston, April 1988, pp. 29–34.

'Who Owns Zora Neale Hurston? Critics Carve Up the Legend', *The Village Voice Literary Supplement*, New York, April 1988, pp. 18–21.

'Reading 1968: The Great American Whitewash', *Zeta* magazine and *Dia Art Foundation: Discussions in Contemporary Culture, 4: Remaking History*, eds Phil Mariani and Barbara Kruger, Bay Press, Seattle, 1989, pp. 97–109.
'Tim Rollins and KOS: The *Amerika* Series', *Amerika: Tim Rollins & KOS*, ed. Gary Garrels, Dia Arts Foundation, New York, 1989, pp. 37–48.
'Variations on Negation and the Heresy of Black Feminist Creativity', *Heresies*, Fall 1989.
'Negative Images: Towards a Black Feminist Cultural Criticism', forthcoming in *Cultural Studies: Now and In The Future*, eds Cary Nelson, Paula Treichler and Lawrence Grossberg, Routledge, New York, 1991.

The three illustrations are by Faith Ringgold: on p. 35, 'For the Women's House' mural, courtesy of the artist; on p. 65, 'Who's Bad? Painted Quilt', courtesy of the Bernice Steinbaum Gallery; on p. 127, 'The Flag Is Bleeding', courtesy of the Bernice Steinbaum Gallery.

INTRODUCTION

Negative/Positive Images

The enormous controversy in the black community over 'negative images' of black men in Ntozake Shange's *For Colored Girls Who Have Considered Suicide* (1976) first made me aware of the peculiar limitations of the notion that only 'positive images' are appropriate to Afro-American cultural production, particularly cultural production by women.

Specifically, I have become convinced that the binary opposition of 'negative' versus 'positive' images too often sets the limits of Afro-American cultural criticism. Mainstream culture habitually assumes that the first job of Afro-American mass culture (or any 'minority' cultural production in which 'race' is an issue) should be to 'uplift the race', or to salvage the denigrated image of blacks in the white American imagination. As a consequence, judgements on the part of both white and black cultural critics of Afro-American cultural production aimed at a black audience tend to circulate around the failure or success of this usually explicit project.

There are, however, several problems with the negative/positive images conception of Afro-Americans in mass or popular culture.

First, since 'racism', or the widespread conviction that blacks are morally and/or intellectually inferior, defines the 'commonsense' perception of blacks, a positive/negative image cultural formula means that the goal of cultural production becomes simply to reverse these already existing assumptions. Not only does reversal, or the notion that blacks are more likeable, more compassionate, smarter, or even 'superior', not substantially alter racist preconceptions, it also ties Afro-American cultural production to racist ideology in a way that makes the failure to alter it inevitable. Because racism provides an already complete and satisfying comprehension of black identity (which is why it persists), one

1

that is presumably continuous with and essential to the rest of the viewer's ideological framework, a temporary reversal of terms – like a media version of Sadie Hawkins Day – not only doesn't challenge racism but may in fact corroborate it.

Moreover, what this tends to mean in terms of television and a show like *The Cosby Show*, for example, is that blacks are shown as characters who possess 'positive' attributes of white culture, which are really the attributes of a hypothetical and impracticable absence (or commod-ification) of culture. 'Culture' is then reduced to a style of consumption that offers up, say, expensive, exotic-looking handknit sweaters, or a brief scene of the Cosbys at a jazz club where a black woman is singing, rather than any concrete or complex textualization of cultural difference. Indeed the show seems to suggest, in its occasional use of Asians and Latinos as well as blacks, that no one is ultimately different, since culture is something you can buy at Bloomingdales, a kind of wardrobe or a form of entertainment.

Secondly, the negative/positive images conception is unable to contend with the important question of how Afro-American culture, which is a product of 'internal colonization',[1] constitutes an important variation on postcolonial discourse. Afro-Americans, as ex-slaves, are not only permanently exiled from their 'homeland' (which now exists most meaningfully only in their imaginations), but also from their bodies. Their labor and their reproduction can be considered to be in a state of postcoloniality – no longer colonized but not yet free. In a manner that may be characteristic of 'internal colonization', Afro-American culture has traditionally seemed fully aware of its own marginality to the white American mainstream. Accordingly, it combined (and often cleverly disguised) its political objections to Afro-American 'invisibility' with a progressive integration and reinterpretation of precisely those qualities and features that first marked the 'racism' of white images of blacks. In other words, black culture continually reincorporates and even appro-priates the 'negative' or 'racist' imagery of the 'dominant' culture.

Its capacity to turn racism against itself, to deconstruct it, is its most consistently recurrent and characteristic feature. Henry Louis Gates describes this process as 'signifying', which encompasses a sequence of imitation and reversal of 'white' culture as the basis for the 'critical signification' of 'black' culture. While Gates generally discusses sig-nifying in terms of literature and literary criticism, the process is even more characteristic of Afro-American popular culture and its mass culture hybrids. Critical signification seems to draw its primary model from the various stages of development of jazz, rhythm & blues, and rock 'n' roll as the offspring of the Afro-American oral tradition.[2]

I am invoking here, as well, Houston Baker's notion that a blues matrix inevitably shaped by the marketplace and by consumption, and therefore by racism, is heavily implicated in all forms of Afro-American culture.[3] The point is that a 'pure' Afro-American culture untainted by the marketplace, or by 'negative' images, is inconceivable. Another influence on these observations is the work of Fredric Jameson since *The Political Unconscious*, where he identifies extremely useful ways of understanding the consumption and production of culture as a complex collective psychological process that can simultaneously reconstitute an effective 'strategy of containment', even as it may articulate a 'utopian impulse.'[4]

Third, the negative/positive images conception lacks the crucial capacity to differentiate between the visual and the textual. The disposition of racism in the texts and images of US culture provides substantially different perspectives and raises different issues. For instance, black women are more often visualized in mainstream American culture – most prominently as fashion models or as performers in music videos – than they are allowed to speak their own words, or speak about their own condition as women of color, as novelists, say. In a continuation of the same process, they are more often listened to as singers or as writers of imaginative fiction than as theorists or as critics. Combinations of racism and sexism are much harder to diagnose in visual modes than in discursive modes, just as they are much more palatable in the form of art or photography than in the form of analysis.

The reasons for this are complex, but the two central ones have to do with the unique psychological role that images play, as feminist film criticism influenced by Lacan might describe it,[5] as well as with their commodification, which compels them to function as a kind of ideological smokescreen – as Barthes describes the role of the image of the black soldier on the cover of *Paris Match* in *Mythologies*.[6] It is crucial to differentiate and diagnose the problem of negation in the visual realm because people, especially black people, know so little, in a conscious way, about how images affect them.

Fourth, and perhaps most importantly, the negative/positive schema discourages us from looking at Afro-American mass and popular culture from the crucial perspectives of production and audience reception. Who produces Afro-American mass culture, how and for what audience? Can this information be used to distinguish Afro-American popular culture from mass culture? Is the distinction viable? Moreover, how does black audience reception affect the production of mass culture, and is it possible to differentiate black audience reception from a mainstream audience? What relationship do questions of consumption and commodification have to the viability of an Afro-American oppositional avant-garde or the potential for continuing or amplifying Afro-American practices of cultural resistance? How does Afro-American cultural practice incorporate or fail to incorporate feminism, anti-racism, gay liberation and other contemporary critiques and issues such as homelessness and Rainbow Coalition politics?

It seems to me particularly instructive that cultural production by black women, particularly black women who identify their views as 'feminist' or 'womanist', has often been denounced for promulgating 'negative images'. Perhaps the most notable cases have been the controversies over Ntozake Shange's play *For Colored Girls Who Have Considered Suicide*, my own *Black Macho and the Myth of the Superwoman*, Toni Morrison's *Song of Solomon* and *Sula*, and Alice Walker's *The Color Purple*. Although it is possible to be critical of the failure of such work to challenge fundamentally mainstream or racist conceptions of black humanity or agency, it is important to observe that so-called 'negative images' will probably be necessary to any kind of reformulation or restructuring of prevailing conceptions of 'race' and 'ethnicity'. They seem particularly necessary to the inauguration of a public black female subjectivity.

Lurking behind the issue of black feminist 'negative images' is an essentialist notion of the truly black or the truly natural woman who would intrinsically know the 'correct' position. Unfortunately, such essentialism is not only a temptation for male or white critiques of black feminism, but for black feminist critiques as well.

Before one can interrogate the negativity of images in black feminist cultural production, one must ask the question: what makes a critical portrayal of a black person a 'negative image' if films like *Blue Velvet* and *Taxi Driver* don't count as 'negative images' of white men but rather as effective cultural expressions of the reification of desire, or even as compelling critiques of dominant ideologies of family and sexuality? Why is Afro-American cultural production by women always seen in some sense as a series of 'negative images', even as it is considered by feminists and other sympathetic audiences as a critique of dominant discourse? This question may be connected to the tendency of a white critical establishment to dismiss the work of black female artists in the visual arts, film and literature as preoccupied at the level of content and, therefore, too conventional in form.

Also of interest is that in the hands of a white, middle-class dominated Women's Liberation Movement in tandem with an advertising industry eager to have the consumer dollars of women newly employed in professional jobs, feminism doesn't necessarily promulgate or advocate equality for all women, especially poor women of color. This problem becomes particularly pernicious in the production of knowledge. Since white, male-dominated, ethnocentric production of knowledge underwrites most prevailing notions of 'reality', including our perception of the economic and political disadvantages of women (and men) of color, it is profoundly disturbing that women of color in particular appear to be barred from participation in it. For the most part, however, only gender is addressed by the Women's Movement as being disadvantageous for participation in producing knowledge. When race is addressed by feminists in cultural studies, it is usually subsumed by class. As a result, feminist academia, as well as the feminist intellectual left, reinscribes the same racist exclusionary criteria as do white, male-dominated academics and left intellectuals, with the further justification that 'the master's tools will not dismantle the master's house'. And as everyone will tell you, black feminism is 'anti-theoretical' and in any case, a separate movement.

An exclusionary feminism need not take the form of an organized effort, since our culture takes for granted the lack of participation of women of color in the production of knowledge. So much so that hardly anyone says a word when Afro-American literary critic Henry Louis Gates assumes the authority to define black feminist literary criticism for a mainstream *New York Times Book Review* audience. While it is vaguely understood that their perspectives inaugurate a newly mainstream 'black feminism', no one questions what Oprah Winfrey's success as producer and talk-show host, or the successes of black women's novels in the Book-of-the-Month Club arena, has to tell us about sex, race and ideology in a postmodern age.

In *Invisibility Blues*, I have gathered many of my previously published essays and articles, dealing extensively with Afro-American culture. Throughout my career as journalist and critic, I have been preoccupied with the question of how black women figure in American culture. In particular, I've been concerned to comprehend their high *visibility* together with their almost total lack of *voice*.

For me the problem of why black women do so little critical writing is inextricably bound up with other more clear-cut Afro-American social problems like illiteracy and the high-school dropout rate, the homicide rate and the incidence of violence in the black community, especially against women and children; with homelessness and overcrowding in public housing, poverty, drug addiction and alcoholism, teenage pregnancy and teenage unemployment. It should be obvious why a community plagued by such problems would have difficulty producing intellectuals, perhaps especially black female intellectuals, because it is upon the backs of the women that the burden of poverty, homelessness and community violence falls most heavily. Like Frederick Douglass in his famous slave narrative, the individual male often need only conceptualize his own escape (no small task really), whereas women may feel obliged, as did Harriet Jacobs in her less famous slave narrative, to provide an escape for her children as well.[7]

Although I didn't grow up poor and I went to private schools, I did grow up in Harlem. But whether a black woman who desires to be an intellectual or a writer or an artist grows up poor or in Harlem or not, there is, I think, a 'Harlem' of the mind that may set the parameters of her endeavors. In particular, the idea that the black community has little need for certain levels of intellectual activity is as compelling among many black women of the middle class as it is among black women of the working or so-called 'underclass' (those who have fallen into the 'black' market economy of drugs and AFDC).

To personalize this a little, because of my own increasing intellectual engagement and my interest in criticism, I find myself highly marginal to most circles of middle-class black women and men. I don't have a single friend or acquaintance, male or female, black or white, who is a medical doctor, lawyer, or judge, or who works in a corporation. This strikes me as a sign of my own marginality to the ruling middle class, despite my ostensible middle-classness. My friends are all academics, cultural workers or artists; black, white and beige.

As a former professor of Black Women's Studies at Buffalo, and as a Professor of English at the Center for Worker Education in New York City, I have taught mostly working-class black women over the last few years, and while I find their perspectives on literary issues engaging, they, too, find my obsession with cultural criticism a baffling one. From their point of view, the problems black people have are clear, and no manner of 'criticism' and 'interpretation' will solve them.

The reflection of this attitude in the sphere of cultural production, however, is that people of color – perhaps especially black people – have very little input in decisions concerning the representation of their problems and their capacity for self-definition and self-direction. Not only are we barred from participation by racist exclusion, we have also barred ourselves from within Afro-American culture by minimizing its importance. Yet it seems to me that as the social level at which representation occurs (the omnipresence of global TV, the computer program and the national and international wire news services) becomes more and more all-encompassing and indistinguishable from the problems themselves, it is increasingly important for people of color to address issues of representation directly, to become actively engaged in criticizing the politics of the production of culture. I consider it a cultural crisis of the first order that so few people of color, especially women, are in positions of power and authority in the production of newspapers, books, magazines, television, films, radio, music, movies, academic journals and conferences, and university faculty and curricula.

Precisely because it is so well known how little control we have over
representation, the first assumption we make regarding any new, well
publicized representation that seems to come from a black author
(especially if that black author is a female) is that the 'black author' is a
puppet of the white power structure and is being manipulated to do us
further harm.

When I interviewed Ntozake Shange in 1976 for The Village Voice, she
was very unhappy with the way the press had been handling her story.
Both the white and the black press were treating her discussion of black
feminism and 'suicide' as though a favorite armchair had suddenly begun
to speak. 'I don't have to take this,' Shange said. 'I'm a writer. I can
write my own story.' Yet little of what she has written since has reached
anything like the audience that was reached by those first stories in The
New Yorker and People.

The more famous and successful Alice Walker becomes, the less we
seem to hear from her directly, although she used to write essays for Ms
magazine on a regular basis. Although she has begun to publish critical
essays lately, in the past Toni Morrison has rarely attempted to explain
her work or her politics in writing, despite the criticism of it as fraught
with 'negative images'. When she does finally write a critical essay, as she
did recently in The Michigan Quarterly Review, she mentions not one
black woman writer besides herself, but instead focuses on Herman
Melville's Moby Dick.[8]

I have come to see the difficulties black women writers encounter as
structural and systemic. Regardless of what the individual black woman
writer may think she's doing, the problem is with black women making
'political' statements in the broadest and deepest sense. Because black
women are perceived as marginal to the production of knowledge, their
judgement cannot be trusted. If, as intellectuals and writers, as some
French feminist critics have suggested, we are all functioning symbolically
as phallocentric, ethnocentric and logocentric subjects, in other words,
as 'white men', black women are the least convincing in this role, the
least trustworthy. As a consequence, black women are not allowed (by
themselves as well as by others) to make definitive statements about the
character of power, agency and resistance within and beyond the black
community. If and when they persist in doing so, the discouragement is
great.

Another way of putting this is that black women's novel-writing has
begun to reach an audience and exert an influence outside of the black
community far surpassed by other forms of black female or feminist
intellectual discourse. That black women should be unable to articulate
their own experience other than in the most allegorical and coded
language ('fiction') has everything to do with how 'race' currently

functions to corroborate and validate their economic and political inequality. I've also come to suspect that recent trends in mainstream feminism and black feminism participate in and encourage this perpetual imbalance in the production of knowledge.

Developments in feminist cultural studies and psychoanalytic criticism, which now seem to me crucial to even the most basic analysis of black feminist discourse in the US, provide nearly insurmountable obstacles to such an analysis as well. Feminist cultural studies is invaluable because of its reinterpretation of the multiple functions and processes of 'culture', and its vitalization of Marxist approaches to culture. Feminist uses of psychoanalytic film and literary criticism seem helpful because of their attention to the psychological impact of the conventional family, femininity, visual reproduction and the unconscious. Yet, as cultural studies and psychoanalytic criticism presume and require familiarity with the major works of such white male patriarchal (and ethnocentric) intellectual figures as Althusser, Raymond Williams, Lévi-Strauss, Lacan, Freud, Marx, Barthes, Derrida, and Foucault, the problem becomes twofold: not only is there the manner in which sexism and racism are reinscribed by these texts, there is the larger problem of risking being unable to communicate with a heterogeneous black and female audience if one takes too seriously one's reference to such work.

Nevertheless, as I become increasingly interested in the cultural problems of black female 'silence', negation and absence, I am inclined more and more to draw upon such intellectual and theoretical explanations of discourse and mass culture in order to describe these problems in a manner that will allow me to transcend the limits of the usual left-academic language. Therefore, I am including in this book two long essays that I have named 'theoretical', and in which I begin to propose a newly oppositional black feminist cultural criticism.

Parts I, II and III of this book, which are entitled 'Black Feminism/Autobiography', 'Pop', and 'Culture/History', consist entirely of essays, articles and reviews which have already been published. While the content here seems fairly self-explanatory, I have a few comments about each of these sections.

The section entitled 'Black Feminism/Autobiography' documents my consistent use of autobiographical material and how I've come to see the experiences of my life through a feminist prism. My tendency to read my life as a feminist demands some further comment only because the assumption still seems quite widespread that being a black woman and being a feminist, especially a feminist who is interested in theories of feminism, are somehow antithetical activities. I see feminism as a way of naming how women all over the world have raised issues regarding female equality, parity and difference. As a black socialist intellectual, I see my work as consistent with most feminist agendas. Although many of those agendas may not be entirely adequate to the problems of women of color, they provide the basis without which it is usually impossible to even raise most issues of women of color.

Perhaps the problem with my wanting to 'theorize' about feminism on the basis of autobiographical data drawn from my life as a black woman stems from the dilemma of the implied reader for the black writer.

Once upon a time, black writers, especially in what was later derided as the 'protest novel' (there were plays, poems and essays in this category as well), seemed to address white readers primarily. Partly in response to this tradition, in the 60s it became popular for black writers to address a black audience and pretend that the white audience wasn't there. Since then, although there has been some relaxation of this code, it has not been fashionable among black writers to express a desire for white readers at all. Yet we are well aware that it is almost impossible to publish without a white audience, especially if you write critical essays. These concerns have caused me to think a great deal about who I desire my reader to be. Quite consciously I write in order to challenge, tease, entertain, educate and enlighten the woman I think of myself as having been when I wrote *Black Macho and the Myth of the Superwoman.* I see that woman as being at the intersection of 'white' and 'black' culture and 'high' and 'low' culture, virtually blinded by white liberal humanist and black nationalist discourses to other ways of seeing the world and other ways of reading texts. I calculate that what will amuse and divert such a reader will also be of interest to the range of readers, white and black, male and female, academic and generic, with whom I seek to establish dialogue.

The second section on 'Pop' documents the tremendous influence that popular culture has had on my work, as well as the realization that surely everyone has made by now that Afro-American culture and so-called popular culture overlap to a fascinating degree in both North American and global contexts.

In the third section on 'Culture/History', for the most part the essays need no particular introduction except that in 'Slaves of History', when I say that there were no slave narratives actually written by black women, I failed to note the very significant exception of Harriet Jacobs' *Incidents in the Life of a Slave Girl.* The oversight was due to the fact that until fairly recently, most historians doubted the veracity of the Jacobs narrative because the writer used the pseudonym Linda Brent, and because of a variety of issues best catalogued by Jean Fagin Yellin in her new edition of this work.[9]

The fourth section, which is called 'Theory', proposes some initial

terms for a left or socialist black feminist cultural criticism, its relation-
ship to black feminist developments in the past, and the usefulness of
postmodern and feminist theory and cultural studies to the discussion of
Afro-American Studies. In this section, I touch upon the work of Stuart
Hall, Henry Louis Gates, Cornel West, Greg Tate, Gayatri Spivak, Hazel
Carby, Hortense Spillers, Bell Hooks, as well as the relevant work of Julia
Kristeva, Roland Barthes, Raymond Williams, Jean Baudrillard, and
Fredric Jameson. The point is not to propvide an exhaustive itinerary of
'white' theory useful to black feminist cultural studies, but to focus on
some of the more suggestive features of recent cultural studies, postmodern and feminist psychoanalytic literary, film and art criticism as they
bear upon the silent image of what I have elsewhere called 'race/
(gender)' as it marks current conceptualizations of women of color.

NOTES

1. Gayatri Chakravorty Spivak, 'Who Claims Alterity?', *Discussions in
Contemporary Culture 4: Remaking History*, eds Barbara Kruger and Phil Mariani,
New York: Dia Art Foundation, 1989, pp. 274.

2. Henry Louis Gates, Jr, *Figures in Black: Words, Signs and the 'Racial' Self*,
New York: Oxford University Press, 1987.

3. Houston Baker, *Blues, Ideology and Afro-American Literature*, Chicago:
Chicago University Press, 1984.

4. Fredric Jameson, *The Political Unconscious: Narrative as a Socially Symbolic
Act*, Ithaca, New York: Cornell University Press, 1981.

5. Jacqueline Rose, *Sexuality in the Field of Vision*, London: Verso, 1986.

6. Roland Barthes, *Mythologies*, New York: Hill & Wang, p. 116.

7. Frederick Douglass, *Narrative of the Life of Frederick Douglass, a Slave,
Written by Himself*, New York: Signet, 1968; Linda Brent (Harriet Jacobs),
Incidents in the Life of a Slave Girl, New York: Harvest Books, 1973.

8. Toni Morrison, 'Unspeakable Things Unspoken: The Afro-American
Presence in Afro-American Literature', *The Michigan Quarterly Review*, 1988,
pp. 1–34.

9. Harriet A. Jacobs, *Incidents in the Life of a Slave Girl, Written by Herself*, ed.
Jean Fagin Yellin, Cambridge, MA: Harvard University Press, 1987.

PART I

Black Feminism/Autobiography

1

Memories of a 60s Girlhood:

the Harlem I Love

All my life I've dreaded being labeled 'one of dem niggas what claims to be somethin' dey ain't'. So let's get this straight from the git, as even those of us on the fringe say uptown. I live in Harlem and have always lived there. My mother was born and raised in Harlem, and my grandmother's family migrated there from Jacksonville, Florida, when she was in her early teens (like many Harlemites my line is best traced through the women). But I've never seen a rat outside of a cage. My mother was never a domestic nor was any other woman in my family since slavery (they claim they were too 'proud'). I've never been raped behind the stairs, never been evicted, never played much in the streets except one month in the spring of '63 before the fun we were having was discovered and my sister and I were shuttled off to the tiresome safety of Oaks Bluff (the Harlem of Martha's Vineyard). I've never worn a doorkey around my neck, never seen my father hit my mother, was twenty when I ate my first pigfoot, and I never went to what my mother contemptuously refers to as 'P.S. 2'.

So, ecstatic fans of 'Harlem on My Mind' and 'Down These Mean Streets', you may not get what you expected! But then Harlem isn't what you think it is anyway. Harlem is mink coats and two-car families, the pathetic humor of the *Amsterdam News* society column and junior executives with Playboy Club keys, as well as no hot water and welfare checks. Harlem is generations old, as well as just off the boat and just up from down south. Harlem is not merely one seething ghetto but a place where people, black people of all different sorts, actually live and choose to live.

When I was a little girl, I was terrified of Harlem, of the incredible poverty that would spring out at me all at once as I turned some unknown corner, of the other girls my own age who, it seemed, were always twice my size, their socks held up by rubber bands, their braids sticking out every which way, just waiting to catch my eye on one of those rare occasions when I raised them: 'What you lookin' at girl?'

There simply wasn't any right answer, just the personal matter of which I considered more humiliating: being pushed down in the snow or having my blouse torn over my nonexistent bosom in front of everybody in a fight that the neighborhood boys would be giggling about for weeks. But I reserved my most violent trembling for getting lost on the subway, getting off at the wrong stop, 116th and Lenox, for example, wandering through what I never then doubted were the devil's own angels, the world's maddest men and women of all ages just standing in the streets, some of them slobbering drunk, some of them junkies, their bodies bent so low in a nod, their noses almost touching the ground, some of them screaming and fighting, any one of them likely to flash a razor at a moment's notice.

Other fears of my early youth included the possibility of being beaten beyond recognition for my grocery money, of being held down while someone forced a needle into my arm – instant junkie. And then there was the constant threat of somehow ending up with ten babies on relief with rats as big as fire hydrants for front room boarders, of ending up a whore out on the street trying to eke out a living for me and my man. These are the kinds of things I spent a considerable amount of time speculating about when I was a kid. After all, I was looking in the neighborhood pimp's face every day on my way home from school. He was right across the street and anytime I wanted to sign up ...

However, none of these things ever happened. My childhood was sheltered, eventless, like most American childhoods. On crisp Sunday mornings we would walk down Seventh Avenue (now renamed Adam Clayton Powell Jr Boulevard) with my grandmother. All along our way to the opulence of Abyssinian Baptist Church, the old men would tip their hats and old women in mink stoles and smart black suits would stop to say hello. We lived on Edgecombe Avenue when I was very little. It was a quiet and clean residential street where gossipy neighbors posted themselves on the benches of the parkside keeping tabs on everyone's comings and goings. When I was a bit older we moved to the big, new apartment house on 145th Street with doormen, two bathrooms, and the safest stairwells in town. There we met our two best friends, sisters like us. We all shared a cab to school in the mornings: they were going to Eron, we to New Lincoln. They later told us they hated us because we were always talking about our trip to Europe. We hated them because they got $5.00 allowance apiece, every day.

At some point or another it seemed as though everyone was coming out – our two cousins, our two rich friends whose parents owned a chain of beauty parlors, every female I knew who was old enough to wear sheer stockings and heels. I was missing out on it all – the clubs and societies like Jack and Jill, and Hansel and Gretel, the cotillions, the gauzy white dresses, the visits to the beauty parlor, the boys in tuxedos, cameras flashing, a mention in the *Amsterdam News*. I finally asked my mother why.

'You're already out,' she said. 'A woman once asked me if you could join Jack and Jill but when she told me what they did – give parties and teas – I told her no.' The first washcloth I ever had was designed to look like a book. My mother subscribed to the school of thought that said anything that didn't have an educational value didn't have any value at all. So, my sister and I saw the Uffizi, the Louvre, the Metropolitan, and the Guggenheim, but we missed the cotillions, the social clubs, the afternoon teas, the dancing lessons, and the Sunday school graduations.

Meanwhile, dope addiction reached epidemic proportions in Harlem in the 60s, and the clean sunlit streets of Harlem's Sugar Hill (as opposed to the valley – all of us hill dwellers knew that the valley was the real ghetto) were becoming more treacherous.

From what I can gather, when my grandmother was coming up, Harlem used to be a much safer and a more congenial place to live. 'If it was hot, you could lay out on the roof all night long, and nobody'd bother you,' she tells me. They had the Savoy with two bands playing every night: the Renaissance, the Lafayette Theatre with plays 'as good as downtown. Nobody had any money so people just had to stick together.' If someone got a relief package, the contents were shared with next-door neighbors. 'If your feet were about to fall clean off – you didn't go nowhere you couldn't walk – you didn't take a bus. Adam Clayton Powell said "Not till they get a black driver".'

The entire family went to the dances, not because the girls needed chaperons, but because, my grandmother says, 'young people didn't have anything to hide from older people like they do now'. A whole gang of them would go roller skating on Sundays after church – Bradhurst was the avenue. Zoom! right down the center of it. The cars used some other street till Monday.

In my mother's youth, Nipsey Russell, Pigmeat Markham and Redd Foxx played Harlem clubs. Duke Ellington lived right around the corner and so did Max Roach. People would beg Harry Belafonte not to bring his guitar to parties, and Sonny Rollins drove the neighbors crazy practicing his scales. The world's best music was a short walk and a drink away – the Club Baron, the Baby Grand, Mintons, Count Basie's. Of course your life might depend on you being able to remember how the territory was divided, what gang's turf you were on now – the Lords? the Comanches? the Royals? And my mother tells me they meant something entirely different when they talked about crashing a party. It meant the party got turned out, there was a fight, someone might die.

Jail was somewhere you never admitted anyone you knew had gone, especially not anyone in your family. History books report that the Great Depression ended in the 40s but in Harlem it continued right through the 50s. Money was something people in the movies had. My mother, an art student, and my father, a musician, both unemployed most of the time, tell me they lived very comfortably on $15 a week when they were first starting out.

Harlem today is something else again, although some things never change, like corrupt politicians and leaders, like the never-ending quest for 'what the figure is today', like mile-long Cadillacs double-parked in front of tenements. There are the innumerable funeral parlors, always the most sumptuous structures in the community, the churches on every block, and the bars on every corner. There's Eighth Avenue, the likes of which I have never seen anywhere in the world. If Eighth Avenue were emptied, you would think no one had lived there in years but, as it is, the streets are extremely crowded twenty-four hours per day with young men, very few women, standing around a fire made in a garbage can, waiting for what I'm not entirely sure. For those who think blacks are really going places, these are the backs they rode on.

But there are also the limousines outside the Lenox Terrace waiting to drive our various public officials to work. There are the doctors, lawyers, and various Indian chiefs, all in Brooks Brothers uniforms, who wear the leather thin on the stools at Jock's (Seventh Avenue) talking money and the pros and cons of black power. There are the neighborhood merchants, mostly black, who never sell rotten meat but who sell for outrageous prices, who know you by name, who discuss the weather and the foolishness of youth as though they were proprietors of general stores in Wisconsin.

But Harlem has changed drastically in my own lifetime, and that's been due to two things which may or may not be related: the prevalence of dope addiction and the fact that Harlemites are no longer victimized only by 'The Man' but also by a complicated network of crooks, hustlers, politicians, and 'leaders' who come from their own ranks.

Dope addiction has meant that the streets are now much more dangerous – that's true for all of New York. Old people never leave their homes at night. Most businesses close around six. By seven any commercial street is completely deserted, and has donned its night-time mask – impenetrable fortress of gates, metal walls, and padded locks. An able-bodied adult male without dependence on dope, wine, or hustling flesh or drugs is a rare sight in certain sections of Harlem.

The higher visibility of the black oppressor has meant that the squalor and poverty is that much more senseless and maddening, that there is a greater sense of hopelessness and despair among impoverished Harlemites, and that self-hatred has returned, feeding upon the unkept promises of the 60s, with roots thicker and deeper than before.

With very little encouragement, anyone who lives in Harlem is likely to get highly emotional on the subject simply because our solutions seem so close at hand, so obvious, so easy, and yet so confoundingly unattainable. Harlem's story is a difficult dose to swallow – the people who could do something won't and if they did they wouldn't be the people who could do something anymore.

(1975)

2

Anger in Isolation: A Black Feminist's Search for Sisterhood

When I was in the third grade I wanted to be president. I can still remember the stricken look on my teacher's face when I announced it in class. By the time I was in the fourth grade I had decided to be the president's wife instead. It never occurred to me that I could be neither because I was black. Growing up in a dreamy state of mind not uncommon to the offspring of the black middle class, I was convinced that hatred was an insubstantial emotion and would certainly vanish before it could affect me. I had the world to choose from in planning a life.

On rainy days my sister and I used to tie the short end of a scarf around our scrawny braids and let the rest of its silken mass trail to our waists. We'd pretend it was hair and that we were some lovely heroine we'd seen in the movies. There was a time when I would have called that wanting to be white, yet the real point of the game was being feminine. Being feminine *meant* being white to us.

One day when I was thirteen on my bus ride home from school I caught a brief but enchanting glimpse of a beautiful creature – slender, honey brown, and she wore her hair natural. Very few people did then, which made her that much more striking. This was a look I could imitate with some success. The next day I went to school with my hair in an Afro.

On my way out of my building people stared and some complimented me, but others, the older permanent fixtures in the lobby, gaped at me in horror. Walking the streets of Harlem was even more difficult. The men on the corners who had been only moderately attentive before, now began to whoop and holler as I came into view. Becoming exasperated after a while, I asked someone why. 'They think you're a whore, sugar.' I fixed my hair and was back to normal by the next morning. Letting the

18

world in on the secret of my native naps appealed to my proclivity for rebellion, but having people think I was not a 'nice girl' was The War already and I was not prepared for it. I pictured myself in a police station trying to explain how I'd been raped. 'Come on, baby, you look like you know your way around,' sneered an imaginary policeman.

In 1968 when I was sixteen and the term black consciousness was becoming popular, I started wearing my hair natural again. This time I ignored my 'elders'. I was too busy reshaping my life. Blackness, I reasoned, meant that I could finally be myself. Besides recognizing my history of slavery and my African roots, I began a general housecleaning. All my old values, gathered from 'playing house' in nursery school to *Glamour* magazine's beauty tips, were discarded.

No more makeup, high heels, stockings, garter belts, girdles. I wore T-shirts and dungarees, or loose African print dresses, sandals on my feet. My dust-covered motto, 'Be a nice well-rounded colored girl so that you can get yourself a nice colored doctor husband', I threw out on the grounds that it was another remnant of my once 'whitified' self. My mind clear now, I was starting to think about being someone again, not some-*thing* – the presidency was still a dark horse but maybe I could be a writer. I dared not even say it aloud: my life was my own again. I thanked Malcolm and LeRoi – wasn't it their prescription that I was following?

It took me three years to fully understand that Stokely was serious when he'd said my position in the movement was 'prone', three years to understand that the countless speeches that all began 'the black man ...' did not include me. I learned. I mingled more and more with a black crowd, attended the conferences and rallies and parties and talked with some of the most loquacious of my brothers in blackness, and as I pieced together the ideal that was being presented for me to emulate, I discovered my newfound freedoms being stripped from me, one after another. No, I wasn't to wear makeup, but yes, I had to wear long skirts that I could barely walk in. No, I wasn't to go to the beauty parlor, but yes, I was to spend hours cornrolling my hair. No, I wasn't to flirt with or take shit off white men, but yes, I was to sleep with and take unending shit off black men. No, I wasn't to watch television or read *Vogue* or *Ladies' Home Journal*, but yes, I should keep my mouth shut. I would still have to iron, sew, cook, and have babies.

Only sixteen, I decided there were a lot of things I didn't know about black male/female relationships. I made an attempt to fill myself in by reading – *Soul on Ice, Native Son, Black Rage* – and by joining the National Black Theatre. In the theatre's brand of a consciousness-raising session I was told of the awful ways in which black women, me included, had tried to destroy the black man's masculinity; how we had castrated him; worked when he didn't work; made money when he made none;

spent our nights and days in church praying to a jive white boy named Jesus while he collapsed into alcoholism, drug addiction, and various forms of despair; how we'd always been too loud and domineering, too outspoken.

We had much to make up for by being gentle in the face of our own humiliation, by being soft-spoken (ideally to the point where our voices could not be heard at all), by being beautiful (whatever that was), by being submissive – how often that word was shoved at me in poems and in songs as something to strive for.

At the same time one of the brothers who was a member of the theatre was also a paraprofessional in the school where my mother then taught. My mother asked him what he liked about the theatre. Not knowing that I was her daughter, he answered without hesitation that you could get all the pussy you wanted. NBT was a central institution in the black cultural movement. Much time was spent reaching for the 'godlike' in one another, the things beyond the 'flesh' and beyond all the 'whitewashing'. And what it boiled down to was that now the brother could get more pussy. If that was his revolution, what was mine?

So I was again obsessed with my appearance, worried about the rain again – the black woman's nightmare – for fear that my huge, full Afro would shrivel up to my head. (Despite blackness, black men still didn't like short hair.) My age was one thing I had going for me. 'Older black women are too hard,' my brothers informed me as they looked me up and down.

The message of the black movement was that I was being watched, on probation as a black woman, that any signs of aggressiveness, intelligence, or independence would mean I'd be denied even the one role still left open to me as 'my man's woman', keeper of house, children, and incense burners. I grew increasingly desperate about slipping up – they, black men, were threatening me with being deserted, with being *alone*. Like any 'normal' woman, I eagerly grabbed at my own enslavement.

After all, I'd heard the horror stories of educated black women who had to marry ditchdiggers and get their behinds kicked every night. I had thought the black movement would offer me much better. In 1968 I had wanted to become an intelligent human being. I had wanted to be serious and scholarly for the first time in my life, to write and perhaps get the chance Stokely and Baldwin and Imamu Baraka (then LeRoi Jones) had gotten to change the world – that was how I defined not wanting to be white. But by 1969, I simply wanted a man.

When I chose to go to Howard University in 1969, it was because it was all black. I envisioned a super-black utopia where for the first time in life I would be completely surrounded by people who totally understood me. The problem in New York had been that there were too many white people.

Thirty pounds overweight, my hair in the ultimate Afro – washed and left to dry without combing – my skin blue-black from a summer in the sun, Howard's students, the future polite society of NAACP cocktail parties, did not exactly greet me with open arms. I sought out a new clique each day and found a home in none. Finally I found a place of revelation, if not of happiness, with other misfits in the girls' dorm on Friday and Saturday nights.

These misfits, all dark without exception, all with Afros that were too nappy, chose to stay in and watch television or listen to records rather than take advantage of the score of one-night stands they could probably achieve before being taunted into running home to their parents as 'fallen women'. They came to Howard to get husbands; if you slept around, or if it got out that you had slept with someone you weren't practically engaged to, then there would be very little possibility of a husband for you at Howard.

Such restrictions are not unique in this world, but at Howard, the scene of student takeovers just the previous year, of riots and much revolutionary talk about casting aside Western values, archaic, Victorian morals seemed curiously 'unblack'. Baffled by my new environment, I did something I've never done before – I spent most of my time with women, often turning down the inevitable humiliation or, worse, boredom of a date (a growing possibility as I shed the extra pounds) even when it was offered to me. Most of the women were from small southern and midwestern communities. They thought me definitely straitjacket material with my well-polished set of 'sophisticated' New York views on premarital sex and atheism. I learned to listen more than I spoke.

But no one talked about why we stayed in on Friday and Saturday nights on a campus that was well known for its parties and nightlife. No one talked about why we drank so much or why our hunger for Big Macs was insatiable. We talked about men – all kinds, black and white, Joe Namath, Richard Roundtree, the class president who earned quite a reputation for driving coeds out on the highway and offering them a quick screw or a long walk home. 'But girl, ain't he fine?' We talked about movie stars and singing groups into the wee hours of the morning. Guzzling gin, cheating at poker, choking on cigarettes that dangled precariously from the corners of our mouths, we'd signify. 'If we could only be woman (white) enough' was the general feeling of most of us as we trotted off to bed.

Meanwhile the males on the campus had successfully buried the old standards of light, curly-haired young men with straight noses. They sported large, unruly Afros, dashikis, and flaring nostrils. Their coal-black eyes seemed to say, 'The nights *and* the days belong to me,' as we'd pass one another on the campus green, a fashionable, thin, colorless little creature always on their arm.

Enough was enough. I left Howard for City College after one term, and the significance of all I'd seen there had not entirely escaped me, because I remember becoming a feminist about then. No one had been doing very well when I had left New York but now it seemed even worse – the 'new blackness' was fast becoming the new slavery for sisters.

I discovered my voice, and when brothers talked to me, I talked back. This had its hazards. Almost got my eye blackened several times. My social life was like guerrilla warfare. Here was the logic behind our grandmothers' old saying, 'A nigga man ain't shit'. It was shorthand for 'The black man has learned to hate himself and to hate you even more. Be careful. He will hurt you.'

I am reminded of a conversation I had with a brother up at City College one mild spring day. We were standing on a corner in front of the South Campus gates; he was telling me what the role of the black woman was. When a pause came in his monologue, I asked him what the role of the black man was. He mumbled something about, 'Simply to be a man'. When I suggested that might not be enough, he went completely ape. He turned purple. He started screaming. 'The black man doesn't have to do anything. He's a man he's a man he's a man!'

Whenever I raised the question of a black woman's humanity in conversation with a black man, I got a similar reaction. Black men, at least the ones I knew, seemed totally confounded when it came to treating black women like people. Trying to be what we were told to be by the brothers of the 'nation' – sweet and smiling – a young black woman I knew had warmly greeted a brother in passing on Riverside Drive. He responded by raping her. When she asked the brothers what she should do, they told her not to go to the police and to have the baby though she was only seventeen.

Young black female friends of mine were dropping out of school because their boyfriends had convinced them that it was 'not correct' and 'counterrevolutionary' to strive to do anything but have babies and clean house. 'Help the brother get his thing together,' they were told. Other black women submitted to polygamous situations where sometimes they were called upon to sleep with the friends of their 'husband'. This later duty was explained to me once by a 'priest' of the New York Yoruban Temple. 'If your brother has to go to the bathroom and there is no toilet in his house then wouldn't you let him use your toilet?' For toilet read black woman.

The sisters got along by keeping their mouths shut, by refusing to see what was daily growing more difficult to ignore – a lot of brothers were doing double time – uptown with the sisters and downtown with the white woman whom they always vigorously claimed to hate. Some of the bolder brothers were quite frank about it. 'The white woman lets me be a man.'

The most popular justification black women had for not becoming feminists was their hatred of white women. They often repeated this for approving black male ears. (Obviously the brother had an interest in keeping black and white women apart – 'Women will chatter.') But what I figured out was that the same black man who trembled with hatred for white men found the white woman irresistible because she was not a human being but a possession in his eyes – the higher-priced spread of woman he saw on television. 'I know that the white man made the white woman the symbol of freedom and the black woman the symbol of slavery' (*Soul on Ice*, Eldridge Cleaver).

When I first became a feminist, my black friends used to cast pitying eyes upon me and say, 'That's whitey's thing.' I used to laugh it off, thinking, yes there are some slight problems, a few things white women don't completely understand, but we can work them out. In *Ebony*, *Jet*, and *Encore*, and even in *The New York Times*, various black writers cautioned black women to be wary of smiling white feminists. The women's movement enlists the support of black women only to lend credibility to an essentially middle-class, irrelevant movement, they asserted. Time has shown that there was more truth to these claims than their shrillness indicated. Today when many white feminists think of black women, they too often think of faceless masses of welfare mothers and rape victims to flesh out their statistical studies of woman's plight.

One unusually awkward moment for me as a black feminist was when I found out that white feminists often don't view black men as men but as fellow victims. I've got no pressing quarrel with the notion that white men have been the worst offenders, but that isn't very helpful for a black woman from day to day. White women don't check out a white man's bank account or stockholdings before they accuse him of being sexist – they confront white men with and without jobs, with and without membership in a male consciousness-raising group. Yet when it comes to the black man, it's hands off.

A black friend of mine was fired by a black news service because she was pregnant. When she proposed doing an article on this for Ms, an editor there turned down the proposal with these words: 'We've got a special policy for the black man.' For a while I thought that was just the conservative feminist position until I overheard a certified radical feminist explaining why she dated only black men and other nonwhite men: 'They're less of a threat to women; they're less oppressive.'

Being a black woman means frequent spells of impotent, self-consuming rage. Such a spell came upon me when I recently attended a panel discussion at a women artists' conference. One of the panel members, a museum director and a white feminist, had come with a young black man in a sweatshirt, Pro-Keds, and rag tied around the kind of gigantic Afro you don't see much anymore. When asked about her commitment to black women artists, she responded with, 'Well, what about Puerto Rican women artists, and Mexican women artists, and Indian women artists? . . .' But she doesn't exhibit Hispanic women any more than she does black women (do I have to say anything about Indian women?), which is seldom indeed, though her museum is located in an area that is predominantly black and Puerto Rican. Yet she was confident in the position she took because the living proof of her liberalism and good intentions sat in the front row, black and unsmiling, six foot something and militant-*looking*.

In the spring of 1973, Doris Wright, a black feminist writer, called a meeting to discuss 'Black Women and Their Relationship to the Women's Movement'. The result was the National Black Feminist Organization, and I was fully delighted until, true to Women's Movement form, we got bogged down in an array of ideological disputes, the primary one being lesbianism versus heterosexuality. Dominated by the myths and facts of what white feminists had done and not done before us, it was nearly impossible to come to any agreement about our position on anything; and action was unthinkable.

Many of the prime movers in the organization seemed to be representing other interest groups and whatever commitment they might have had to black women's issues appeared to take a back seat to that. Women who had initiative and spirit usually attended one meeting, were turned off by the hopelessness of ever getting anything accomplished, and never returned again. Each meeting brought almost all new faces. Overhearing an aspiring political candidate say only half-jokingly at NBFO's first conference, 'I'm gonna get me some votes out of these niggas,' convinced me that black feminists were not ready to form a movement in which I could, with clear conscience, participate.

I started a black women's consciousness-raising group around the same time. When I heard one of my friends, whom I considered the closest thing to a feminist in the room, saying at one of our sessions, 'I feel sorry for any woman who tries to take my husband away from me because she's just going to have a man who has to pay alimony and child support,' even though she was not married to the man in question, I felt a great sinking somewhere in the chest area. Here was a woman who had insisted (at least to me) upon her right to bear a child outside of marriage, trying to convince a few black women, who were mostly single and very worried about it, that she was really married – unlike them. In fact, one of the first women to leave the group was a recent graduate of Sarah Lawrence, her excuse being, 'I want to place myself in situations where I will meet more men'. The group eventually disintegrated. We had no strength to give to one another. Is that possible? At any rate, that's the way it seemed, and perhaps it was the same on a larger scale with NBFO.

Despite a sizable number of black feminists who have contributed much to the leadership of the women's movement, there is still no black women's movement, and it appears there won't be for some time to come. It is conceivable that the level of consciousness feminism would demand in black women wouldn't lead to any sort of separatist movement, anyway – despite our distinctive problems. Perhaps a multicultural women's movement is somewhere in the future.

But for now, black feminists, of necessity it seems, exist as individuals – some well known, like Eleanor Holmes Norton, Florynce Kennedy, Faith Ringgold, Shirley Chisholm, Alice Walker, and some unknown, like me. We exist as women who are black who are feminists, each stranded for the moment, working independently because there is not yet an environment in this society remotely congenial to our struggle – because, being on the bottom, we would have to do what no one else has done: we would have to fight the world.

(1975)

3

Baby Faith

The rumor was that Harlem Hospital maternity had sent some families home with the wrong babies that year, so babies had to be named before their mothers left delivery. But my grandmother Willi Posey was depressed and uninterested in naming her newborn baby girl. In an effort to rouse my grandmother's spirits, and bestow upon the child the quality she was most likely to need, a nurse suggested helpfully, 'Why don't you name her Faith?' It was, after all, 1930, the height of The Great Depression. Although my grandfather had one of the rare good jobs a black man could have in the period – he drove a truck for the Department of Sanitation – my grandmother, who was always ambitious, faced her future as Harlem housewife and mother of three through the grief of having lost a two-year-old son to pneumonia only six months before. Yet she stirred herself sufficiently to give to my mother her own first name, Willi, as a middle name.

There's always been a gift among the women in my family for making things. We trace it back to my great-great-great grandmother Susie Shannon and her daughter Betsy Bingham, both house slaves and quilt makers in antebellum Florida. Skipping the generation of my great-grandparents who were preachers and teachers, it survived in my grandmother Willi Posey, whom I called Momma Jones, as part of the generation that came North. Once her children were grown, she worked sewing in the factories in the garment district, while launching herself as a prominent Harlem clubwoman and fashion designer. When I was little, she was always quitting her job downtown because of some white male boss whose authority she could not abide, always sewing or cutting a pattern or fitting a dress or a suit on a model or a customer. All of us – my mother, my aunt, my sister and I – modeled in her fashion shows. These lavish, musical extravaganzas – more social than financial successes – showcased my grandmother's penchant for the theatrical.

The work of my mother Faith Ringgold as feminist performance artist, painter, soft sculptor and quilt maker seems the culmination of this tradition. At various times, all of us have been her collaborators. Momma Jones, in particular, made Faith's tankas (cloth frames) for paintings, clothing for her soft sculpture, costumes for her performances, and taught her the rudimentary skills of quilt making. My childhood evenings were often spent in a circle of women, drawing, cutting, sewing – making things.

But along with my mother's and my commitment to black feminist goals, there has emerged in my family an increasing fascination with naming, storytelling and language. Perhaps the ultimate manifestation, thus far, has been Faith's own increasing reliance on storytelling in her art, from the picaresque black feminist tale of 'The Who's Afraid of Aunt Jemima Quilt' to the autobiographical photo-essay of 'Change: Faith Ringgold's Over 100 Pounds Weight Loss Story Quilt' and Performance. Both performance and quilt feature photographs and text illustrating the 'changes' wrought upon her body and spirit, as sister, wife and mother, from childhood to the present.

Like Milkman's search for Pilate's 'gold' in Toni Morrison's *Song of Solomon*, which leads him to uncover the conundrum of names in his family, we knew that the feminist notion of history, continuity and tradition, was a way to remember what we could no longer afford to forget about the patterns of being a black woman. It wasn't only that naming ourselves had been a heady privilege for blacks ever since the collective 'mis-naming' of slavery. It was also that we would no longer be Alice Walker's 'Saints' in search of our mothers' gardens. We weren't rural, but urban, nor bound to the land or religion or anything but each other. Momma Jones never kept a garden, but she wrote all the time – letters to her family, notes to herself, plans and sketches for future fashions – in a large, imperial hand. Yet it never occurred to her to organize these materials because somebody might want to read them.

Quite early, my sister and I were persuaded that the world was most profoundly known through the accretion of language, the nuances of interpretation, anecdotal accumulation and overlay. Although Faith grew up hearing the story of how the nurse had named her, Momma Jones didn't tell her that her middle name was Willi. Faith thought her middle name was Elizabeth until her marriage in 1950 required that she obtain a copy of her birth certificate. I grew up hearing my mother tell this story about Momma Jones, who never explained. It was part of an endless performance of stories about life on Harlem's Edgecombe Avenue and beyond, that were told and retold by Momma Jones, Faith, my Aunt Barbara and my stepfather Burdette Ringgold. Not only did visitors bring newer, less familiar stories but, thanks to the intellectual curiosity of my then proto-feminist mother, I had access to a vast store of Afro-American music as well as books.

As infants, my sister and I often accompanied my mother to the 42nd Street Library, our own copies of 'The Cat in The Hat' or 'Eloise' in tow. (Kenneth Clarke's research had resulted in black dolls, but not yet black books for children.) Momma Jones began teaching me how to read when I was three. Later, I remember visits to the bookstore offered up, along with the movies, as the ultimate weekend entertainment. 'Why' questions were chased down and settled with books and music, as well as stories. From their first appearance, James Baldwin's books — which would subsequently inspire Faith's first series of political paintings on the Civil Rights Movement — were primary texts in our house, along with the records of Dinah Washington, Billie Holiday and Nina Simone.

Again in Harlem Hospital, fifty years later, another Faith Willi was born in our family to my sister Barbara Faith Wallace, PhD student in theoretical linguistics at the CUNY Graduate Center. The cold, grey dawn of March 1, 1982, Faith woke up abruptly to announce that Baby Faith had arrived within minutes of her birth, which a call to the hospital soon confirmed. Barbara shared a hospital room with five other women, all black and Latina. Each woman held a baby, gingerly, in her arms. But the room was absolutely silent except for Barbara chattering away full speed to the new Faith Willi as though it were not a new conversation but an old one interrupted.

At the time, Barbara and I were living together in what had been Momma Jones' apartment in the Lenox Terrace across the street from Harlem Hospital. Momma Jones had died in her sleep at age seventy-nine in October the year before. My sister Barbara and Faith had found the body, as well as the blue wool panels of a winter maternity coat she'd been making for Barbara, spread out on a cutting table in the living room.

It had not been a good year for any of us. My sister had suffered a difficult divorce. Pregnancy would indefinitely delay her PhD, although she had been awarded an MA and an MPhil that June in a ceremony that Momma Jones had attended. The first draft of my novel was rejected by my publisher, and I suddenly realized that, for financial reasons, I would be unable to continue graduate school in American Studies at Yale.

Having recently finished her first quilt, 'Echoes of Harlem', as collaboration with Momma Jones, Faith eagerly pursued her interest in this medium. Although she was well known across the country as a feminist artist, with no dealer and no gallery, she was making very little money from the sale of her art. My Aunt Barbara, an elementary school teacher, who had once dreamed of a PhD in education at Columbia

University and who encouraged my interest in writing with introductions
to Langston Hughes' 'The Sweet Flypaper of Life' and Ann Petry's The
Street, would die of a heart attack brought on by acute alcoholism only
six months after Baby Faith's birth. She had never reconciled herself to
Momma Jones' death.

Prompted by recent speculation that the fetus was receptive to
conversation, my sister and I had talked to Baby Faith in the womb
throughout Barbara's pregnancy. As writer and linguist, we were eager
that Baby Faith would share with us the mystery of words as soon as
possible. Thus we continued a family tradition at least one generation
old. When Barbara and I were born, in 1952, both Faith and her sister
Barbara were college students majoring in education at the City College
of New York and Hunter College, respectively. As a result, Barbara and I
were endlessly probed and tested.

Now we anticipated observing and studying Baby Faith. And she did
not disappoint us. Every day was a small adventure. The first time she
smiled, I initially mistook it for a burp. During our weekend candlelight
dinners, we propped up the five-month-old Baby Faith in her carriage, a
steak bone in her hand, so that she might enjoy the conversation. An
endlessly expressive 'Dah' was her only word. In tribute, Faith did the
'Dah series', six large abstract paintings that channeled the emotions of
losing her mother and gaining a first grandchild in a single year. Faith
and I collaborated on the Dah Performance number 1 in surrealistic
masks and costume. The six-month-old Baby Faith watched from the
front row and was unafraid.

Every day, I grow less certain of feminism's definition, of the
usefulness of confining it to narrow, monological explanation. Surely it is
process, ethos, movement, archive and article of faith all at once. Its
range is simultaneously psychological and international. Black feminism,
then, is perhaps her-story, whatever it calls itself, in order to make the
world inhabitable for the Faiths, Willis and Micheles, who would make
things with their hands, and with language, and with all of their being; a
unique caliber of self-expression and fulfillment; to each her own niche.

Four years later, Faith now has a dealer, the Bernice Steinbaum
Gallery in SoHo. In a recent one-person exhibition, she displayed quilts
of an unprecedented range, incorporating autobiography, fictional
narrative, performance, photo-essay, painting and sewing. She has lost a
hundred pounds, a pivotal feat of self-love in itself. From January to
June, she is a tenured professor of Visual Arts at the University of
California in San Diego. The rest of the year she spends making art, that
now sells quite well, in her beloved Harlem. She has been awarded two
honorary Doctorates of Fine Arts from the Moore College of Art ('86)
and the College of Wooster ('87).

I teach Afro-American Literature, Women's Studies and Creative Writing at the University of Oklahoma. I write fiction about black girls with strong mothers, fiction which has not yet found its place. Continuing the work I began in Black Macho and the Myth of the Superwoman, I also write about Afro-American culture and literature, and its particular ambivalence towards what Toril Moi has called 'Sexual/Textual Politics'.

My sister Barbara now teaches third grade at P.S. (Public School) 200 in Harlem. She has switched her dissertation topic from theoretical linguistics to sociolinguistics. Although she says that feminism conflicts with her religious beliefs, she says her research will focus on black English as spoken by black women who were raised in Harlem. Barbara says that most black people speak some degree of black English. Recent studies identify three levels – basolect, mesolect, and the acrolect, which includes, Barbara tells me, 'most professional, middle-class, occasional black English speakers like you and me and our mother Faith Ringgold'.

Which causes me to recollect the curious half-Southern, half formal speech Momma Jones sometimes used when talking to strangers, and the way people were always unable to tell the voices of my Aunt Barbara, Faith, myself and my sister apart. Barbara points out that studies of black English are rarely done on women: 'Linguists have concentrated on men's language because men were the linguists. But women teach children how to speak. In the first five years we are the dominant figures in children's lives'.

In July of 1983, Baby Faith was joined by a baby sister Theodora Michele, named after a great-grandmother who is still living and me. On March 1, Baby Faith's fifth birthday, I called their family long distance. After several resounding 'Hi's' from the 1½-year-old Teddy, I spoke to Baby Faith. I asked her how she felt on her birthday.

'I'm proud of myself, happy,' she said. 'I know how to tie my shoes. I know how to read easy books. I'm teaching myself how to read. Sometimes I draw a picture of my family. I help my mother with Teddy. I pass her the diapers. I make milk for Teddy.'

'What do you want to be when you grow up?' I ask her. Perhaps to Barbara's credit, this question is not a familiar one. But finally, she says, 'I want to be a nurse, and I want to be a lawyer when I grow up. Also I want to be an artist like grandma and a writer, too'.

The last time I'd seen Baby Faith had been a year ago, when I visited her in Harlem. She gave me several pieces from a large stack of her drawings, and dashed off a pencil sketch – a 'portrait' of me, I think, while I sat there, which she then promptly signed Faith Willi Wallace-Gadsden.

'How will you be all those things at once?' I asked.

'If I lose one job I can go on the other,' she explained reasonably.

'Are you a feminist?' I asked her.

'What's a feminist?'

'Well, a feminist is somebody who believes in the equality of women to men.'

'What's equality?' she asked me.

At the time, I was unable to come up with an answer, perhaps because of the alienation of the telephone, the long distance call, which has linked me to my family these past years. But what I should have done was what Momma Jones or Aunt Barbara or Faith might have done – tell her a story, or perhaps there's an easy book ...

POSTSCRIPT (1989)

In 1988 Faith won a Guggenheim fellowship and has been engaged in many exciting projects and commissions, perhaps chief among them her participation in a benefit for Bishop Tutu, sponsored by Michael Jackson. Her contribution to this effort was a special painting/quilt devoted to Jackson's 'Bad'. In it she deals with her notion that when you're black, good is never good enough. Thus 'bad' is what you need to be in order to overcome the dangerous forces that compromise your effectiveness. In the corners of the painting, she writes the names of notorious 'bad guys' like Rosa Parks, Fannie Lou Hamer, Zora Neale Hurston, Bishop Tutu, Martin Luther King, Michael Jackson and myself.

Also, Faith has done 'Church Picnic', a painted story quilt, and a new acquisition of the permanent collection at the High Museum in Atlanta. The image shows a vast array of black people attending a church picnic in Atlanta around the turn of the century. The story focuses on the black community's problem in dealing with a couple who fall in love and choose to marry, despite their class differences and despite the objections of their respective families. Faith suggests that the underlying struggle here is really about how the black community will define its relationship to freedom and emancipation.

So far, we've engaged in one collaboration called 'Dream 2: MLK and The Sisterhood', a story quilt which shows Martin Luther King with Coretta King, Fannie Lou Hamer, Rosa Parks and Ella Baker, and which includes a text by me first delivered as a speech commemorating his birthday as an official holiday in Flint, Michigan. The quilt will appear in a special issue of The Sunday Washington Post Magazine devoted to the anniversary of Martin Luther King's death on April 4th.

I am no longer teaching at the University of Oklahoma. I am now teaching Women's Studies and American Studies at the University of

Buffalo–SUNY. Although I've written very little fiction this year, I have been writing essays on Zora Neale Hurston, Michael Jackson, Spike Lee and what I call 'Variations on Negation: The Heresy of Black Feminist Creativity', which will appear in the Winter '89 issue of *Heresies*. I am also very close to completing my Master's in English at CCNY.

My sister Barbara has just had another baby named Martha. She took a leave of absence from the doctoral program at the City University of New York Graduate Center in order to do so. Although she advanced to candidacy in 1977, and they customarily permit candidates only eight years in which to finish up, they had recently granted her another two years. In the fall, then, she'll have another year in which to complete her dissertation, but she also has the responsibility of three children and will soon return to teaching a 7th grade class at P.S. 175 in Manhattan.

Needless to say, I think my sister's ambivalence about getting a PhD runs deep. In fact, I think she has babies *instead* of PhDs. But I have no children and I have suffered from the same problem, having attempted to pursue graduate degrees on four separate occasions – first in Creative Writing at CCNY, then in English at NYU, then in Afro-American Studies and American Studies at Yale, and now in English at CCNY.

Perhaps our ambivalence has to do with the pressures incumbent upon black female speech (and writing) described by Bell Hooks in an essay called 'Talking Back'.[1] In this essay, Hooks illustrates in poignant detail, drawn from autobiographical reflection, the three levels of speech that occur among black women: (1) speechlessness, the plight of female children (who should be seen and not heard), the mad and the dead; (2) self-reflexive speech, that speech which is only listened to by other black women, but ignored by almost everybody else including black men; (3) and 'talking back', that speech, which usually must be written (in order to become history), that transcends and transforms the barriers of race, class and sex to address the world.

This third category of speech is the kind that generally gets you in trouble precisely because it problematizes the invariability of classifications of difference. It is also unavoidable in any process of black female intellectual self-formulation. Although such self-formulation is not *required* as part of the graduate education we usually receive, the ritual of education inevitably raises the spectre of such process. The problem then becomes how to pursue a degree as part of a graduate education (in history or literature, philosophy or linguistics) which inevitably denies the significance/presence of the black intellect, in a demonstration of precisely that intellect (female no less!) which the structure of that education denies. These obstacles appear not only in the form of the antipathy of our frequently white male professors but also in the form of financial and child-care restrictions and limitations. I also think that the black community – from family to church to boys on the corner to the men in our lives – exacts a high price for 'talking back'. And most of us are unwilling, or unable (after a while, it becomes difficult to tell the two apart) to pay it.

(1987)

NOTES

1. See Bell Hooks' *Talking Back, Thinking Feminist, Thinking Black*, Boston: South End Press, 1988, a collection of her personal essays.

4

For the Women's House

In March of 1971, Faith Ringgold, artist, teacher and lecturer on Black Art, won an award from the Creative Artists Public Service Program (CAPS). She decided that with the money she would do a mural for the Women's House of Detention on Riker's Island. On January 18, 1972, 'For the Women's House' was presented to the female inmates.

A discussion of this work with Faith Ringgold follows:

MICHELE: What made you decide to do a mural for the Women's House of Detention?

FAITH: My first ideas were to do something about women and to put it in a public place. I asked some colleges but when I spoke to the Deans I would get a lot of 'Who are you?' It was just like going to museums. Then I asked myself, do you want your work to be somewhere where nobody wants it or do you want it to be somewhere it is needed? Then I thought, a women's prison would be the best bet because nobody wants to go there, therefore they'll let me go there. Isabelle Fernandez from the CAPS program assisted me. I met with the warden and supervisor who were both women and eventually with the architects and representatives of the Correction Department. Finally the project was finalized and the mural was installed. So it turned out that it wasn't easy to do a mural there but it was possible to do it there. There were no power plays and confusion, although there was a lot of bureaucracy and institutional standoffishness.

MICHELE: Did your idea of doing a mural for the Women's House, rather than for a men's prison, meet with any resistance?

FAITH: Oh yes I got a lot of 'why don't you go to the men's prison, it would be so much easier. What difference would it make?' Well, I knew there was a difference because I was aware that the problems of rehabilitating women are different. The stigma attached to having been

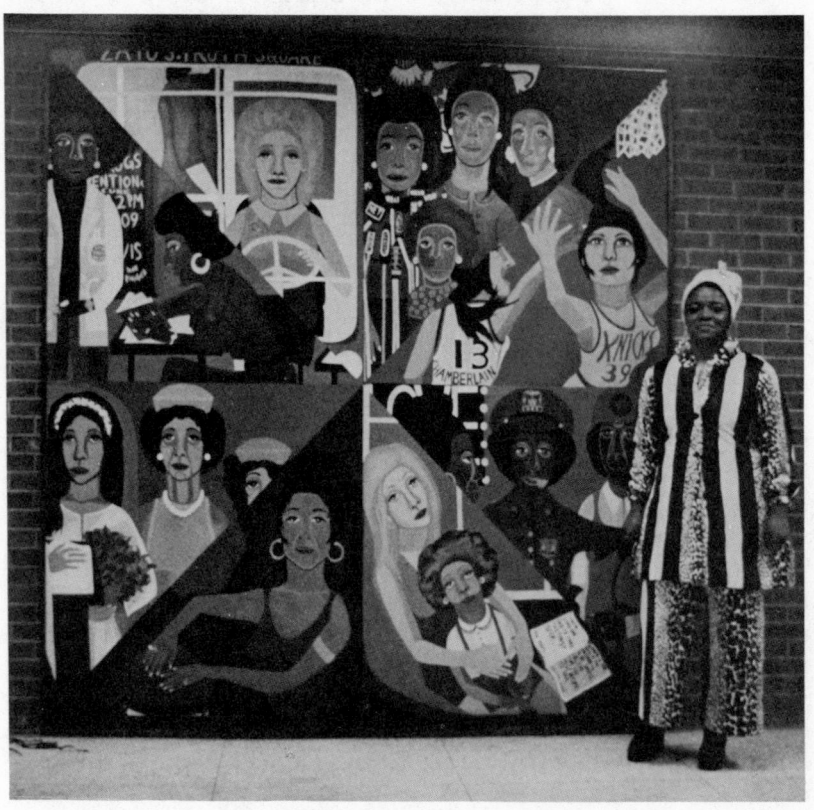

'For the Women's House' by Faith Ringgold

in jail for a woman is still a very threatening one because of the idea of how dare she not be a good wife and mother. She goes to jail because she is not able to play her traditional role as a woman.

MICHELE: I understand that you asked the inmates what they would like to see in the painting. What did they say?

FAITH: They said they wanted to see justice, freedom, a groovy mural on peace, a long road leading out of here, the rehabilitation of all prisoners, all races of people holding hands with God in the middle, 85 per cent black and Puerto Rican, but they didn't want whites excluded. There was a kind of universality expressed by their feelings.

MICHELE: How did you come about the decision to make everybody in the mural a woman?

FAITH: I had decided that I was going to do a feminist mural, which meant that it was going to be about women being equal. Then I decided that, if I put men in it, it would be read wrong in this society where everyone thinks of men as being superior to women. If I put men in a subordinate role then they'll say, 'oh that's propaganda'. That's the kind of painting I might do later but not for an institution where people are captive audiences, as it were.

MICHELE: The mural is 8 x 8 foot and the design is BaKuba, of an African tribe called the Kuba. The mural divides into two 4 x 8 foot oblong rectangular canvases each of which is divided into two 4 x 4 foot sections, each of which in turn is divided into two triangles, which means that the painting is split into eight triangular sections. In each of these sections, a different aspect of the existence of woman is depicted. The first section shows an older white woman driving a bus, the 2A which is bound for Sojourner Truth Square. Why did you choose to show a woman driving the bus?

FAITH: The busdriver is a fiftyish lower-class white woman. Even though she's got the race thing together, she falls low on the class and the sex, so she gets to drive a bus. However, busdriving is not a bad job for a woman. It's a way in which she can make quite a lot of money without an education so that she can take care of herself and her children, send them to college or whatever. It's a job that doesn't demand a great deal of physical prowess and it is a pleasant job in some respects. I think women would be less threatened by the job than men are. Men often get very angry with us when we don't know what stop to get off or on. Women are more accustomed to being asked silly questions. I wanted to show more women going to work, doing things, but I didn't want to become too literal.

MICHELE: Why did you give the viewer such a close-up view? You could have just shown the bus at some distance with the sign saying 'To Sojourner Truth Square' visible.

FAITH: Yes, all of them are close-ups because the faces are very important. I never knew why I always used to paint big faces and heads and littler bodies until I became aware of African sculpture and found out that all natural peoples make a big thing of heads because the head is the seat of character, and I guess I follow in that tradition. It is much more Greek to make a big thing of bodies, but the body doesn't serve any kind of a function of a spiritual nature; the body is for doing and the head is for thinking and being which is why I have always focused on facial expressions.

MICHELE: The next section shows a black woman doctor from the Rosa

Parks Hospital teaching a class on drug rehabilitation.

FAITH: What I'm really saying here is that teaching is a woman's profession. But just to put a teacher there would not be saying anything because everybody knows that women get a chance to teach in CORE programs run and set up by men. I am saying that the whole teaching thing needs to be changed and that women can do that because women are teachers. Teaching shouldn't be a profession. Your profession should be something else you teach about. She is a teacher and a doctor, and she comes in because our schools need the best possible experts to come in and tell the students about everything. This would make school totally interesting to children, and it would get rid of this notion that whoever is left with the children (teachers and mothers) is a drag. The children would know that here we have a doctor who is out in the world and she comes in to tell us about narcotics. That's something we ought to listen to. Plus it makes the doctor understand that part of what you do is with the children in the schools, and this should be followed through to all professions.

MICHELE: The next section is the controversial wedding scene. We see only the hand of a woman priest on a holy book before a Puerto Rican woman about to be given away by her mother in marriage.

FAITH: I think it's natural for any mother to want to give her daughter away. I know the father is supposed to give you away, but when I got married I was angry with my father so I didn't let him give me away, and I have found that there are a lot of people who have had this problem and there is always a big hustle to find a man to give the bride away. Maybe you didn't like your father, or he wasn't close to you, or he's dead. (An old friend of ours had been separated from her husband for years when her daughter got married. Suddenly her husband appeared talking about how he had to get ready to give his daughter away. She told him, 'You gave your daughter away twenty years ago'. That stuck in my head.) Whoever has been taking care of you all these years should give you away.

The hand on the Bible is also the hand of a female priest which I think has got to happen sometime soon. I feel that if anyone must wear the cloth, it should be women who are unblemished by killings and war and have real empathy: and if they want to do it, they should have the opportunity.

MICHELE: It doesn't seem like a hard thing for me to figure out that when getting married, the groom stands on the left side of the bride. However, some people seem to have been confused by the presence of a woman on the right side of the bride.

FAITH: Certain sectors feel that there is creeping lesbianism throughout this mural, and their biggest evidence is that this woman is marrying this old lady next to her. In any kind of painting where people are confronted with images that are about themselves, people come with their own prejudices and limitations and they relate to the painting in terms of what their own life experiences have been, but that doesn't have anything to do with the way in which I have portrayed it. That's their hang-up, not mine.

MICHELE: In the next section, there is a Chinese woman dressed in leotards playing the drum, while another woman dances behind her. I guess you're aware of the sin attached to a woman touching a drum, particularly a drum like this which is obviously African, or some kind of ancestral drum.

FAITH: Making music is big entertainment in this country. I believe women should and would be musicians if they had the opportunity. I made a woman drummer because the drum (a traditional African instrument) is one of the most masculine of all instruments. But it's ridiculous to *make* anything masculine ... except males.

MICHELE: At the top of the second half of the painting a black woman is shown who has obviously just won the presidential election. She is standing before a lot of microphones with two women beside her and a little girl in front of her. Why is this woman's hair straightened as opposed to many of the other black women in the painting?

FAITH: She represents the middle-class black woman who will run for office, and in order to run for public office and win, one needs votes. In my painting, the power is in making a woman president, and a black woman at that. If Shirley does become President, she is representative of this class of woman. And next to her she has her sidekicks, because women need their support also, and her child is there because she is also a wife and mother. Possibly her husband and other men are cut out on the other side. She is not overly pompous; I wanted to make her a real person.

MICHELE: The next section shows two women playing basketball. One woman has the name Chamberlain spelled out on her shirt with the number thirteen. The other woman has Knicks spelled out on her shirt. What's the significance of number thirteen?

FAITH: That's Wilt Chamberlain's number.

MICHELE: Aren't the Knicks an all-male team? Why didn't you make up a name for the women's team in your picture?

FAITH: Because then you wouldn't have taken it seriously. You would have thought, 'Oh, this is the Butternut team from around the corner with the Church'. I'm talking about real professional ball which women can play. Some of them can play with men. All women are not 5'2" and 130 lbs. Some are 6'3" and 200 lbs or whatever, and instead of growing up feeling uncomfortable about their builds and trying to suppress the idea that they want to play ball, they should be able to play. Sports are a whole good money-making, prestige-building, image-making avenue closed to women. Although sports are not my thing, I recognize that they are powerful.

MICHELE: In the next section there is a policewoman conducting traffic with a whistle in her mouth, and I know that you went to a great deal of trouble to duplicate that shield that police wear. To the left of her there is a black woman hardhat with lunch pail and newspaper. There is another black woman with her hair in a bun, and behind her there is a neon sign which says 'Love'. The fact that she has her gun visible in a holster separates her from other policewomen.

FAITH: One thing you know when you call 911 is that they're not going to send a woman; and why not? If you're afraid that some dangerous criminal is going to beat the woman up, then let the men and women go together in teams. I think that people would feel a good deal more secure if there was a woman around when the cops busted in. When I tried to find out what police wear, wow, did I run into a lot of different stickers and things – talk about fetishes! The crap you wear varies according to rank, and whether you sit on a motorcycle or a horse and so on. It's a whole heavy male ego bullshit thing, when what it's really all about is that you have a gun and are sanctioned to crack somebody over the head. Guns are just another extension of the male genitals, just like the drum. Women just need to start using them. I think everybody would take guns much more seriously if women wore them. (The community service man in my local precinct told me that he didn't know whether women from the House would be eligible for jobs on the force because of their records. I told him that some of the women have not been tried yet; and, furthermore, the Knapp Commission Investigation has turned up many of New York's finest who have admitted to crimes in the name of the law, and they are getting paid and are still on the force. So perhaps we need to re-evaluate the criteria for service on the police force.)

As far as the female construction worker goes, the black women (who take much less dope and drink much less liquor and who are much less likely to be docile about doing nothing in their community) haven't got the slightest notion that they should 'Build Baby Build', which is what it says on her hat. There are cranes to lift heavy things, and she can certainly lay bricks and do different things. Some people are going to say, black men can't even get into these unions. If the able-bodied-looking men who fill Harlem's bars and street corners would pass up the man with the pot and the heroin, then I might be able to sympathize. Because if he would stay sober for one day, he'd have these jobs because there would be so many able-bodied, bright, alert men around that you would have a revolution immediately. However, in the meantime, let the women who are of sober mind and body do the jobs, since what is most important is that the children be fed and sent to school; and the children are with the women anyway and the men are on the corners ...

MICHELE: In the last section, there is a young white woman without a wedding band and an obviously part black child is in her arms. She is reading to the child from a book with a quote from Coretta King on one page and a quote from Rosa Parks on the other.

FAITH: Unwed mothers are a reality, and there is no such thing as an illegitimate child, although sometimes we have illegitimate parents. It is unfortunate that all children don't have the right to equality in this society, but one thing we can do is stop calling children illegitimate. This section also points out that the mothers of many black children today are white. This white woman is paying her dues; we don't have to condemn her. She is already condemned to paying for having dared to have that child. Rather than stressing the importance of the father who is absent, let us stress the importance of the mother who is present. And look what she's doing. She is teaching the child about her history. One quote is Coretta King's, which says that if the nation is going to have a soul then the women must be that soul. And one from Rosa Parks, the most bedamned woman in the whole history of the Civil Rights Movement, the woman who started the movement. Today she gets to be Representative Conyers's secretary, which is ridiculous. She started the movement while he was in diapers, and now she gets to be his secretary. What picture in Alabama, Mississippi or Georgia could be worse? She is the nigger of the movement, as are all black women; we get to play only nigger roles ... I couldn't give her a wedding band because then everyone would have thought she was just some middle-class white woman married to a black doctor or lawyer or something.

MICHELE: In this mural your rendering of things becomes more literal than in your former paintings. However, the viewer is still disoriented by these triangular close-up sections where one can see neither floor nor ceiling. Why did you choose to do this painting in this way?

FAITH: I don't want anything in my paintings that doesn't have a message involved in it. I don't demand that the message be interpreted exactly as I intended, but the idea is to confront the viewer and get the viewer involved with the idea that my art is something to be dealt with; and that my art is all about you – you the person who is looking at it. I usually make certain words and things upside down and sideways. This is done to involve the viewer physically and to upset the notion that paintings are just 'pictures of' something. However, 'For the Women's House' was done with a desire not to upset; I didn't want to add to their problems. I wanted it to be uplifting, inspiring,, forward-moving, hopeful; I wanted it to give the women some reason to be proud of themselves and to believe in themselves.

MICHELE: Why are you a figurative painter?

FAITH: I guess I am a figurative painter in the sense that my people have figures. However, what I really am is a people painter. I am concerned with the heads of people rather than the rest of the body which just tells us what people are or are not doing, how they are or are not dressed, and whether they are well-proportioned or sensually well put together, and so on. If you ask me why I paint people, that is because I have certain messages that I want people to be aware of; and in order for me to convey my messages to them, I have to come through them. So I do people that are people because I don't want people to say, 'Oh, that's Martin Luther King' or somebody. It isn't someone else. It's you.

MICHELE: You have got women of all races and all ages in this mural and they are doing a lot of things that women still have never been permitted to do under this or any other government. However, they are all 'working within the system'. Why?

FAITH: What I have painted is not the system as we ordinarily know it. This is obviously a new kind of society that we don't know anything about, a society where women are allowed to take aggressive roles, are allowed to fulfill themselves. I think it's unreal to say that you don't want to have anything to do with existing institutional structures because all our people are in those institutions. So we may turn our backs on the prisons and say they're oppressive, part of the oppressive bureaucratic system that runs this country and say we don't want to have anything to do with it. But I'm afraid that there are a great many women who can't say that because they've been arrested and they are in those institutions. How about the thousands of kids in the public school system? Brandeis, the high school I teach in, is exactly like the Women's House, no difference. We can turn our backs but the children are still there. The old people are still in the old folks' homes, the people are still in the mental institutions. No matter how revolutionary you may think you are, everybody makes some kind of concession to this government when 15 April comes. There is very little we have to do, you know, that will land us right out in the middle of the painting, getting to see exactly what is going on out there, because we'll be right out there with it, in prison.

MICHELE: It seems to me that the most important criterion for a successful society is that it meets the needs of its people, and the realization of many of the things going on in this painting would be a step in that direction. And if a society is meeting the needs of the people, what difference does it make whether you call it the United States or the United Peoples' Republic or whatever. You are dealing with correcting the situation from where we are now, which is important because the revolution is too abstract – as it has turned out, far more abstract than any of us might have suspected. Therefore, the revolution has been too conveniently removed from our daily actions.

FAITH: Some people say that they don't believe any woman should have to do housework, but in any kind of society there are going to be those people who would rather spend their energies in one direction rather than another. For example, not every woman wants to write like you do; they would much prefer to do something else. Let us find out what that something else is and give them the opportunity to do that. Some people want a limited involvement in certain things that have to do with work. They would prefer rather to keep a garden or something, and there are men who feel that way too and have been oppressed into thinking that they must strive to be heads of corporations.

MICHELE: But men can also keep gardens if they wish and call themselves gardeners.

FAITH: It does seem that men are able to give titles to what they do, whereas the activities of women are all loosely gathered under 'house-wife'. So what we are really talking about is choices.

I thought, how do we deal with narcotics? Should I show women capturing a large load of drugs? But a lot of 'revolutionaries' wouldn't like that, since they are selling it and using it. Furthermore, is that what it's about, or is it getting people's heads together so that they know not to drink Clorox [bleach]? 'Cause that's what we did, like I was taught and I taught my children 'never drink Clorox', so we didn't grow up feeling like that was something we ought to do. But if somebody had gotten a nip of it and found out it made you high, Clorox might have been the thing instead of heroin.

I'll grant you one thing – that if this painting had not been going to a prison then it would have been different; and I can't even guarantee that that difference would have been better for the women, because those women out there are not necessarily revolutionary.

MICHELE: How did you know that the women would want to see an all-female painting? What made you think that they didn't want to see a mural of nude men or something?

FAITH: I didn't. If I put men in the mural, it would have had to be in an oppressive role or in a lying role. If I had shown a man, woman and child, that's not real and those women out there know better. There is a great upheaval between men and women in this society today. Maybe I could have done that two years ago.

MICHELE: Like a sister who is an inmate out there told me, when I asked her what she thought about the fact that there were no men in the painting, 'There's women in this prison. Ain't no men in here'. A lot of women might be in prison because of something their man told them to do.

FAITH: Yes, and they were deserted too.

MICHELE: Are you happy about the painting?

FAITH: Yes, I'm very pleased. If I hadn't done it for the Women's House, then it would probably have been more political. But these women have been rejected by society; they are the blood guilt of society, so if this is what I give them, then maybe that is what we should all have. Maybe all this other stuff we're talking is jive because these women are real. They don't have anything to be unreal about. If they want to do something, they do it; that's why they're in jail. We dress ours up and decide we'd better not do it.

MICHELE: What are you going to do now?

FAITH: This mural is just part of a series called 'America's Women'. I want to do more with women, dealing with their ages, races and classes, because no matter how old you are or what color you are, or how much money you have, you're still a girl. You may be a 'rich ole girl' but you're still a girl.

MICHELE: What are you doing next in the prisons?

FAITH: We're getting together a group of artists and concerned people to go into the prisons at least once a month and perform services and bring the women things they need. The group is called 'Art Without Walls'. I have been asked, also, to do a mural for the Adolescents Remand Shelter, which is also out on Riker's Island.

(1972)

5

A Women's Prison and

The Movement

Since the battle of Attica, a lot of artists have been making a mad dash for the prisons, that is, the men's prisons. The feeling seems to be that political prisoners can only be male, and that feeling is shared by a shocking number of women, as well as men. While the women's prisons remain forgotten, the male artists are obtaining money from other men to rush out to the men's prisons with their programs, the female artists holding up the rear – needless to say, without pay.

Eventually, it begins to occur to a woman that something ought to be done about the *female* inmates, particularly since, at least in my mind, there is some doubt as to whether all male inmates (especially those that rape, murder, assault, and steal from women) are really political prisoners. Certainly, they *are* political prisoners, but should they be put before women inmates who are political prisoners in a much more vivid sense? Let's face it, women go to prison for one reason – men. If a woman decides that she doesn't want to be tied down, doesn't want to do anything in particular, just wants to bum around for a while, she will end up in a mental institution if she's white, and in a jail if she's black. A woman can never afford to be so unclear about what she wants to do because if she doesn't know, there is a man that will know for her and, eleven times out of ten, that ain't good.

If you should decide that you really want to do something for women inmates, how do you go about it? You immediately think, 'I'll ask around and find out what everybody else is doing'. What you will find is that everybody else is doing absolutely nothing. There is no structure set up to rehabilitate women in or outside of the prisons. There is nothing nothing nothing happening for women prisoners: I repeat – nothing. Suppose you don't believe me. Then call the Fortune Society or some other organization that claims to help all former inmates. A white woman will answer the phone. But don't be fooled, she is fully authorized to speak for the black men who run things. She'll tell you that they don't have time for women prisoners, of whom, at least in the Women's House, 95 per cent are black, Puerto Rican, and so on. If you don't want to, don't just take her word for it. Ask to speak to the man and he'll hit you with the real dope – it is impossible to rehabilitate female inmates. Now do you understand? Maybe you want to get in touch with the Women's Bail Fund. Fine, if you want to devote your major time to freeing leftist women, while Mary who is sick and has a baby on the outside and who is in jail for assaulting a police officer (she slapped a cop in the face) remains in prison. And if that does not appeal to you, then you better realize that you are going to have to start from the very beginning.

About four or five months ago, some of us got lucky. We got hooked up with Faith Ringgold, painter and educator, who had done a mural for the Women's House of Detention. She knew some of the prison officials and she knew the warden. She wanted to start a program to bring art to the women's prisons. We all got together, decided on a name, 'Art Without Walls', and planned for five workshops – art, poetry, dance, yoga, and a rap session. Representatives were chosen who met with the warden, arrangements were made, everything was set. We were to go out every Sunday at three and leave at five, calling in the names of the people who were going on the Thursday before.

Pessimist that I am occasionally, I smelled trouble from the 'git go'. It seems that there was something basically wrong with the very type of woman who was drawn to such a program. She's a pretty common kind of a creature – incompetent, but an eager do-gooder. She's got guilt enough for one hundred Ku Klux Klanners. She's politically uncommitted. She's on the verge of feminism but somehow never quite makes it over the hump. Her most distinguishing feature – she wants to know more about 'what the blacks are into'. In fact, the truth is that she really doesn't want to work in a women's prison at all, but she knows that if she joins a male-dominated program, she'll never get to do anything except type up more proposals for money and lay the men. So she works with the women, hoping that what she will achieve there will carry her to greater heights – the men's prisons.

Why is the do-gooder usually white rather than black? The black woman in jail seems to be too huge a dose of reality for the black woman outside. But for pure, unvarnished good luck, that would be her in prison: and what every black woman knows is that, if she slips up just a little, she can still end up there in two seconds flat. Under such circumstances, it is difficult for the black woman to feel sympathy for those sisters who didn't possess unearthly strength, who refused to play the game, who 'fucked up'.

Are men drawn to a program for women inmates? White men in small numbers, partly because the guilt trip in the men's prisons is so heavy that they can't bear up under it. Further, they, like the white women, aren't allowed to do very much, except supply the money.

As for the black man, he seems to be completely repelled by the idea of working in the women's prisons. I closely observed the few who did come out with the program now and then. Outside of one young student, none returned for a second visit. It seems that they were very disturbed about how close the women were to one another and about the not inconsiderable lesbian activity. They would spend all their time trying to convince one woman inmate after another that this was horribly, horribly wrong, and that they should be ashamed of themselves. It was just too much for them. On the ride back to the city, I would sneak a glance at their faces; sometimes I would even talk to them, ask them how they felt about the program. 'Oh, I'll be back, I'll definitely be back,' they would say. 'We've got to get these women's heads together, get their heads together.' You could see the confusion and horror in their faces; and I knew how each of them felt, kind of like the first time I noticed a brother giving me an intense, hot hate look because *he* was with a white sister. You could see in their eyes that all they wanted to do was get far far away from that all-woman world, never, never to return.

No doubt about it – the people in the program were wrong from the very beginning, but 'Art Without Walls' happened despite that. You're probably thinking that any program is better than none. At first I thought the same, but now I don't know. The problems got heaped pretty high during the ten or more weeks the program existed.

WORKING COLLECTIVELY

The first controversy was over who should sign in for the group. At first it was just assumed by Faith Ringgold who did, after all, know the warden and know the prison officials and did obtain clearance for the program. Quite naturally the prison officials wanted someone who was responsible, and whom they could find if anything went wrong; and there were a lot of things that could go wrong with twenty some people going in and out of a prison every week. But it wasn't long before the cry of pig was raised against Faith. She was taking over, setting herself up as the leader, not working 'collectively'. She backed down, and from then on a different person signed in almost every week. The first thing that happened was that each one of us had to sign up at the reception center;

then we had to sign in again when we got to the Women's House; then the checklist didn't have all the names on it (and if you weren't on the checklist you didn't go out). Meanwhile, all of this new procedure was robbing time from the program.

Then there was a controversy over money. At first, no one wanted any. Then people slowly began to realize that the program was turning out to be very expensive. It was decided that there would be an attempt made to acquire funds, and that was when all hell broke loose.

We had to incorporate, and, in order to do that, we had to have a board of directors. No one on the board of directors could be a 'pig'. In other words, we could only consider people for the board who were not rich and not famous. The function of a board of directors is to help an organization obtain funds, stability and recognition. A board member achieves this end by using his or her connections. Who has those kinds of connections? Rich and/or famous people.

We had to have officers. Faith Ringgold could not be the president or hold any other official position, since she somehow fell into the 'famous' category. However, the membership was aware that without her the organization could not continue to exist. So what they did was elect me president because I am twenty (young and dumb), I am black (blind and honored), and most important, I am Faith Ringgold's daughter. Realizing that the job was just a glorified secretary, that I would receive no cooperation, no assistance and no credit from anyone, but wanting very much to set the organization on its feet, though knowing that that would be impossible, I, like an ass, accepted the position.

We had to decide who was going to be on the proposal, who was a member of the organization, in other words, who was going to get paid once the money came through. If you know anything about this grant thing, then you know that once you get the money, as far as the funding agencies are concerned, you can go fly a kite with it, build a home on the shore, go to Bermuda, whatever you want. In fact, that is exactly what they want. It's all 'keep quiet' money anyway. Once a person was placed on our payroll officially, they wouldn't have to do a damn thing if they chose not to; or, worse yet, they could stand around and block everybody else. Well. The group wanted everybody who had even hinted that they might be interested in talking about going out to the Women's House to be placed on the proposal.

THOSE WHO CAN, SHOULDN'T

Where did all this shit come from, you might ask. It's all from one basic pile, and the name of that pile is *Those Who Can, Shouldn't*. The particulars go like this.

'Art Without Walls'' active membership was largely composed of white women (and I noticed that the men rarely came to meetings), latecomers to the Civil Rights Movement, latecomers to the left, still dazed by the appearance of feminism, generally inept and unsuccessful. They thought that in the women's prison, they would make their statement – a fantastic new dance technique or an exhibition or something. But just as they were incompetent in the past, they continued to be incompetent. The women inmates were not fooled by their spurts of enthusiasm, for they are seasoned experts on human nature.

Further, these do-gooders were feeling a lot of guilt, as one might imagine was justified, but that wasn't the point. The first thing you are supposed to think about when you are trying to do service for someone is what will add to that service. Guilt is not going to get those women out of jail, is not going to teach them a skill, and, generally, is not going to assist them in any way. That being the case, the only thing to do is to get rid of it, or indulge your guilt on your own time – it's too expensive.

For example, a woman inmate would start to tell a story that was truly horrible. The do-gooder would stop to listen: she would be paralyzed by guilt. Another Sunday had passed, the woman inmate had not learned anything about art, anything about how to stay out of prison, had only learned that people are as full of shit as ever. The female do-gooder goes home feeling empty, disgusted with herself, realizing that she has done nothing to improve the lives of the women in prison, frustrated, and guilty more than ever, naturally. The do-gooder comes to the conclusion that she cannot teach a woman prisoner anything. She decides that what she has to do is bring revolution, not art, to the prisons; men's phony revolution, that is. At that point she begins to encourage her fellow do-gooders to do the same. She frowns upon anyone doing anything constructive. For example, when I stated that the aim of the organization was to prepare women inmates for professional work in art fields, members of the group objected. 'Don't impose your middle-class values on the beautiful savage' was the tone. After the do-gooder has failed, no one must succeed. In other words, those who can, shouldn't.

FEMALE INMATE, LATENT FEMINIST

In the course of trying to bring male pseudo-revolution to the women's prisons, the do-gooder ran into another problem – how to deal with the latent feminism of the female inmate. It is very difficult to get a woman inmate to fall for a bullshit male left line that was tired to begin with. They see right clear through it immediately. But they do know, perhaps better than any of us, that men and women are having some enormous problems relating to one another normally. They do know, deep down inside, that men are the reason they are in prison. They do know that they have been deserted and cast aside by their own black men. (I am sure you already know that when a black man becomes a Muslim, before or during incarceration, he becomes a part of a subgroup of Muslims inside; and when he is released, the mosque welcomes him with open arms. However, a Muslim woman is forgotten by the temple. In the Women's House, Muslim women renounce their faith because they have no support on the outside. The Muslim policy is that women have no business in jail anyway, or at least that's the way it seems.)

If you were to visit the women's prison, you would probably be shocked by the lack of hostility, the amount of warmth that is there; and racial bigotry is at a minimum. There is an awareness of prejudice, of the problems dividing the races, but there is also an awareness of the fact that all women are oppressed, whether white or black. The black woman inmate knows that the black man put a lot of her white sisters in jail.

In this drugged, deaf-and-dumb society, it is shocking to find people who are reacting to you and demanding that you react to them, as the women inmates do. As a matter of fact, it is very hard to get used to it, and you have to pull yourself up to it. Many of the women on the program never did get used to it.

Some of the inmates are having sexual relationships with one another, and, when they leave the prison, some of them will continue to do so, some of them will not; and those that will not, as far as I can determine, will not be hung up about it. Women have always done what they have had to do, and that was that. However, it is obvious that the special closeness and warmth and honesty between sisters in prison will disappear as soon as everybody hits the streets, for the men will be dividing them again. That warmth has to be preserved – not necessarily the lesbian activity, but the warmth. If such a bond existed between women all of the time, they just might be able to survive out of prison.

But that bond was just exactly what upset the do-gooders most. They couldn't deal with it. 1. Here they were trying to talk male revolution to the women inmates, and the women inmates were past all that, well on their way to feminism. 2. I suspected from the way a lot of the do-gooders seemed to be constantly getting involved in problems with the inmates propositioning them (why couldn't they simply say no?) that many of these do-gooders were lesbians themselves. Whether they were lesbians or not, the important thing is that it was increasingly difficult for them to face the lesbian activities of the inmates every Sunday. 3. The do-gooders, both lesbian and non-lesbian, were playing male roles, which is to say that they took the same position with respect to the inmates as would a man. They saw themselves as very different – they being superior and the inmates inferior – and all their actions had the effect of maintaining that difference. They used the powerless position of the inmates to make themselves look better, to distinguish themselves from the other women there and other women in general. There were lesbian inmates who were playing a similar role – and this made for the only hostility among the inmates. If you add that element of hostility to what the do-gooders brought in, then you will have some idea of the strain there was at times in the program. 4. All of this wasn't exactly conducive to warmth and honesty and unity.

The do-gooders were horrified by the fantastic independence of the women inmates, who brought to light the possibilities of a world actually dominated and run peacefully and satisfyingly by women; and every time someone got a peek of such a world, it seemed to just knock them senseless. No one was capable of admitting it, but that was the horror no one would verbalize; it made everybody try their damnedest to doom the program to failure.

As could be expected, all of these goings on frightened me considerably. Before long 'Art Without Walls' had collapsed. The prison would not continue to allow the program to come out. Their official reason was that they did not have the staff although they did allow a few of the workshops – the most unproductive and most reactionary ones – to come out separately. Strangely enough, none of these workshops was taught by black women. Ho-hum.

INMATES HELP INMATES

With my mere twenty years of life experiences behind me, what I really wanted to do was run. Instead, I chose to attempt to analyze the situation in the manner that I always do when movement things get fucked up, which is often. I try to be objective. I ask myself, 'Are blacks inferior? Are women really inferior?' I calmly answer, 'No.' 'But then what went wrong here?' I ask. 'You are dealing with rehabilitation,' I say to myself. 'You know male former inmates. How did they do it?' 'Why, they did it for each other,' myself says to I. And that is the answer – women inmates must do it for themselves. Only women inmates can help women inmates. White women, white men, black men and even other black women are all well aware of the problem, but none of us carries the solution. All any of us can do is try to put women inmates in a position to help other women inmates.

How? First you encourage the woman inmates' feminism as the only means by which they will be able to survive. You encourage their feminism because that will be what will enable them to stick together in a world that degrades and humiliates women, particularly black women. Feminism will be the thing that will enable the woman inmate to break the bonds of the shame that bounces them back to jail time and time again and keeps them there.

Second, you somehow set up an organization that will be financially solvent, and you set it up in such a manner that former women inmates will be able to assume all the positions in the organization as they are ready. What does this organization supply them with? They need two things from us – jobs and skills. Those two things will strengthen their feminism more than all the words in the world. Jobs and skills are pretty tall orders, even for women outside – then how do you do this for a woman who has just come out of jail? The former woman inmate cannot work on many of the jobs that women have always taken (because of her record). Further, the woman in prison is the woman who would not stay home and play nice-nice or work as a secretary or a maid and eat shit her whole life. If she is given the skills of an artist, then at least she can feel independent, at least she can feel self-confident about her worth. She'll know she can create something besides a baby; it's something she can do by herself, and art is a hustle anyway: it's something a woman can fight with. You can change people with it and you can stay out of prison with it, as did a lot of male former inmates who now earn livings as artists because they learned how in prison.

Third, you have to find some people to work with the program. They have to be women and they have to be feminists. It is better that they have a hard line on drugs and that not many be lesbians. Why? Because the overwhelming majority of women inmates are addicts. If a do-gooder doesn't know how she feels about drugs, or starts talking about 'hard' and 'soft', the situation becomes impossible. Reformed alcoholics never drink, no wine, no beer, no nothing, and that's the way it's got to be for addicts in a lot of cases. As for lesbianism, most women inmates do not identify as lesbians. Since the former woman inmate is not about to reject men, it is much more realistic to examine with her ways that one might go about relating to a man more positively, in other words, stop him from running over her. If a woman inmate is a lesbian, then naturally she needs the help of other lesbians. However, she does not need to be encouraged to play the male role, and of that you have to be very careful. (Do you know that there are female pimps?) A good-doer should either be black, or know something about black people. There is no time for people who are doing research on the race. These women are not guinea pigs. A good-doer should be capable, know her art, know how to teach it. The women inmates know when you're bullshitting.

So we were out on our asses, and a couple of do-gooder, do-nothing women are allowed to stay. What do we do now? It would have been nice to work in the prison, but it seems that that was not going to be possible. The prisons are just like any other governmental system, like the board of education, like the board of health. They don't want anything to happen, they don't want anyone to do anything because then it becomes too obvious that no one else is doing anything. The system cannot absorb, cannot afford productivity. It's a question of honor at this point, like the Vietnam War.

So we decided we were going to have to work outside of the prison. We would set up a kind of halfway house where women inmates could live, and we would set up workshops supplying the women with professional training in the arts. The program will expand according to the needs of the women. Former inmates will assume positions from the top down as soon as they are able or willing. The program will be run by feminist women until that happens, and being twenty, I think it will work. The program will be called 'Art Work House', and we are trying to get a loft and some money for it now – not to mention some feminists . . .

(1972)

6

The Dah Principle:

to be Continued

It was in 1981, one of those hot, sticky days that makes summertime the bane of all New Yorkers. Faith had just arrived home from MacDowell, an artists' colony in New Hampshire. She had barely said hello before she rolled out the eight large canvases that comprised the *Emanon* series (then still untitled), and the five small canvases that made up the *Baby Faith and Willi* series.

As the most figurative, I felt a communion with the *Baby Faith and Willi* series almost immediately. Their poignant musicality was self-evident in the lyrical use of browns, reds and blues. Their soft silver painted canvas frames only served to heighten this effect. They were simply blues pieces. That is to say, they were confirmation/celebration/ mourning pieces in recognition of the death of Faith's mother and my grandmother, Willi, and the birth of her first grandchild and my only niece, Baby Faith, both of which occurred within a time span of six months.[1]

It was as if Faith's experience of death and birth, neither of which can ever be talked about or thought of in a way that resolves, had been sifted through a dream – and she did, in fact, dream of both subjects often. Shadowlike heads floated through the pictorial space. The images were evocative, mysterious, yet as telling in their lack of detail as in their shimmering formlessness.

But the *Emanon* series, which was entirely abstract, was harder to accept. Her previously strict avoidance of anything like free abstraction had not prepared me for this sudden transition in her work. On the contrary, I thought we had settled the issue long ago when we had agreed that abstract painting was severely limited in its ability to depict emotional states, or much of anything else for that matter, that the nature of abstraction was essentially what everybody had always incorrectly attributed to crafts – it was decorative, inconsequential.[2]

This is not to say that Faith didn't admire and draw inspiration from some abstract art. Who could fail to note the engaging specificity of say, Mondrian's *Boogie Woogie* series, or Ad Reinhardt's *Black Paintings*, which prompted Faith's development of *Black Light*, or, more recently, the manner in which feminist artists (such as Catti) and black artists (such as Joe Overstreet) have engaged in a reinterpretation of abstraction that reflects their necessarily critical approach to formalist assumptions. But abstraction had never been Faith's particular choice for a combination of reasons.

What then had prompted her to reconsider? What had caused this radical shift away from the focus of the painting of the preceding years – often highly polemical, politically articulate and involving the re-evaluation of materials, techniques and 'distribution systems' from an 'Afro-femcentric' perspective? Again, it had a lot to do with the death of her mother and the birth of Baby Faith. From a practical point of view, Faith was no longer able to draw upon the sustenance of her collaboration with her mother, which had been so critical to the energy of this previous work. Further, she needed to find new means of expressing the new emotions she was feeling, of describing her encounter with the infinite/unknowable.

When pressed for explanations, Faith insisted that she could not explain *Emanon*, that she could only tell us that they were from deep in her soul, that they consisted of images that she could not avoid, that she had to paint them exactly as she had seen them.

My stepfather, Birdie, looked at the canvases and said, 'Mommy, you were very close to yourself when you were doing these paintings.'

'Yes,' Faith said and smiled. 'That's it exactly.'

But my stepfather and I came to love *Emanon* deeply, and to resent their absence when they were on tour. On one such occasion, when Faith was away as well with the paintings, Birdie commented, 'You kind of get used to having them around, don't you?' He has always been a master of understatement. I knew exactly what he meant.

Again, the musicality. Faith was invited to do a performance piece in conjunction with her first exhibition of *Emanon* at Joe Overstreet's and Corinne Jennings' Kenkeleba House on the Lower Eastside. In the organic way in which Faith's process always seems to permeate our family life, we all got involved. I found myself insisting upon a certain kind of music, which Birdie helped me to select.

We played hours and hours of Thelonius Monk, Miles Davis, Sonny Rollins, John Coltrane, Billie Holiday, Aretha Franklin singing Dinah Washington's songs, Dinah Washington herself, Nina Simone, Sarah Vaughan. And as we played this magical selection of music, we talked on and off of old times, some of them before I was born, of my natural father Earl Wallace, who was a classical and jazz pianist and the childhood companion of both my mother and my stepfather, of the musicians who gathered in our home on Edgecombe Avenue then to make music or get high, of their often tragic, often painful lives, of the nowhere/anyhow of the 50s, but also of the unremitting, unquestionable beauty/rightness of their aesthetic conceptions. It was during this procedure that the *Emanon* series got its name.

'I want to call it "Untitled",' Faith said. 'I don't want to call it anything.'

'Why don't you call it Emanon?' Birdie suggested. 'That's what Dizzy Gillespie did when he didn't want to be bothered with a title. Emanon spells no name backwards.'

Through this process, which included pondering Faith's unfathomable conception, our consciousness was not only raised but somehow, as well, we entered the space Faith had created. We came to understand that you don't just look at these paintings and count the colors, or rest. You have got to *feel* and listen to them.

In the performance piece, *Emanon I*, that Faith and I did with the help of a tape that included classical jazz and rhythm & blues, we tried to recreate the energy of those family meditation/memory sessions. Baby Faith, who was seven months old, was situated in her stroller almost in the center of the action. She looked at Faith and me dancing in our colorful robes and our African-like masks decorated with red and orange raffia, and she smiled. We had expected her to be afraid, but instead she listened to the music, cooed, clapped her hands and moved her feet to the rhythms. She was a participant. Her mother Barbara, my sister and Faith's daughter, stood beside her triumphant.

And then Aunt Barbara, Faith's sister, died, which meant that Faith had now lost all of her original immediate family. Aunt Barbara had loved Billie Holiday, so that's what we played at her funeral. We continued to listen to Billie for many days and nights afterwards on through the mournful season misleadingly referred to as the Christmas Holidays.

It reminded me of when Dinah Washington had died, shortly after having moved from the apartment in Harlem that we had come to occupy. For a long while afterwards, we played her music around the clock, in mourning yes, but also because her spirit had so recently flowed in the space in which we now lived, which we could not ignore. That was our introduction to our neighbors who, attracted by Dinah's inimitable voice, often knocked on our door to ask, 'Have you seen her?' I was eleven then and enchanted. So much art, it seems, requires living with.

So now we looked at those *Emanon* paintings, educated as we had been, once again, by the valley beyond the shadow of death, and we listened to Billie slow drag her way through her later performance (it was this work particularly that attracted us), and we thought of Aunt Barbara, who had never gotten over my grandmother's death, of Momma Jones (we grandchildren's name for Willi), of Faith's brother, Uncle Andrew, who had died at thirty-six, of Faith's father, Big Andrew, who had died it seemed not too many years back (it was ten), of my natural father Earl, who had died when I was thirteen, of the sense of having survived a war that one gets from being part of a Harlem family, of all the moments of death and birth that life has a way of pressing upon one, and I think we became different people. Those *Emanon* paintings began to look like great stained glass windows, as if they had sun and air in them instead of paint. They were not only new space but the possibility of space itself. Their essence was one of passages. Bigger than themselves.

But their airy optimism no longer reflected Faith's perspective. She began to paint again. This time, Faith said, her intention was to be discordant, to release herself from the desire to circumscribe or dictate the imagery, making the character of this work distinctly improvisational. The control came in the choice of color and the frequency of its occurrence. Her generous use of a metallic silver and gold made sound impressions that caused me to identify the end result with the creative journeys of Ornette Coleman, John Coltrane, McCoy Tyner, David Murray and Betty Carter.

We were all together when Faith began to work on the *Dah* series. More often than not, Baby Faith was running around or seated on the floor near Faith, playing with her toys. I was trying/not trying to work on my novel. Barbara was stopping by to discuss her dissertation on Masai grammar. It seemed like Birdie was always looking for dinner. To the extent that anything can make an impression upon such a busy environment, *Dah* caused a revolution in our household. As the images emerged, in the surprising way that flowers unfold as they bloom, it was clear that they would be much harder and uncompromising than anything we had seen in *Emanon*.

Everyone had an emotional reaction to this work, which both delighted and aggravated Faith. Barbara said the paintings look troubled. My stepfather just shook his head. Sometimes I slept in the room with them. They made frightening images in the dark that disturbed my sleep.

Baby Faith seemed to be the only one who knew what she was looking at. When two of the canvases were finished, she pointed a stubby finger at the painted surface and confidently announced, 'Dah!' which was how this work got its name.

Dah was Baby Faith's first word, the only word she ever used for what seemed a very long time. From the way she used it, it was clear she thought it covered everything. 'Dah!' she would insist over and over again until she had us, too, talking about Dah, no longer trying to figure out what it meant because, once you caught on, it was so obviously an affirmation/presumption of the creative imperative. Of its chaos/struggle/ sweetness. And after living with the *Dah* series and beginning to hear their music, I too began to see Dah, not to understand Dah, because you don't understand it anymore than you can understand anything really critical about the nature of the emergency called life. I don't think I need tell you but I will, the *Dah* series has now become a family standard too. Which, in this case, is another way of saying the road to recovery.[3]

(1984)

NOTES

1. You will find a lot of slashed words here as I grope for a language appropriate to Faith's current work.

2. Years earlier, Faith had done a series of highly formal, highly controlled abstractions called *Windows of The Wedding*, working with African Kuba design of eight radiating triangles. Faith used them to create environments for her soft sculptures, assuming that even these abstractions could not stand alone.

3. After I had referred to something called a Dah principle as the essence of creativity in describing Faith's *Dah* series for the catalogue to accompany the 'Jus Jass' exhibition of 1983 at the Kenkeleba House, Corinne Jennings pointed out to me that there was, in fact, a Dah Principle in the Congo, used to describe the nature of creativity.

7

Homelessness is Where the Heart Is

In Alice Walker's novel about the 1960s, Meridian is a black woman who becomes a civil rights leader by default. Everybody else has been martyred, turned cynical or graduated to black power. Bald, impoverished, emaciated, sickly, and virtually homeless, Meridian doesn't know how to quit. As the book opens, she is leading a demonstration protesting the segregation of a surrealistic local museum, or circus sideshow, in a small Southern town.

Twenty-five years before, Henry O'Shay, a white man and the present proprietor of the museum, had caught his wife Marilene 'cheating' on him with another man. He strangled her and threw her in a salt lake. Years later, he retrieved her permanently preserved body and placed it on display. 'One of the Twelve Human Wonders of the World', 'Preserved in Lifelike Condition', 'Obedient Daughter', 'Devoted Wife', 'Adoring Mother', 'Gone Wrong', the legends read on the side of the circus wagon that houses the corpse. Although exposure to the salt water had turned her skin dark, Henry suggests that viewers consider Marilene's long red hair as verification of her white race.

Meanwhile, segregation of those who attend the exhibition is not based on race but rather on keeping those who work in the guano (fertilizer) plant, and therefore smell, away from those who don't. Of course, most of the workers at the guano plant are black, and the segregation of plant workers covers their children as well. The children want to see the show, however, so Meridian – in pursuit of the letter of equality in the blatant absence of its spirit – is ready to lose her life to gain their admittance to the museum.

Herein Henry O'Shay's museum is revealed as a version of the crucial institution in Western culture: the mausoleum of dead ideas of aesthetic beauty, patriarchal authority, white supremacy and capitalist logic. Yet this project, in one form or another, is always ready to take on new life in the form of commercial or popular spectacle – I'm thinking of the Ollie North saga serialized on TV last summer – dulling our senses while consolidating our society's entrenched unwillingness to address the vital dilemmas of race, class, and sexuality in a constructive way. Walker signals to those of us who are black the danger that the final prize of 'equality' may be an endless rehash of patriarchy's lifeless and sordid melodramas.

Yet it is unclear whether we are supposed to regard Meridian's troubles as allegorical or concrete. Her homelessness is not called 'homelessness'. Her madness is not called 'madness'. Her feminism – being unwilling to play the role of wife and mother and determined to take her vocation seriously – is not called 'feminism'. While Meridian's plight vacillates between the existential and the heroic, the problems of self-definition she faces, concerning work, shelter, friends, family, morality and vocation, preoccupy the thoughts of many women (and men) of color these days. Yet the black community's faith in the transcendent virtues of the patriarchal still has us believing that what matters most is who your parents were. If you were born to the wrong parents with the wrong genes and the wrong habits, your longing for reformation and reconstruction will be continually thwarted, as much by the attitude of the world towards you as by your own programmatic convictions concerning your aptitude for change.

A tall white businessman once explained this to me on an airplane somewhere in the Midwest. He wasn't drinking, for he had once been an alcoholic. While he had managed to save himself from a 'useless life', there were others who didn't 'stand a chance'. If your mother was an alcoholic and your father was a junkie and you were therefore somehow genetically predisposed to poverty and public assistance, this man maintained, Alcoholics Anonymous wouldn't be able to help you. I was even enjoying the conversation until I began to think how this man might view the secrets of my family history. That I was a black female author on my way to do a college lecture, wearing my 'middle-class' face, automatically meant to him that I had no connection to the 'underclass' he thought he was describing.

But my father, a jazz pianist, had died of an overdose of heroin when I was thirteen, as had my only uncle, a gang leader, when I was nine. My aunt, a teacher, and my maternal grandfather had died of alcoholism. My paternal grandfather, perhaps the family's most likely positive masculine role model, an atheist and a socialist, is said to have turned down an opportunity to be a Rhodes Scholar because he preferred being a horticulturist (a gardener) to being a lawyer. He attended college in

Jamaica, taught at a girls' school where he was fired for fraternizing with the students, was dishonorably discharged from the military in the 1920s for 'inciting the troops to rebellion', hoboed his way across the US during the Depression and refused to work a desk job even when he could get it. When I first knew him during my childhood in the 50s, he enjoyed painting murals in Harlem apartment building lobbies and singing calypso to his own accompaniment on guitar. In his final years, he spent his time studying several African and European languages, doing the family gardening and working on and off as a messenger until he died in 1979.

Suppose Nature really meant everything, as this pillar of contemporary white patriarchy was suggesting? Moreover, had I ever heard anybody black propose a hipper way of understanding an individual and/or collective capacity for growth that didn't propose, as well, some airborne faith in Allah or Jesus Christ or 'Mother Africa'? Such thoughts made me squirm in my seat, order another drink, light another cigarette. When would my genes betray me, I wondered? When would all this madness and self-destruction win out? The day finally arrived in 1981.

That fall, my maternal grandmother, Momma Jones, died in her sleep, my sister announced she was pregnant with her first child (which for me was a kind of disaster because I knew this meant she probably wouldn't finish her PhD), my first novel was rejected by my publisher, and I had a 'serious nervous breakdown' in the middle of my first semester in the PhD program in American Studies at Yale. Because I was highly allergic to psychotropic drugs – including the so-called wonder drug lithium, which nearly killed me – my stay in Harlem Hospital was prolonged and complicated. There was an entire month during which I languished on a medical ward in a semi-conscious state of which I have no memory.

Meanwhile, my family, who had never approved of Yale (too Waspy), closed up my New Haven apartment and moved my things into storage in New York. I signed over my power of attorney and, although I was still the author of a successful book, I was as economically indigent as the average teenager, a condition not uncommon among mental patients. Yet I came out of the hospital January 4, 1982, my thirtieth birthday, feeling lucky to be alive, born again. Having narrowly escaped death – an intern from Peru had taken me off drugs despite the disapproval of his superiors – I felt tempted to turn to religion, so certain was I that I had transcended the past.

But Momma Jones was still dead. Barbara was still having a baby, for whom, as it turned out, I would be principal caretaker for the better part of the next two years. Key members of the generation of black intellectuals that preceded mine still resented me for my book. And there seemed no way to resume my studies at Yale or anyplace else, or to go on with my

career as I began the endless and unsuccessful rewriting of my nov
would trap me for the next five years.

I supplemented my small income from writing, lecturing,
consulting by working as a typist for a clerical temporary agency. I ..ed
first with my sister, then with my parents for the next two-and-a-half
years. Not a week went by that I didn't argue with them about the past,
why I had done this, why I hadn't done that, how I had come to be
'friendless and broke'. Meanwhile, many of my fellow inmates on the
psychiatric ward were released into the streets, having long ago run out
of family to take them in.

There was no transcending the past so long as I remained in the
Harlem of my birthplace, so long as I remained at home. Yet getting my
own apartment in New York seemed financially out of the question. So I
dreamed a black woman's dream that made no sense at all. I would
change my name, get on a Greyhound bus, and get off wherever it
stopped, begin a new life in a new place – like John Garfield or Henry
Fonda in some formulaic 1930s movie – washing dishes or slinging hash
at a no-name diner.

In an essay, 'Helping and Hating the Homeless: The Struggle at the
Margins of America' (*Harper's Magazine*, January 1987), Peter Marin
provides a preliminary breakdown of the categories of people who make
up the 'homeless' in the US. He includes: (1) Vietnam veterans (who
make up half of the males); (2) the mentally ill; (3) the physically
disabled and the chronically ill; (4) the elderly poor; (5) individuals and
families 'pauperized by the loss of a job'; (6) families headed by women;
(7) runaway children 'many of whom have been abused'; (8) legal and
illegal immigrants 'who are often not counted among the homeless', and
so on.

My favorite category on his list is 'alcoholics and those in trouble with
drugs (whose troubles often begin with one of the other conditions listed
here)' because finally Marin begins to provide some sense of the layering
of unfortunate circumstances that make 'homelessness' into the most
visible pathology in a domestic urban scene where, increasingly, people
who are not wealthy risk losing their homes. But Marin's favorite
category appears to be what he refers to as 'traditional tramps, hobos,
and transients, who have taken to the road or the street for a variety of
reasons and prefer to be there'. Marin's point is to defend the option of
marginality, the right to choose homelessness: 'We must learn to accept
that there may be people', he writes, 'who have seen so much of our
world that to live in it becomes impossible'.

I think I understand what he means about the need for a way to drop
out, but I don't believe there ever was, except in the movies, an

economic and social demilitarized zone to which people could escape. In fact, it seems more and more as though such notions of frontier were always exploitative, elitist and the exotic side of imperialistic. Just who is included in Marin's confident reference to 'our world'? When he writes of 'traditional tramps, hobos, and transients', I think of Red Skelton in a clown costume with a day-old beard pencilled in, or Meryl Streep and Jack Nicholson stumbling from public shelter to tavern, working through their middle-class angst, in the 1940s world of *Ironweed*. I don't think of Grandpa Bob, who hoboed because he couldn't get the kind of work he wanted as a horticulturalist just because he was black. I don't think of the 1980s in which AIDS, crack, the lack of affordable housing, hospitalization and health care, diminished employment opportunities and welfare benefits make poverty and homelessness inevitable for more and more people who don't 'have it all together'. Our world is their world, too.

So this is no confession. I'm not sure what happened to me, whether I truly went insane or I was merely fed up with the hypocrisy of everyday life, as Marin might suggest, since psychiatry now strikes me as both a laughable profession and a dangerous practice of social control. Perhaps it is more important to realize how madness is one very effective means by which poor and/or dependent populations contain themselves and are contained by others. 'Crazy' is a word I hear being used more and more often to describe what people do to one another and themselves in their 'leisure' time, perhaps in order to accommodate, simultaneously, the limited choices and the much more extensive choicelessness of our present living arrangements.

I'm thinking of the Steinberg and the Chambers cases, especially of Hedda Nussbaum's broken nose and the videotape of Chambers mocking his lethal act of 'rough sex', both of which were shown again and again on television. I'm thinking about the violence that people of color visit upon one another and themselves that receives much less national coverage, but that gets lots of airtime on local news shows across the country, especially in small towns where the diverse ethnicity of nearby cities is still considered an aberration. Most of all I'm thinking of Tawana Brawley, who was surely raped and defecated on by somebody. It infuriates me to hear the television or *The New York Times* pose the question, yet again, 'What really happened to Tawana Brawley?' As though our electronic and print media, our court system, our local and state governments, our police, as well as the 'community' forces that purport to have Tawana's best interest at heart, had ever been remotely interested in the plight (or the dreams) of the teenage black girl – much less as she might articulate it in her own words.

Although I feel fairly certain that the medical establishment's notion of madness is self-serving, exploitative, socially constructed – as Thomas Szasz, R.D. Laing, Wilhelm Reich, Michel Foucault, and a host of others have suggested – I do believe in madness at the level of individual consciousness, because I don't believe that everything and everybody makes sense. Perhaps madness exists in place of individual consciousness for some of us. In its most severe forms (barring the furthest reaches of the biochemical which, however, I don't pretend to understand), I see it as the inevitable by-product of imposing conventional and/or patriarchal notions of family and morality in all sorts of dysfunctional ways – one reason why women have always been the particular target of the institutionalization of mental health.

To be specific, my sojourn among mad people of color and their numerous administrators (mostly not of color), the journey I traveled from psychiatric to medical ward in Harlem Hospital, one of the largest, multiracially run state hospitals in the world, has made apparent to me the need for a rigorous critique of the black family. It is impossible for me to imagine any longer that white supremacy, patriarchy, and capitalism form a simple, coherent unity or sequence. While there is no question in my mind that they are connected in some 'crazy' way, these connections don't entail that they can be dealt with in tandem or by one set of measures. To know that each of them is endlessly specific and contextual is much more important than determining which has more impact, in some abstract sense, or which came 'first'.

Patriarchy, in particular, can seem woefully irrelevant to our political and economic existence as black people, to our so-called 'extended families', our frequently female-headed families, and our large numbers of under-employed, incarcerated and drug-addicted men. But the ideal of the patriarchy is kept alive, nevertheless, in the rhetoric of our leaders, who rely on nostalgic and conservative notions of 'the strength of the black family' as the inevitable source of high SAT scores, widespread drug rehabilitation, safe sex, college diplomas, the elimination of the welfare rolls and child abuse, and all the myriad benefits of 'life, liberty, and the pursuit of happiness'.

Even in some of our most rigorous and well meaning Afro-American intellectual and activist traditions of protest and self-improvement, the secret ingredient more often than not has been some black approximation of patriarchal authority and know-how. Nor am I advocating dispensing with the assertion of black male authority and power as a goal of black liberation. As long as white male authority and power exist, such tactics will be indispensable to Afro-American and African survival in this country and the world. Rather, I am proposing the aggressive development of a feminist critical sphere – a heightened critical awareness on the part of black men and women of the inherent and inevitable shortcomings of masculinist authority as a crucial way of conceptualizing the downward mobility of the masses of black children (of whom I am one) unlucky enough to be born to fathers who don't know how, and may never learn, to take advantage of affirmative action.

(1988)

PART II

Pop

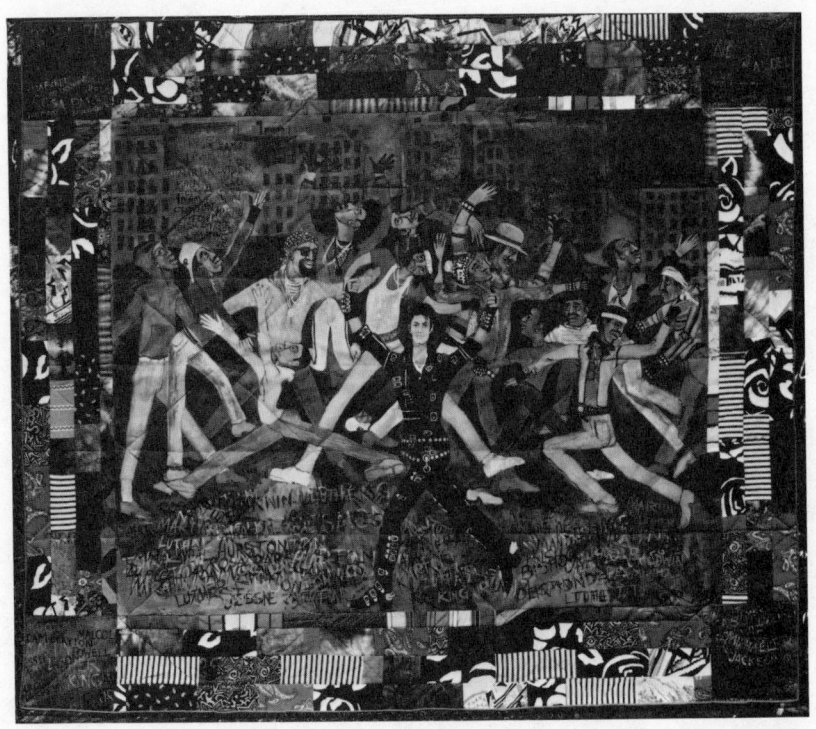

'Who's Bad? Painted Quilt' by Faith Ringgold

8

Blues for Mr Spielberg

I first saw *The Color Purple* Christmas Eve in a theatre in Oklahoma City. It was the same theatre in which I had seen *A Passage to India*, another book adaptation stressing the surrealism of the minimally civilized and the incomprehensibility of women. I watched in mute astonishment the same grand sweeps of the camera over lush landscapes and masses of dark faces, the same trivialization of nonwhite culture and female pain. It was even worse than I expected.

In the theatre I'm surrounded by white people in baseball caps and cowboy boots, the uniform in these parts, and there's a lot of frantic guffawing every time Mr goes upside Celie's head. It starts at the beginning of the film, when the adolescent Celie emerges from behind a bush, hugely pregnant, and it doesn't stop. The members of this typically Oklahoman audience seem to feel the film has been made for their amusement and approval, a comic *Birth of a Nation*, confirming their suspicions about how little black people matter. They don't have to deal with Spielberg's attempts to make witty jabs at racism and sexism – like placing Mr in the slavemaster role as he dramatically separates Celie and Nettie – so they don't. They side with the film's humor and titillation, just as they probably sided with Archie Bunker when he battled that show's liberal superego, his son-in-law. Except here there's no liberal superego.

When I heard that the director of such wistfully hegemonic film fables as *Close Encounters of the Third Kind*, the boy wonder of pop culture, Steven Spielberg, would direct *The Color Purple*, I was immediately alarmed. For all its ostentatious success in the marketplace, Alice Walker's novel is experimental. Its point of view is that of Celie, whose real-life counterpart would ordinarily be perceived as radically marginal, even in the black community itself. Walker's object, I assume, is to arrive at a feminist vision of black community that rejects the foregone conclusions of the upwardly and outwardly mobile bourgeoisie – a major concern of Afro-American feminist literature. Since Spielberg was unlikely to be familiar with this concern, I braced myself for the inevitable shock, the blunt edge of uninformed translation.

After all, I am deeply susceptible to paranoia. I am black, a woman, an ex-New Yorker, and my presence in hypnotically tranquil Oklahoma has done nothing to reduce that susceptibility. At first it was Indian Territory, once envisioned as the promised land by blacks hoping to escape racism in the western migration of the 1870s. This image of frontier soon dispersed under the hoofs of the Boomers, who rushed in before the official opening of the territory to white men; the Sooners, who rushed in before statehood; and the sundown laws ('Nigga, don't let the sun set on you' signs at either end of a town) that rushed black folks out of white towns and into their own separately incorporated black towns. Now Oklahoma is about 7 per cent Native American (although many Oklahomans claim partial Indian ancestry) and 6 per cent black; vastly barren and oil-well laden, usually balmy, and strikingly under-populated with three million people. There's no such thing as a crowd in Oklahoma, except at football games.

Occasionally, from my perpetual stance as outsider, I am able to weigh the pros and cons of Oklahoma. Sometimes I see it as the typical American heartland of wife beating, unexpected violence, people who insist on radio talk shows that they don't want or need seat belts, car insurance, or AFDC; other times, as a land of panoramic sunsets, southwestern hospitality (which is muted and practical), bumper crops of marijuana, liquor by the drink. But increasingly I notice that the scarcity of blacks and the docility of the women make racism and sexism the always already said, as implacable as Oklahoma's omnipresent red dirt.

This is my second year teaching Afro-American literature, feminist literature, and creative writing at the University of Oklahoma in Norman. I explain feminism, blackness, and the improbable creativity of both to Oklahoma youth. Lately this job has involved explaining Alice Walker's *The Color Purple* – or more precisely, putting up with in-creasingly enthusiastic explanations from the book/movie's vast local audience. This audience includes not only most of my students, but also fellow faculty. In restaurants, in the gym, in the hallways before and after class, they smile knowingly and ask me, 'How do you like *The Color Purple*?' giving me no more than two beats to answer – presumably I like it – before they launch into their own feelings. Since I alone, of all the beings in their universe, teach Afro-American literature, it's unthinkable that I won't understand the rare communion they feel with this book/ movie. In these dog days of the movie's success, they seek no enlightenment from me, only confirmation. I'll admit to immediate suspicion of white readers in Oklahoma who tell me they love Celie, since it seems to me they spend their lives avoiding Celie and her problems. On the other hand, life is one thing, novels and movies are another.

Walker's portrait of Celie is part of an ongoing series of attempts by black authors – Toni Morrison, Ntozake Shange, John Edgar Wideman, David Bradley, to name a few – at providing alternatives to reductionist interpretations of black community by social scientists, both black and white. Such efforts are the product of an extended internal debate within the black artistic and intellectual community, beginning with various assertions of a black aesthetic in the 60s. These authors are trying (despite the dismay of a frequently baffled black middle-class readership) to locate and define a presently inarticulate black center. The goal is an imagination through which the seeming chaos, brutality, and sensualism of the black community will not only make sense but also generate its own aesthetic and spiritual possibilities.

In most influential twentieth-century Afro-American literature, portrayals of black community are deeply ambivalent. On the one hand, the community may offer certain protections and compensations. On the other, the community is a result of segregation and poverty, not fraternal feelings or collective purpose. And so the protagonist, usually radically individualistic, either endures some degree of spiritual alienation from the community as the price of creative identity or is destroyed/consumed. Even when deliverance comes, it is apt to be in the form of exile, hibernation, catastrophe, madness, or death.

The critique of Western patriarchy – which describes the enterprise of Afro-American writers since the 60s as well as anything else – runs all the deeper in recent literature by Afro-American women. Perhaps it's because we are the most disenfranchised by patriarchy; we are not only victims of the master's manipulations, but also suffer at the hands of all his symbolic intermediaries – black men and white women, for instance – who would instruct us how to please him. Although this literature by black women may appear obsessed with the day-to-day shortcomings of black male behavior, its real point is to clarify black men's failure to see beyond the meager compensations patriarchy offers them in exchange for most of their, and our, dignity and freedom. Similarly, these writers depict white female characters, rarely creatures to be admired, usually trapped in their peculiarly feudal relationship to the seat of power.

More to the point, this literature is about reconstructing black female experience as positive ground. One metaphor for this enterprise is the black woman's blues. The black female blues singer as a paradigm of commercial, cultural, and historical potency pervades twentieth-century Afro-American literature by women. Beginning with Zora Neale

Hurston's use of lines transparently derived from blues lyrics in *Their Eyes Were Watching God*, I don't think I've ever read a book by a black woman writer that does not include some reference to the fact that Afro-American women have sung the blues for a living, and sung them well. Among younger black women writers, in particular Gayle Jones, Ntozake Shange, and Gloria Naylor, black woman's blues is an explicit source of content and form.

Another metaphor is lesbianism – an option in Naylor's *The Women of Brewster Place* and Shange's *Sassafrass, Cypress and Indigo*, as well as informing an infinite array of otherwise inexplicable innuendo in works by older black women writers. Further, there is by now a tradition of black feminist lesbian poetry, beginning with our most celebrated black lesbian poet, Audre Lorde. Like abstinence (which gets scant tribute in this literature), lesbianism functions in these works as a choice that says I love who loves me, and I won't love who doesn't love me. Singing the blues and lesbianism, as opposite ends of the same act of self-affirmation – ranging from the material and symbolic to the personal and sexual – are critical to defining the spectrum of possibilities for black women beyond servility and self-abnegation.

In *The Color Purple*, Walker draws from a tradition of black male and female variations on the call-and-response patterns of the blues. These patterns set up an exhaustive dialogue about how male–female relations in the black community reflect material conditions, political impotence, and white male supremacy. The dialogue reappears in black literature. Among black women writers, the key figure is Zora Neale Hurston; *Their Eyes Were Watching God* responds on many levels to the black male writers of the Harlem Renaissance, then offers a new call that recognizes previously unconsidered dimensions of black female experience and black community. In *The Color Purple*, Walker responds to Hurston's call by refiguring Hurston's figure of black women as the mules of the earth.

For Walker, lesbianism, which is never called that in the novel, becomes a kind of developmental narcissism, essential to Celie's discovery of orgasm, and so to her accomplishment of self-esteem. If orgasm is half as important to women as male writers like Mailer, Miller, and Reich have claimed it is to men – and I think it is – then the theme is critical to any discussion of female power. In black feminist literature that engages with the black woman's blues, lesbianism, like the male–female dialogue, is part of the larger issue of desire. But Walker's revolutionary reconception of the subject in the first half of *The Color Purple* is undermined in the second half, with its abrupt and premature solutions.

Walker's previous novels – *The Third Life of Grange Copeland* and *Meridian* – explore the cruelty of male–female relationships and parent-

hood under the pressures of poverty and racism in a perversely patriarchal black community. Each of these novels has its provisionally
satisfactory resolution, but what's really compelling in both books is
Walker's discourse (particularly in *Meridian*) on the inability of the Civil
Rights and Black Power movements to solve the moral and ethical
problems of sexism. Enter *The Color Purple*, the closest thing to a utopian
Afro-American novel I've ever read. The idea (it's just that skeletal in
presentation) that supports the utopian vision is that the black woman's
perspective – the archetypal experience of her oppression as lived by
Celie – is critical to realizing a feminist ideal of community. Most of the
characters end up miraculously transcending the alienation and disfigure-
ment of polar male–female roles. This approach, which Walker calls
'womanist' instead of feminist, softens men, strengthens women, and
turns economic, political, and racial frustration into manageable units at
an astonishing rate.

The Color Purple is not a realistic novel; its primary concern is not with
characterization or individual growth. Rather, in a narrative that harks
back to such literary traditions as the fable and the romance, community
is redefined in blunt strokes. Walker defines God as a personal spirit
without gender, undermining the cornerstone of white Western patriarchy; she presents female orgasm as an experience critical to adult
female self-esteem; finally, she proposes constructive, profitable creativity
as the way to transcend pain, keep track of history, and turn the negative
into the positive. These themes are interwoven in the book. The
traditional image of God as a stern, elderly white patriarch is reconceived
as the cushy inside of a clitoral orgasm, the appreciation of the color
purple, public acts of female creativity. The patriarchy's sexism, crimes of
the father against the daughter, are transcended – the depth of female
experience takes their place – because the daughters have grown up to
mother the world.

Needless to say, this is all a bit of a fantasy, which granted is no
particular sin in the writing of fiction. It seems to me that in most cases
the truth of experience is aggravatingly pointless, resistant to didactive
messages (Martin Luther King Days and space shuttle explosions
notwithstanding), that the essentials of life are stubbornly material and
costly. God seems dead in precisely the same way my grandmother died
five years ago and I can no longer ask her what she thinks about
anything.

It seems not accidental that Walker's vision should have met with
such an enthusiastic reception – a Pulitzer Prize, mammoth sales among
black and white readers – precisely at the moment when black
community is in profound crisis, with accelerating rates of high school
dropouts, imprisonment, teenage births, unemployment, impoverished

female-headed families (all symptomatic of resistance by both conservatives and reformers to empowering women). For the American public, surrounded by so many alarming fluctuations in the reign of patriarchy, *The Color Purple* must have been reassuring to read. Given the chance, it implies, women won't lead so much as nurture. Furthermore, the characters are black, rural, and situated in a nebulous version of the 30s and 40s (no signs of the Great Depression, for instance), rendering the immediate prospects of matriarchy safely remote.

In the movie, we have the response to Walker's call. Spielberg juggles film clichés and racial stereotypes fast and loose, until all signs of a black feminist agenda are banished, or ridiculed beyond repair. Amid crackling thunder, numerous melodramatic partings and reunions, garishly picturesque blacks grinding it up wall to wall in Harpo's juke joint, we are treated to the epic version of *Amos 'n' Andy*, the cellulite-ridden backside of *Gone With the Wind*, *Porgy and Bess*, and *North and South*. The touches of undigested Charles Dickens and Flannery O'Connor don't make the mixture any more palatable. Upwardly and outwardly mobile are back on the menu.

As for Alice Walker's experimental content, all but a shadow of its feminism has vanished. For Spielberg, matriarchy is a disjointed fantasy of female power that exists in a vacuum and appears, inexplicably, like Topsy, who 'jes grew'. Celie is not so much marginal as simply an old-fashioned underdog. In the book Celie, victimized by the death of her mother, forced separation from her sister, incest, an abusive marriage, and battering, is resurrected by her admiration for Shug Avery, a locally prominent blues singer. Shug symbolizes the black female creative tradition of such blues virtuosos as Ma Rainey, Victoria Spivey, Bessie Smith, and Billie Holiday. The point is not their saintliness, or even their heroism, but their cathartic assimilation of experience. Shug abandons her children but nurtures the women around her. Her knowledge of love's disappointments becomes her ability to write and perform the blues.

At the bottom of her constructive power is a vigorous sexual desire that will not consent to abstraction. Celie is a virgin, Shug tells her, because she's never known orgasm, despite having borne her stepfather two children and being virtually raped by her husband. Shug confers transcendence on Celie through lesbian sexual initiation. Then Celie and Shug communicate their transcendence to the women and men around them – Harpo, Sofia, Mary Agnes, Mr,.even across the ocean, it seems, to Nettie, the Reverend, and Corinne, who are struggling with African patriarchy and colonial imperialism.

In the movie, Shug (played by Margaret Avery like Lena Horne's

Good Witch of the West in the film *The Wiz*) seems less the embodiment of the black female blues spirit than some ahistorical hybrid of the Cotton Club and the Ziegfeld follies. Celie obviously loves Shug, but it's Hollywood love, a series of chaste kisses. 'Smile, Miss Celie,' Shug insists repeatedly. Am I the only woman for whom such a demand recalls all those endless childhood-into-adulthood requests to smile, just smile? Shug seems oblivious and indifferent to Celie as she goes off on another singing tour, even though Celie has confided that Mr beats her when Shug's not around.

In the movie, God the father is not deconstructed but re-verified, contradicting the book in spirit as well as content. Shug is preoccupied with the disapproval of her minister father, who will not speak to her because she sings the blues and because she's borne Mr children outside marriage. Their rapprochement provides the film with its climax. First, Shug gets married – the film hints she's done so to please her father. Then she stops singing the blues, mid-song, and turns out a jam session at Harpo's juke joint, where she is reigning queen, to join her father's congregation in a raucous rendition of Andre Crouch's blatantly contemporary 'Speak Lord'. Speak Lord? Simultaneously, Mr sees the error of his ways – God knows why – and goes to the immigration board to verify the citizenship of Celie's sister Nettie and Celie's children, who have been raised in Africa.

There are lots of little white patriarchal interventions all along the way. In the book Sofia is the epitome of a woman with masculine powers, the martyr to sexual injustice who eventually triumphs through the realignment of the community. In the movie, she is an occasion for humor. She and Harpo are the reincarnation of Amos and Sapphire; they alternately fight and fuck their way to a house full of pickaninnies. Harpo is always falling through the roof he's chronically unable to repair. Sofia is always shoving a baby into his arms, swinging her large hips, and talking a mile a minute. Harpo, who's dying to marry Sofia in the book, seems bamboozled into marriage in the film. Sofia's only masculine power is her contentiousness. Encircled by the mayor, his wife, and an angry white mob, she is knocked down and her dress flies up, providing us with a timely reminder that she is just a woman.

Somebody recently explained to me that a certain woman writer was not really a feminist, although she said she was, because of her apparent ambivalence about it. To which I responded, is there any other feminism but the ambivalent kind? The alliance of black feminist forces and Hollywood is documented in the December issue of *Ms*, where Walker is still a contributing editor. A cover story by Susan Dworkin tells us that among Walker's advisers were Barbara Christian, preeminent black feminist literary critic and professor at UC Berkeley, and Quincy Jones, the black pop composer and reigning master of crossover music.

Perhaps because of Jones' role as producer of USA for Africa, the ordinarily movie-shy Walker thought his involvement in the project guaranteed its artistic and political integrity. Apparently, Spielberg won her over just as easily when he first proposed making the film. 'What impressed me', Walker is quoted as saying, 'was Steven's absolute grasp of the essentials of the book, the feeling, the spirit.' She concludes, 'We may miss our favorite part' (the understatement of the year), 'but what is there will be its own gift. . . .' Which only goes to show that few display the old feminist fervor and purism anymore. Flo Kennedy's 'Kick ass and take names' is forgotten while 'out of the streets and into the suites', also Flo's, assumes the authority of divine providence in the never-never-land of famous feminists. 'Let's make a deal,' we say in the 80s, and Walker has made hers. Predictably, some blacks – probably not a majority – wish she hadn't.

Also predictably, the movie – with its villainous, sinister male characters and its obscenely virtuous female characters – has given rise to controversy and debate within the black community, ostensibly focused on the eminently newsworthy issue of the film's image of black men. But in a way, all the indignation misses the point. Artists always turn the experience of other ethnic, national, and sexual groups into suburbs or outposts of their own; inevitably, Spielberg has made black men into icons, through which he projects his ambivalences about masculinity and male–female relations.

What's really at issue here is that visions of the black experience from a black perspective rarely receive wide distribution in this society. Which means that when a vision like The Color Purple's gains prominence, we may have to live with it for a long time, in good weather and bad, together with the various rumbles of the landlocked national ship. It's happened before, and it will keep happening as long as black access to the media is severely circumscribed. Every time a book or television show or film breaks the customary silence and sparks the national imagination – like Soul on Ice or Roots or For Colored Girls or even my own Black Macho – the sheer scarcity of such texts forces us to ask what this one will do to our situation. Inevitably, we regard the new, uninvited addition to our cultural baggage with suspicion, particularly when a figure like Spielberg plays porter.

Perhaps because there seemed to be no black women whatsoever on the screen a year or two ago, I was not much bothered by Sheena, Queen of the Jungle, in which the former model Elizabeth, Princess of Toro, played some kind of combination mammy-witch doctor. In fact, I was relieved to see so many black people finally on the screen, regardless of the context, which in this case was a minstrel version of East Africa. But when *Gentlemen Prefer Soldiers* (or whatever it was called) won the Oscar for the superb black actor Lou Gossett, I knew we were in for some major revision in the role of black male actors in American film.

Ever since then, I've been watching black male actors blossom into sidekicks, variations on Huck's Jim, in the *Star Wars* and *Rocky* sequels, *Places in the Heart*, *The River*, *Trading Places*, and *White Nights*, and black women actors get lighter and lighter — à la Lonette McKee in *The Cotton Club*, whose character passes for white — until they almost dematerialize. Now and then a black woman pops up in a surprising place, like an afterthought on sexism — Tina Turner in *Mad Max*, Grace Jones in *View to a Kill*, the maid in *The Purple Rose of Cairo*, Iman in *Out of Africa*.

For me, the bitter humor of all this has been the backswiping at black women artists, starting with the ludicrous casting of Patti Labelle as the 40s Southern blues singer in *A Soldier's Story*. Hollywood seems determined to deepen the black woman's blues while turning it into a joke. At least black men can look to whatever hope John Sayles' *Brother from Another Planet* may represent; on the other hand, it worried me a lot that the most sympathetic and interesting black male character I've almost ever seen in a movie (I can't think of even one competing example) was entirely unable to speak in any language.

The fact is there's a gap between what blacks would like to see in movies about themselves and what whites in Hollywood are willing to produce. Instead of serious men and women encountering consequential dilemmas, we're almost always minstrels, more than a little ridiculous; we dance and sing without continuity, as if on the end of a string. It seems white people are never going to forget Stepin Fetchit, no matter how many times he dies.

Not that these images of comic servility are completely inappropriate. The behavior they portray was born of a concrete economic, political, and historical situation, first known as slavery, then Jim Crow, then de facto racism, and it's an important component of any true story about American blacks. What's infuriating in a movie like *The Color Purple* is that the shine of the coon and the humorlessness of the buck are given full time, while the material conditions that produced these responses are not depicted at all. I suspect that blacks who wish to make their presence known in American movies will have to seek some middle ground between the stern seriousness of black liberation and the tap dances of Mr Bojangles and Aunt Jemima. Even then I'm not sure they'll find it. From my vantage point in 'the heart of the heart of the country', I've learned what it really means to be a minority. It means you'd better melt quickly or reconcile yourself to being a footnote.

Perhaps now there'll be more money for independent black filmmakers who will provide us with multiple, simultaneous variations on the theme of black experience. Then again, perhaps when Whoopi Goldberg and *The Color Purple* win a few Oscars, that will be our cathartic racial experience for this half decade and we'll return to our customary slumber. For it's my conviction that the token exception – in this case a film about blacks taken from a black woman's book – only proves and strengthens the rule, the unmarked case: white films about white subjects designed to question, challenge, and stimulate white audiences.

I went to see *The Color Purple* again the day after New Year. This time there was a modest line in front of the theatre. The audience was larger and predominantly black, a rare phenomenon in Oklahoma. The laughter was obviously less sneering, more sympathetic, although the kissing scene between Celie and Shug still got titters. I, too, was more relaxed now that there were no surprises. I can't deny the movie's entertaining. There's a peak experience a minute, so there's plenty to watch.

As I left the theatre for popcorn, I heard a middle-aged black couple acting out their own little drama in the back row. As Mr committed yet another injustice against Celie, the woman said, with great annoyance, 'Shit, I wouldn't take that mess!' The man laughed nervously and responded, in what was clearly meant to be a soothing voice, 'It's a movie, baby, you know, *just* a movie!'

(1986)

9

Michael Jackson, Black Modernisms

and 'The Ecstasy of Communication'

According to a recent quantifying study of MTV, videos featuring white males take up 83 per cent of the 24-hour flow. Only 11 per cent of MTV videos have central figures who are female (incidentally, the figure is even lower for blacks), and women are typically, like blacks, rarely important enough to be part of the foreground.

E. Ann Kaplan

We must therefore begin to think of cultural politics in terms of space and the struggle for space. Then we are no longer thinking in old categories of critical distance but in some new way where the disinherited and essentially modernist language of subversion and negation is conceived differently.

Fredric Jameson

Any evaluative interpretation of Michael Jackson's recent contribution to the music video scene must constantly struggle for space alongside considerations of consumerism and televisual postmodernism. But perhaps it is precisely these conditions that provide the ground for a different conception of 'the disinherited and essentially modernist language of subversion and negation'. Music videos are a prime example of how consumer society or late capitalism has co-opted the alternative and/or the oppositional in a once avant-garde rock'n'roll/rhythm & blues aesthetic. A hybrid of music performance documentaries and television ads, music videos not only sell us what we expect to be free, namely our own private and unfulfillable desires, but they also make it increasingly impossible to distinguish between the genuine mass appeal of an artist and the music industry's simulation of that appeal.

Further, the encroaching 'postmodernism', or nonsensical redundancy and fragmentation of the televisual medium, particularly in its music-

video format, implies a lack of 'interpretative depth', which Marxist critic
Fredric Jameson describes as 'the idea that the object [is] fascinating
because of the density of its secrets and that these [are] then to be
uncovered by interpretation. All that vanishes.'[1] Here Jameson refers to
a postmodern aesthetics marked by its rejection of historical sequence
and individual subjectivity as supreme organizational principles. In other
words, music videos are irreversibly implicated in what Jean Baudrillard
would call 'the ecstasy of communication', in which 'all secrets, spaces
and scenes' are 'abolished in a single dimension of information'.[2] So we
might reasonably conclude that there's nothing to say.

Yet despite music-video consumerism and televisual postmodernism's
powerful deterrences to interpretation – especially the kind of interpretation that bestows value – there are extenuating circumstances
indicating that Jackson's videos may be capable of playing a key role in
evolving public discourses of race, sex, and class. First, Jackson is a black
performer. Given his race, he has achieved an entirely unprecedented and
gargantuan fame in a previously white supremacist music industry, which
routinely objectifies and colonizes the Third World and people of color.
He may in fact be, as his own media hype never tires of suggesting, the
new Elvis Presley or the new Beatles. Or perhaps he might have been –
as Jesse Jackson might have been president – if not for racism.

In any case, not only does Michael Jackson's extraordinary fame and
wealth mean that he may be able to supersede previous (dispersed and
inarticulate) standards of industry control, Jackson's videos are also first
rehearsed in a special format, independent of the unrelenting twenty-
four-hour flow of videos, music news, and DJ chatter on VH1 and MTV.
These peculiar shows constitute a curious new form of television program
as unnameable as it is unspeakable. None of this means that Jackson
escapes the corrupting influence of the commercial. Rather, I am
suggesting that Jackson, both because of his race and his extraordinary
success (even if it is equal parts hype and reality), has reached the stage
at which we can usually expect an artist, consciously or unconsciously, to
show signs of public resistance to his own formulaic social construction.

As for postmodernism, Jackson's status as a black male is even more
important in understanding his case as an exception to the rule. The past
for Afro-American culture, particularly that oral 'tradition' (which
includes jokes, stories, toasts, black music from spirituals to funk, and
black English)[3] pursued by the black masses has been precisely a
postmodern one inevitably inscribing (and inscribed by) our absence
from history, the dead-end meaninglessness of the signifiers, 'equality',
'freedom', and 'justice', and our chronic invisibility to the drama
of Western civilization and European high culture. It should thus
come as no surprise when the telltale 'schizophrenia' and 'pastiche' of

postmodernism are considered by some black artists to be characteristic of the enemy within, or racism internalized. In contrast, the most enlightened trends in contemporary Afro-American culture are in consistent pursuit of meaning, history, continuity, and the power of subjectivity. I am calling these various, heterogeneous, and sometimes conflicting efforts, Black Modernisms, of which Jackson's recent performance is perhaps a new type.

There aren't too many people in the media who agree with me. In fact, it is precisely the breadth of the Michael Jackson controversy that has drawn me to this topic. Where does this controversy focus its attention? Is it on his videos, his music, his wealth, his fame, his sexuality, his race, his lifestyle, his aesthetics, his unwillingness to be interviewed, his family, his plastic surgery, his skin lightening and hair straightening, or is it some ineffable combination of any or all of the above? Why, at this moment, at the peak of his career, is he being attacked and criticized on all sides? Why not attack Bob Dylan, who is also more wealthy than political; Prince, who also exhibits signs of ambiguous sexuality and plastic surgery? Is it because Jackson's album announces that he's 'Bad'? Why was his sister, Janet Jackson, not attacked when she announced that she was in 'Control' on her album, in the process utilizing many of her brother's stylistic trademarks? What is the criticism really about? Where does it come from? Could it have to do with Jackson's participation in what E. Ann Kaplan describes as a 'second, softer androgynous group' of rock performers (that includes Annie Lennox, David Bowie, and Boy George), which is 'not so concerned to stress the masculine that lies beneath the feminized veneer' and is 'less obviously (and manipulatively) erotic'?[4] Could it be that we find it intolerable to hear a black male speak from this position, especially now that his recent videos substantiate that he thinks of himself as speaking for/to the black male?

More than once in the supermarket checkout line, I've noticed covers of The Star and The Enquirer that exhibited an intense preoccupation with the question of whether or not Jackson has ever had sex with a 'girl'. These headlines offer one sign of how Jackson has lately been marked 'other' in the entertainment industry. Another kind of sign has been the way The Village Voice – or young, hip, left-liberal opinion in general – has turned against him: 'There's no longer any question that Michael Jackson is America's pre-eminent geek,' Guy Trebay wrote recently. In the same issue of the Voice, black cultural critic Greg Tate described Jackson's plastic surgery as the 'savaging of his African physiognomy' in an article entitled ' "I'm White!" What's Wrong With Michael Jackson.'[5] But all this criticism seems to circle around the same problematic of racial and sexual difference, the inauthenticity and untrustworthiness that are implied when such issues are invoked by a black male (instead of, say, Diahann Carroll), because 'Michael just looked too much like a woman to strut around like a homeboy in chains,' as one of Trebay's respondents said of Jackson in the video *Bad*.

A recent *New York Times* article, written by Jon Pareles and entitled 'A Political Song That Casts its Vote for the Money', attacks Jackson's work directly, apparently ignoring his persona. Pareles characterized Jackson's *Man in the Mirror* as 'the most offensive music video clip ever' because 'its particular sales pitch is that buying the song equals concern over issues....' Part of Pareles' complaint is that the video wouldn't arouse would-be censors: 'there's not a whiff of sex, no blood and little violence'. And, 'Mr Jackson doesn't show up either.'[6] In a consummate gesture of objectivity, Pareles pretends to be color blind, but in the process he only renders invisible (i.e. irrelevant) Jackson's race, the races of people who suffer 'the homelessness and poverty' that he says the video only 'glances at'), and the video's unmistakeable preoccupation with racism and white-supremacist values. Perhaps this is why Pareles thinks the video, like the song, 'points no fingers, reveals no underlying causes, assigns no blame, suggests no action'. Perhaps this is also why Pareles didn't see Jackson in the video, for he is certainly there in one of the final frames, laughing, a small figure in red in a sea of Japanese children, who appear to be tickling him. Jackson, as was explained in *The Making of Thriller* video, is very ticklish.

The refrain of 'Man in the Mirror' is 'I'm starting with the man in the mirror. I'm asking him to make a change. No message could have been any clearer. If you wanna make the world a better place, take a look at yourself and make a change, change, change, change'. Certainly not a revolutionary lyric (what is a revolutionary lyric?), but, significantly, it is sung by an artist who has been transfixed by the hands-on mutability of his own face (as his extensive plastic surgery demonstrates) and his own image (as he demonstrated also in *Thriller*, in which he turns into a werewolf). We have in these lyrics, no doubt, an objectification of the self, in that he is addressing himself, along with other men, in the third person. But while we might reasonably expect the video to elaborate on this potentially narcissistic text, instead, for the first time, Jackson is the smallest image in his own video, the least imposing figure, so much so that Pareles missed him entirely. For the mirror is the television screen itself.

The video, directed by Don Wilson, is, as Pareles says, 'a smoothly edited, slightly tricked-up montage of news footage'. But it does not, as he also says, 'demonstrate remarkable – I'd say monumental – gall, insensitivity and megalomania'. Or is that finally racism speaking? The images are, in sequence, white police beating black South Africans in a riot, two successive images of mostly black and nonwhite homeless people, four successive images of starving brown children in Ethiopia, a swarming mass of mostly black people in a Civil Rights march. Up until now, all the images have been in color except for the first of South African violence, which was in black and white. The next image, which is important, combines, for the first time, color and black-and-white film. It features a solitary figure of a black boy dancing in what appears to be an urban riot. On either side of him there is fire. The fire is colorized.

Pareles also apparently missed this image, or considered it unimportant (probably because he's never been a little black boy, never expects to become one, and never will have to worry what may happen to one). Yet it is the first to combine colorization and black-and-white film. Like Michael Jackson, the boy dances, and the dance intersects ambiguous emotions of joy and despair, recalling to me children caught up in political/religious violence from Soweto to the West Bank. Moreover, that this child dances alone amidst fire makes this frame crucial to the video's self-understanding. This frame is followed by a headshot of Bishop Tutu crying into clasped hands, two more shots of the homeless, then a headshot of Lech Walesa – the first facial shot of a white male – which dissolves into a shot of a Solidarity rally. This is followed by a shot of an unidentified black male yelling something in the context of what appears to be Civil Rights violence, a Ku Klux Klansman in full attire, then a side view of a bus in black and white, which has written on the side of it, 'We Hate Race Mixing'. Then the back of the bus is shown, with 'Hate Bus' written in colorized red, then a black-and-white Hitler with a colorized armband, which Pareles describes as 'red, like a soda-pop commercial'.

Pareles is right enough to point out that, as we listen to and watch the video Man in the Mirror, we are snapping our fingers and tapping our feet to world hunger, violence, man's inhumanity to man and woman. But isn't that what we're doing anyway when we rock 'n' roll? Or when we engage in any cultural activity that inevitably masks the seriousness and gloom of our global plight? Moreover, would it be considered such monumental bad taste if Man in the Mirror were made by David Bowie or Mick Jagger or even Stevie Wonder? Pareles' flight from the letter of racism and the way it intersects with sexism (or, in this case, homophobia) allows the importance of a little black boy dancing his way to global multiracial and androgynous interpretations to escape him.

Perhaps this is the time to emphasize that the critical refrain of the lyrics is couched in the past tense: 'No message could have been any clearer' the words of the song say. Is this megalomania or history? After pointing the finger at racial bigotry and economic marginalization as epitomizing the administration of men (class distinctions become ethical and moral ones), Man in the Mirror focuses upon children (who dance) as the hope of the world. Perhaps the suggestion is somewhat lame in a First World in which black discourses are consigned to an awkward, unwanted, and self-reflexive postmodernism (which exists in autistic relationship to Western modernism). But this is new speech from a position once silent. That position speaks for a multiracial, androgynous (non-patriarchal) future in which children no longer dance to the tune of class or religious (the same thing?) violence. The important thing to notice here is not the inevitable closure, but rather the very existence of the discourse in a First World in which blacks still fail to occupy positions of power in the media or academia, still fail to shape the interpretation of events, or the interpretation of interpretation. Is Jackson – or Don Wilson in Jackson's name – attempting an historical understanding of racial hatred? Who is this Don Wilson? Is he black? Is his mother black? Who is speaking here? And from where?

> All functions abolished in a single dimension, that of communication. That's the ecstasy of communication. All secrets, spaces and scenes abolished in a single dimension of information.
>
> Jean Baudrillard

Despite Baudrillard's 'ecstasy of communication', American television still keeps one unfathomable secret: this country's Afro-American presence. Almost everyone on television has blond hair. But watching this year's Grammy Award ceremonies – which promised to emphasize Jackson's participation – you got an entirely different impression. Precisely because of the record industry's history of apartheid and the crucial role that Afro-American music has played in the genesis of all American forms of music, blackness is an ongoing crisis in the discourse of this annual program. Here the order of spectacle (or 'entertainment') is substituted for the politics and/or history of heterogeneity.

The host was the white comedian Billy Crystal, an excellent choice (since he is known for his impression of Sammy Davis, Jr). In his comedy monologue, he told us about his father's intensive involvement with (black) jazz greats. Then he launched into an impression of an old-time (black) jazz musician that sounded vaguely like Louis Armstrong. Thus, Crystal consolidated his mediational role in the drama of racial differ- ence. This racial sketch inaugurated an endless stream of musical categories – Latin Pop, Latin Traditional, Traditional Gospel, Pop, R&B, Reggae, Rock, Contemporary Gospel, Country and Western, Folk, Classical, etc. – each featuring presenters carefully chosen for racial, sexual, age, and aesthetic balance. It seemed as though even the decisions about whether presentations of particular awards should be made on or off the air were weighed in terms of creating impressions of fairness and equality (but then this is probably the paranoia of invisibility speaking). Overall, dare I say that the process was tense in its misrepresentation of an egalitarian televisual practice? As one would imagine a one-day special-session United Nations of Music, there were repeated standing ovations from the industry audience.

The location was Radio City Music Hall in New York City. The racially insensitive Mayor Koch occupied a prominent seat. Blacks did much of the entertaining for the Awards Ceremony, which is kind of interesting since blacks actually received very few awards. Whitney Houston sang 'I Just Wanna Dance With Somebody', backed up by a veritable rainbow coalition. George Benson sang 'On Broadway', Cab Calloway sang 'Minnie the Moocher', Latin drummer Tito Puentes accompanied a black Celia Cruz, who sang in Spanish. The white performers – Lou Reed, who was backed up by one black and one white female; David Sanborn, who was accompanied by two black guitarists, and Billy Joel – all sounded black. Billy Joel's Ray Charles-like piano playing and singing 'A New York State of Mind' was particularly striking in this regard. When Run DMC descended upon this spectacle from the audience – three slightly overweight black boys rapping, signifying, making a music of the unmusic of political marginality, and looking very much as though they knew they were assaulting the sensibilities of the Grammy audience – the exorcism of New York City racial tension seemed complete.

Then a very strange thing happened, which either threatened or confirmed the provisionality of the peace, the falseness of the synthesis. Jackie Mason, an elderly Jewish comedian, came out and did the only other comedy monologue in the show. It was supposed to have been an excerpt from his album, which was nominated in the comedy category, but some of its improvisatory elements revealed an 'entertaining' banter that came dangerously close to piercing the unknowing of the 'political unconscious' and revealing all. Mason began by lamenting his never having won any kind of award. Then he said he would take an award from anybody, even the Ku Klux Klan. He said this was a joke.

And perhaps Mason thought it simply was a joke (funny to whom?) and not racism, as if the two weren't binary oppositional faces of the same systemic dilemma. What do North Americans joke about, anyway? Hasn't the joke always been the outhouse of the racial/sexual, what Julia Kristeva calls 'the abject'?[7] In his comedy routine, Mason's shtick is that he plays a bigot – a Jewish Archie Bunker – with a particular focus on Jewish/Gentile animosities. Ordinarily, in moments of ideological tension in cultural spaces (remember the early Telethons?), sex is the icebreaker. But at the Grammies, already racially coded, Mason was almost irresistibly drawn to the off-color humor of race. Characteristically, he chose to focus on somebody in the audience.

That person, as the camera quickly revealed, was Quincy Jones, perhaps the most powerful black male in the music industry, the single figure who has most clearly transcended all the barriers and made good the promise of the Civil Rights Revolution. In recent years, he has produced and scored the movie *The Color Purple* and produced a succession of commercial hits for Michael Jackson. Perhaps Mason was trying to 'roast' the industry's most successful producer or perhaps he really didn't recognize him, but he proceeded to heckle him in the following way:

> Mister, are you a black person or just a Jew with a tan? It's not nice. I don't pick on black people. I have the highest respect for black people. You know the reason I have the highest respect for black people, Mister? Because the black people are finally making progress, the progress they deserve all these years in this country. And this is a show that proves it, this is where it's happening. This is where it's at. Thank God for them. I'm not like these fake Civil Rights crusaders, who tell you 'Black People are as good as anybody else!' They sit in the back of their cars and when they see a black person walking towards the car they tell you to lock the door, 'Lock the door! Lock the door! Click it! Click it! They're as good as anybody else. Are they coming back? Click it! Click it!' Why do you think black people dance so good? Wherever they go, they hear clicking and clicking.

Then Mason did a little dance to demonstrate Afro-Americans' skill, derived, as he said, from their keeping pace with the incessant clicking of exclusion and social death. 'I was in favor of black people when they started making fires twenty years ago,' Mason went on to say. 'They were 100 per cent right for making fires because they never had true equality in America.' Which made me think of the young boy dancing amidst fire in *Man in the Mirror*. But, as Mason felt compelled to remind us, 'they only succeeded in burning their own houses down'. On the other hand, Mason continued, Jews set smaller fires, 'and every fire shows a profit'.

What was Mason doing? I don't know; televisual 'fact' melts before the eyes. I only know that Mason seemed somehow responsible for everything important that subsequently happened that night. First, Crystal parodied Jimmy the Greek's racial wisdom as Mason left the stage: 'Jackie was bred to be a comic,' Crystal said. 'In the old days, they would get a comedy writer to breed with the funny man ...' But the apparent inscription here of 'racism' as just another 'harmless' item on the menu of American comedy only continued the practice of mythologizing history and 'nature'.[8]

Much later, during the presentation of an award, Little Richard playfully declared himself the unacknowledged originator and architect of rock 'n' roll. Then during another award presentation, Joe Williams sang 'Everyday I have the Blues' to the accompaniment of Bobby McFerrin's basslike scat singing. These gestures seemed to be poised between strategies of black postmodernism – in which the critique of racism is effaced by the autism of aesthetic demonstration – and old strategies of black modernism, which propose to reconstitute the critique as an aggressive dialectic.

On the other hand, Jackson's performance at the Grammies, which I count among the black responses to Mason's inscription of racism, seemed to announce a new black modernism in that it is critical of racism, even as it formally challenges conventional hierarchies of class, race, sexuality, and aesthetic mastery. Jackson began by lip-synching to a recording of *Man in the Mirror*, accompanied by black gospel star Andre Crouch and his largely black female choir. But then Jackson didn't stop. The tape of the music ran out, the microphone was off, and Jackson was left singing soundlessly in one of those moments of televisual aporia that the industry abhors. Then the microphone was switched on: Jackson's singing and the background singing were live now. He whooped, he jumped in the air, he shook his hands frenetically, and, showing most of the classical signs of 'getting happy', as it is referred to in the black church, he fell on his knees. Crouch left his position on the stage and walked over to Jackson, evidently to help him to his feet, and then stopped. What did he see? That Jackson didn't need any help? That it was all an act? Or that it was a deliberate spectacle in which Jackson was now having his say, just as Mason had had his? Crouch danced away lightly. Jackson began to shout and exhort the people to 'stand up', which this standing-ovation-loving audience seemed suddenly disinclined to do. But Jackson wouldn't stop until they stood up. The black female choir moved forward, clapped harder, sang louder. 'White man's gotta make a change,' Jackson cried almost inaudibly. 'Black man's gotta make a change.' Needless to say, Jackson won no Grammies this year.

The one by whom the abject exists is thus a *deject* who places (himself) separates (himself), situates (himself), and therefore *strays* instead of getting his bearings, desiring, belonging, or refusing. Situationist in a sense, and not without laughter – since laughing is a way of placing or displacing abjection. Necessarily dichotomous, somewhat Manichaean, he divides, excludes, and without, properly speaking, wishing to know his abjections is not at all unaware of them. Often, moreover, he includes himself among them, thus casting within himself the scalpel that carries out his separations.

Julia Kristeva

Have you ever wondered about Michael Jackson's education? Have you ever had a problem understanding the words he sings, or the words in black rock 'n' roll in general? My mother, who is a total fan of Jackson's, says he makes up words. But isn't that what black singers have always done? Ella Fitzgerald and Louis Armstrong simply made 'scatting' official. Henry Louis Gates calls this aspect of black culture 'critical signification'.[9] It is a process in which black culture 'signifies' on white culture through imitating and then reversing its formal strategies and preconditions, thus formulating a masked and surreptitious critique. The perfect example is the relationship of 'jazz' to white mainstream music. But what I'm beginning to wonder is: how 'critical' is it?

Bad, on the other hand, is deliberately and forthrightly critical of the world we live in. Very elaborate for a video, it attempts to address problems of class and race, and diminish or marginalize problems of sexuality and gender. First, the camera fixes on Jackson's face in a shot that reminds me of Dracula. I half expect him to reveal fangs, as in *Thriller*, but he doesn't. Filmed in black and white, the video continues by suturing together, in classic filmic mode, an alienated Jackson at a white, all-boys prep school called Duxton, somewhere within commuting distance of urban New York. His train ride home illustrates the unspeakable psychological distance he feels from his white classmates, who are playing with him one moment and literally dissolve the next. Then a subway ride – in which the camera pans a row of subway riders, mostly black and all female, except for one elderly white male – slowly eases him back into the ghetto.

When he gets home – a small, poorly furnished ghetto apartment – he is greeted by a note from his mother, which is read aloud by a female voice who tells him that she's at work and there is food in the refrigerator (there are no women in this video except the women we see briefly on the subway). The camera pans the walls, which are covered with photographs of adult black men (many recognizable R&B performers), perhaps one of whom is his father.

In short order, Jackson's character joins his black male friends in the street only to have elaborate communication problems, as though he hasn't seen them in a long time. They make fun of his speech. They also think he's making fun of theirs. That Jackson's character occupies a position outside the power of language to describe is thus established. Then his friends expect him to join them in their usual pastime, robbing people. First, they try to rob a drug pusher, but the drug pusher has a gun. The image presents the only full shot of an adult black male character in the video, as he pulls his coat back to reveal a gun stuck in his pants.

Then Jackson's character – identified only by the nicknames 'Home Boy' and 'Joe College' – and his black friends go into a subway station to rob people on their way home from work. Jackson's character dissents.

There is a break in the action and Jackson, who had been dressed in a drab sweatshirt with a hood and a jacket, now reappears in color, fully made-up, hair elaborately done and gleaming, in a black outfit that features multiple metallic fixtures, which I think of as industrial nipples. He is joined by a collection of male dancers of various races – he is flanked by an Asian male and a white male. Together they dance a very athletic dance that attempts to substitute discernibly masculine gestures for the feminine gestures of an old-fashioned chorus line. Besides the refrain, which says, 'You know I'm bad, I'm bad, you know it, you know it,' Jackson also sings, 'The word is out. You're doing wrong. Gone lock you up before too long. Your lying lies don't make you right. So listen up, don't make a fight. Your talk is cheap. You're not a man. You're throwing stones out your hand.' Once the dance concludes, his ghetto friends are quiet, yet impressed. They show mute indications of making peace with him. As they leave, the color images vanish and we pan to Jackson standing alone in a sweatshirt again.

First, the obvious: the video seems to be grappling with Jackson's problematic professional identity in relation to a world of white, established wealth or cultural hegemony, and a world of black homelessness and poverty. In the process, it constructs a third racial view. Alongside the white and the black, there's Jackson's new (fantasy) race, exemplified by his dancing and singing 'I'm bad' with a team of multiracial male dancers. Meanwhile, the video revels in the full splendor of his plastic surgery, his processed hair, his skin peelings to lighten his complexion, all of which can be seen as Jackson's attempts to alter his racial characteristics towards this 'third race'.

Less obvious: the video also struggles with Jackson's problematic personal identity in relationship to a world that insists upon distinct and meaningful sexual difference. The absence of women in this video signals that the inscription of sexual difference will occur among men. But it also means that Jackson's subjectivity is doubly split in a perfect illustration of Jackson's proposal in Man in the Mirror. The first split is: 'Home Boy' (black), who goes to private school (white) in order to learn to speak, vs. the rich black boy (Jackson), whose roots are in a black oral tradition, which doesn't speak, but who performs in the context of a white postmodern culture, which speaks only to deny his history. The second split is: Home Boy's fantasy of a utopian revolutionary consciousness (boys dancing) that would transcend the real (material) conflict between himself and his friends vs. the real Jackson in an actual performance. It is appropriate to speak of such doublings precisely because videos are hybrids of music performance documentaries and television ads, and also because Jackson probably has more control over his own videos than he knows what to do with. Not only is the Bad video selling the consumer

88   INVISIBILITY BLUES

the album, it is also selling the commodified Jackson to the generic
Jackson (black males collectively) as a utopian vision that challenges the
diverse appropriations of black and white postmodernisms.

In *Rocking Around the Clock*, E. Ann Kaplan identifies five basic
categories of videos: romantic, socially conscious, nihilist, classical, and
postmodern. *Bad* reveals traces of all these categories (that Martin
Scorsese was its director suggests this video's complexity). But it also
seems to cross two kinds in particular: the socially conscious and the
classical. The 'socially conscious' video, Kaplan says, is characterized
thematically by a problematic love interest, with sex as a struggle for
autonomy, by parents and public figures as forms of authority, and by the
presence of a cultural critique. The 'classical' video is characterized
thematically by love in the form of the male gaze, with sex as voyeuristic
and fetishistic.

Both parents and public figures were present as vicarious authority in
the scene that shows 'Home Boy' in his apartment – these are his
mother's voice and the photos of the black male R&B stars. Of course,
the visualization of ghetto conditions shapes the cultural critique, and
presumably the fact that he stops his ghetto friends from robbing a
Puerto Rican male signals redeeming socialization. The fantasy dance in
the subway I see as an articulation of a problematic love interest and sex
as a struggle for autonomy. It is clearly defiant, ostentatiously unre-
quited, and obviously a struggle for aesthetic, professional, sexual, and
racial independence, or autonomy, in the most profound sense. At the
same time, 'love in the form of the male gaze' is present in the illicit
voyeurism of the camera when it surveys Jackson in his performance
outfit or as we watch Home Boy's friends watching the sexually
ambiguous Jackson and his team of multiracial boy dancers in full color.
Moreover, 'male as subject, female as object', which Kaplan identifies as
the form of authority in a 'classical' video, undeniably points the finger at
Jackson, in the fictional performer mode of the video, as the female
(white?) locked inside the subjectivity of Home Boy (black male), who is
locked inside the subjectivity of the real Jackson (androgynous and multiracial), the producer of this and all his texts.

Sexual difference, racial difference, and class difference, especially in
concert, are not subjects the televisual medium can deal with forthrightly
(who can?). Nevertheless, *Bad*, in an anachronistic and dialogical
attempt at concealment, reveals the grounds for a new interpretive space,
and the possibility of a new 'modernist language of subversion and
negation' that subverts postmodernism from inside its last secret.

In conclusion, I would like to historicize my interest in Jackson. My
mother, Faith Ringgold, was asked to donate a work of art to a benefit

auction for Bishop Desmond Tutu being sponsored by Jackson. As her contribution to the benefit, Faith chose to do a mural/quilt presentation of *Bad* with Jackson in the foreground. Still living in Harlem, in an apartment fourteen flights directly above the subway station where *Bad* was filmed, Faith is convinced that Jackson has made a worthwhile critique of the values of black boys in the streets. In her video, which documents the making of her 'Bad' quilt, we have a provocative intersection of the power of performance and the performance of interpretation.

On the one hand, the image shows the 'Bad' dancers led by Jackson no longer in the subway station but upstairs in the streets of the ghetto dancing. On the other hand, these could be generic black male youths engaged in frantic physical activity of unclear intent. They could be fighting, or are they throwing off the mantle of drug addiction, under-education, and repression, shirking the rage that blocks their progress in school, and multiplies the precarious homes of their numerous offspring, exorcizing the inarticulate and unspeakable that paves their way to the prisons? Or are they dancing at the end of racism's strings?

In her video, Faith talks about badness as part of that 'struggle for space' Jameson considers essential to the reconceptualization of cultural politics. She describes her images by saying,

> I could use these so-called bad guys and play them against Martin Luther King, Bishop Desmond Tutu, Zora Neale Hurston, people like Nelson Mandela, Winnie Mandela, Rosa Parks (whose names are written in the borders of the quilt), and Michael Jackson himself, because these are the people who are really bad in that they are able to defy very destructive forces in order to help not only themselves but other people. That is what is *really* bad.

In a possibly related gesture, Martin Scorsese includes himself, briefly (almost an invisible mega-second), in frontal and side photos on a 'Wanted for Sacrilege' poster also marked 'Bad' in bold letters.

For me, the key thing is that the perception of Jackson (and of every other aspect of black culture) is shaped by a world process of information gathering, dissemination, and interpretation (spanning mass media and academia) that notoriously marginalizes people of color. Jackson appears to be groping for an individual solution to a global problem as he attempts to generate somewhat primitive or naive historical readings from a position (that of black male pop star/black male in the street/black male of ambiguous sexuality) in cultural discourse ordinarily experienced by mainstream (white) culture as profoundly silent, nonexistent, and unspoken for. That he should have the energy to engage in such a project – despite the Pepsi commercials, despite the sexual anxieties he seems to arouse in a fairly large proportion of the heterosexual male audience over thirteen – strikes me as good, which is to say bad.

(1989)

NOTES

1. Anders Stephanson, 'Regarding Postmodernism: A Conversation with Fredric Jameson', *Social Text* 17, Fall 1987, p. 30.

2. Jean Baudrillard, 'The Ecstasy of Communication' in ed. Hal Foster, *The Anti-Aesthetic Essays on Postmodern Culture*, Port Townsend, Wash.: Bay Press, 1983, pp. 126–34.

3. Lawrence W. Levine, *Black Culture and Black Consciousness: Afro-American Folk Thought from Slavery to Freedom*, New York: Oxford University Press, 1977.

4. E. Ann Kaplan, *Rocking Around the Clock*, New York: Methuen, Inc., 1987, p. 102.

5. *The Village Voice*, September 22, 1987, pp. 15–17.

6. *The New York Times*, March 6, 1988, p. 32.

7. Julia Kristeva, *Powers of Horror: An Essay in Abjection*, New York: Colombia University Press, 1982.

8. Mason has since said in a *New York Times* interview that the lights prevented him from seeing who Quincy Jones was. His target was supposed to have been 'anonymous'.

9. Henry Louis Gates, Jr, *Figures in Black: Words, Signs, and the 'Racial' Self*, New York: Oxford University Press, 1986.

10

Invisibility Blues

Once again, the talking heads at the news program 'MacNeil-Lehrer' have rewound and are playing for the umpteenth go-round their so-called discussion of Jesse Jackson, the-cause-not-the-campaign, the-man-who-can't-win, the mystery meat in the party's platform who will blow-the-chance-of-a-Democratic-victory-in-November. Needless to say, they pointedly neglect to make reference to a Rainbow Coalition. It often seems to me that the so-called media pundits must sleep in coffins at night, and never venture beyond Greenwich, Connecticut during the day. Where else could they be getting their information?

Consider the *Sunday New York Times* 'Week in Review' on Jackson's triumph in Michigan: 'Still, let it be recorded that for at least one week in American history, in a middle-sized Midwestern state, a broad range of white voters took the presidential candidacy of a black man with utmost seriousness.' 'Let it be recorded' by whom? How did it get to be 'American history' when it just happened? Why is it only the disposition of 'white voters' that 'American history' needs to record? Is the use of the verb 'to take' to be understood as a Freudian slip of the political unconscious?

Perhaps most objectionable is the underlying assumption of white-bread discourse, which is that while the writer is perfectly willing to consider the Jackson candidacy – despite the fact that Jackson is black – the most racist voters in the party are not. Therefore, the proposition must be shelved indefinitely because, as everybody knows, racism expresses the will of the party, the will of the people, and is the only show in town. Which is exactly the attitude I expected the nearly lily-white mass media to take. In 1985, blacks held 3.5 per cent of newsroom jobs, 'hispanics' 1.7 per cent, and the notorious 'other' (whom postmodernists claim encompasses everybody but them) a whopping 1.1 per cent according to the American Society of Newspapers. These figures appeared in *Newsweek* in late 1986, in an article emphasizing the lack of minorities – blacks really – in media management. The article was called 'No Room at the Top'. But the story between the lines was that the media were the US private industries with the least progressive affirmative action profile. 'Nearly 60 per cent of daily newspapers employ no minorities at all', *Newsweek* said then. 'Magazines are even worse; TV and radio only slightly better.' I don't imagine the situation has improved since.

As Jackson's comet refused to die a 'natural' death, the media kindly manufactured a climax for him – the way you compose a suspense novel – and then the antagonist *has* to die because the plot dictates it. But it's not over yet. As James Baldwin put it in *Notes of a Native Son*, 'This world is white no longer, and it will never be white again'.

CROSSING THE FINISH LINE

Every time the media start their woefully inadequate coverage of the Jackson campaign – the dichotomizing of Jews and blacks in New York was particularly painful – I am reminded of the day the Kenyan ran in and won the New York Marathon. I am no sports follower, and Gene, my spouse equivalent, and I were about to run ourselves, but because the 19-inch screen Mitsubishi color TV is the central thing in our tiny New York apartment – kind of like an altar – we had a habit of turning it on to verify that there was nothing worth watching before we made any major moves. We did so as usual on Sunday morning – well, we know what's on Sunday morning – but what we saw and heard that day was spellbinding, like watching a real-life illustration of invisibility. For the last several miles of the race, the Kenyan was in the lead by half a mile. Or so it seemed on the screen via one camera, which showed the Kenyan running alone and via another camera, some place else entirely, which showed a gaggle of white male runners-up.

Yet a flock of white male commentators endlessly speculated on the probability of his losing. They considered it from every angle and still it made no sense. Did they imagine he would drop dead from blackness? Just as he was about to cross the finish line – and these white male reporters were forced to acknowledge that clearly he would be the winner – the camera left him. We never saw him cross the finish line, although our eyes were riveted to the screen waiting for them to come back to it. Okay, we told each other, they made a mistake. They're upset because a black man has won the New York Marathon for the first time. But we were not down in Plains, Georgia somewhere talking to members of Jimmy Carter's church. They'll catch themselves soon enough. They'll show a playback or slow motion or something. We watched in disbelief as the white men narrated the second-and third-place finish of white male runners-up, then the finish much later of the white female winner. Does that mean winning is all in the eyes of the beholder or the cameras? I don't know.

I only know that MacNeil-Lehrer and even Charlayne Hunter-Gault are disappointing. Yes, even Hunter-Gault, although she's the black woman who once integrated the University of Georgia in the Civil Rights Movement. For years I've been holding onto the fantasy that Gault was being snide and cynical beneath her modified Southern accent. Such as when she questioned white male economists closely during Wall Street's so-called 'Black Monday' about where was their 'trickle-down' now? Of course, that 'Black Monday' business made me and every other black American wonder whether it was 1887 or 1987. But did Gault say something about how blacks are tired of derogatory references to the color black?

Taking any pride at all in black tokens is much like waiting for Tonto to walk away from the Lone Ranger, or wondering when Rochester will quit Jack Benny's employ, which is how a whole lot of us who aren't white managed to enjoy these programs in the 1950s and 1960s. But this isn't the 1950s. What is a black viewer supposed to wish for Oprah Winfrey, Bill Cosby, Eddie Murphy, Action Jackson, Spike Lee, and Prince? What's changed? Has Tonto walked away from the Lone Ranger yet? Has Rochester handed Benny his notice? And what, if anything, has this tokenism on a grand scale to do with who makes information?

Any black writer less fashionable than Alice Walker or Toni Morrison would be unlikely to be asked to cover the Jackson campaign for a major magazine like *Playboy* or *Vanity Fair*. And even if Morrison or Walker were willing to do it, they would probably catch unmitigated hell about syntax, ideology, and 'black pride'. What's more, there really is a 'trickle-down' to small and progressive publishing and the alternative press. Once upon a time, people like James Baldwin, John A. Williams, and Gordon Parks were asked to write stories for big magazines, but racism appears to be this continually escalating ideological economy with a mind of its own.

It shouldn't be necessary to remind anybody that during slavery blacks were forbidden by law from reading and writing. Simultaneously, the philosophical wisdom of Western civilization, Henry Louis Gates tells us in his introduction to '*Race*', *Writing, and Difference*, was that the black 'race' was constitutionally unable to read and write. We find ourselves in a situation in which, from university to network, it's still assumed that we have no written language.

So it really puzzled me when all the white male critics started bitching about how *Cry Freedom* was a bad movie because it made Stephen Biko's character seem subsidiary to Donald Woods'. It trivialized and sentimentalized Biko's voice, I recall both *The New York Times* and *The Village Voice* saying. Rather, I thought that Attenborough, for perverse Anglo reasons of his own, was drawing the obvious connection between conditions for blacks in South Africa (media representation, political underrepresentation, and poverty) and comparable circumstances for blacks in the US. Moreover, that Biko's message came to the world via the intervention and interpretation of a white male, that a white male starred in the film version of Biko's story, strikes me as exactly the situation we find ourselves reaping the benefits of in US mass media today. The thing to criticize most about the movie is that it seemed far too much like the United States to ever be South Africa.

NO ROOM AT THE INN

Secretary of Education William Bennett, who was quite emphatic in his recent criticism of curricular changes at Stanford University on the 'MacNeil-Lehrer NewsHour', charges that 'racism' and 'sexism' are irrelevant in the context of studying Western civilization. Somehow for him the very words themselves are tainted. Of course, this makes perfect sense to James Lehrer, who interviewed him. In fact, 'racism' and 'sexism' are irrelevant in every context, as far as they're both concerned.

The first moment at which I really began to understand this attitude was on 'Washington Week in Review' when Carl Rowan was given the unpleasant task of trying to explain to a panel of white journalists why Supreme Court Justice Thurgood Marshall had said that Reagan was a racist president. Oh, no, no, no, no, they all insisted, Reagan is not a racist. Not racist, not racist, no, no, they all chanted. Because, after all, nobody is actually racist. Except some anonymous white everyman out in the middle of Michigan, who single-handedly shaped the media's coverage of 'the presidential campaign of a black man'.

Bennett is not entirely wrong to want to have such words as 'racism' and 'sexism' dropped from the language. To suggest that not only dead white men have written (and will always write) the crucial text is to threaten the entire notion of knowledge as something timeless, universal, and, therefore, on another plane, above the historical and intimate concreteness and specificity of 'racism' and 'sexism'. Bennett realizes that there isn't space enough for everybody, not only in the economy but on the book list. Furthermore, if everybody can sit at the table, there won't be any room left at the inn, and pretty soon people will be doing what? Sleeping on subways and eating out of garbage cans? The distinctions and dichotomies between classics and kitsch, winners and also-rans, are necessary in order to preserve order as we now understand it.

It's not just a matter of white people at the top and people of color at the bottom (although that's often the way it turns out); it's about the notion of order as an arrangement in which some people are always better off than others because it helps foster the inexorable self-loathing that keeps everybody in his or her place, paying taxes for cops and robbers shenanigans and awaiting the inevitable exposé on the televised hearings.

CATCHING UP, THE EXISTENTIAL PLIGHT

I teach Afro-American literature, feminist literature, and creative writing in the American Studies Department at SUNY–Buffalo. It's a pretty unusual place, I suppose, in that it attempts to straddle the dream and the reality of American pluralism. The dream is the Rainbow Coalition in academia, although it sometimes appears that all the constituents would prefer to remain separate. The reality is that minority people – Puerto Rican, Native American, US, Afro-American, and Women's Studies Programs, and a Women of Color component – need to start getting doctorates so they can head some of the programs, obtain some of the grant money, do some of the research, and write some of the books that shape the academic enterprise and, ultimately, influence the global production of knowledge that keeps us all enthralled.

The department is in the process of defining the requirements for the PhD. I'm the token non-PhD involved in all of this. We're trying to make sure that book lists facilitate the integration of programs necessary to students at the PhD level, that the oral and written exams are doable, and that minority students are encouraged to achieve professional competence and intellectual rigor. It is difficult for me to get excited about all this, because every day I understand a little better why I don't have a PhD, even though I've tried; why black women, as a rule, don't pursue doctorates; why even when they do, they are often indefinitely delayed.

My Aunt Barbara began her college education in 1942 at Hunter College when she was sixteen (the family pitched in to pay her tuition), completed her bachelor's in nutrition and became a dietician, presumably in 1947, then – while working – did her master's in Education at Hunter College at a time when the City University of New York was not keen on admitting black students. I don't know precisely when she completed her master's, but remember her briefly pursuing her PhD at Columbia, then dropping out because a professor accused her of being illiterate, although I always thought she spoke the most precise English and read more books than anybody I ever knew. She was not what most people would consider to be a brave person, and she never got over that or a lot of other things. As an elementary school teacher, she grew to hate the public schools. About five years ago she drank herself to death.

Many of the people in my family – starting with my great-grandfather who was a teacher in Palakta, Florida and the son of ex-slaves – have graduated from college, although somehow it's never brought us much security, or even the certainty that the next generation would be educated. When he died suddenly at an early age, my great-grandfather's oldest children had to come home from school. None of the six ever finished college. My grandmother dreamed of college for her children instead of for herself. Although my mother and my Aunt Barbara both graduated from college, my uncle never went at all. He became a gang leader called Baron and died of a heroin overdose when I was nine. In my father's family (from Jamaica), the record is just as tattered. Financial ruin, ignorance, and despair seemed to follow us around like badly trained pets wanting food and water.

I was lucky. My grandmother began to teach me how to read before I went to school. My youngest sister, named after Aunt Barbara, would play on the floor around our feet, reciting from memory the words of the stories I was reading. Because I went to private schools and because I was raised in a home where reading and writing were valued above all else, I received a rigorous basic education.

Then I began to attend the City College of New York. In the 1970s, CCNY was undergoing dramatic political upheaval partly due to the open admissions struggle of the late 1960s. The student body was shifting in composition from white to black. Although I was in the English Department, where most black students still feared to tread, the education I received was nevertheless shaped by fluctuating standards.

I graduated from CCNY in 1974 with a BA in English and Writing without ever having studied any English Literature written prior to 1800. Although I received very classy training in creative writing from the likes of Donald Barthelme and John Hawkes, if it had not been for my private high school education, I would never have read Shakespeare or Chaucer,

Beowulf or the Romantic poets. As for the Latin and Greek of Virginia Woolf's and W.E.B. Dubois' lamentations, there was never any question. Milton was out.

When I became a book review researcher at *Newsweek* in the fall of 1974, I realized that there were words commonly used by writers and fellow researchers that I neither knew how to pronounce nor how to use in a sentence. I began to read a lot, for now I vaguely began to comprehend why my favorite teacher at CCNY had begged me to seek a minority scholarship to Harvard. My reading clarified a lot for me, although not yet the importance of reading itself.

So in the search for validation, I landed in the PhD program in American Studies at Yale, where I was lost before I started. I had never heard of Cotton Mather, Jonathan Edwards, Max Weber, Thorstein Veblen, John Dewey, or C. Wright Mills. I had never read John Blassingame, John Hope Franklin, or W.E.B. Dubois. I had read Alice Walker, Kate Millett, James Baldwin, Norman Mailer, and a great many novels, but that seemed to count for nothing. While I could write reasonably well, and I read a lot, the words seemed to escape me when it was time to talk to fellow graduate students. I was morbidly afraid that when I opened my mouth, I would show my bottomless ignorance and make a fool of myself. So I kept to myself and read voraciously but came to loathe the superbly well-educated, articulate whites who shared my classes. I feared I would never catch up. When the fear became too much for me – I was no brave person either – I dropped out. But the project of catching up will always describe my existential plight.

CULTURAL DETENTION CENTERS

Even at SUNY–Buffalo there seems little recognition that increasingly graduate students – especially students of color – need reasons, connections, and explanations if graduate study is to make sense to them. They need to know that people of color have written books, have been intellectually engaged. On the other hand, standards of professional competence, the study of the classics in the field, and intellectual performance should not be dismissed in some misguided liberal attempt to make it easier. Or as Donald Lazere says in *American Media and Mass Culture*, 'Pending revolutionary reversal of white and black hegemonic roles in American politics and culture ... leftists might better direct their criticisms at forces excluding poor minorities and whites from literate culture, rather than minimizing the value of that culture as some leftists do.'

It's not a matter of being for or against Western civilization. We are all victims of it. It's time to consider that the classics may, in fact, make more sense to some of us as records of blindness to the plight of the world's majorities, than as sublime masterpieces. Or as Walter Benjamin once suggested, 'There's no document of civilization which is not at the same time a document of barbarism.' That doesn't mean, however, that we don't need to read and analyze them. It means that we need to keep our eye on the ball.

The important thing to change is the way minority people lack access to the primary means of social communication at every level from mass media to academic publishing. They neither own nor manage – except in the case of marginal institutions – publishing companies, magazines, television stations, film studios, museums, theatres. 'Cultural detention centers' is how Ishmael Reed characterizes their abuse of power in *Mumbo Jumbo*. Blacks are discouraged from service as writers, editors, curators, and directors in these cultural detention centers. As perpetual objects of contemplation, contempt, derision, appropriation, and marginalization, Afro-Americans are kept too busy to ever become producers. Further, the educational system, which doesn't take seriously their educational potential, especially as writers, sabotages them from kindergarten to college. Since the Civil Rights revolution, even more so. Either what they have to learn turns them off, or they're turned off by the spirit in which it is offered.

My sister provides an apt illustration. She advanced to candidacy in theoretical linguistics seven years ago, then later switched her field to socio-linguistics: black English as spoken by black women in Harlem where she lives. Still, with three small children and teaching full time at a public school in New York, she's unable to finish. Not coincidentally, she refers to the ill-behaved, mostly black, children at her school as 'heathens'.

Access is denied from inside the black family as well. Poor, uneducated families may regard intellectual activity as, ipso facto, elitist. Middle-class black families may have the equivalent attitude (especially for girls), regarding advanced intellectual activity as unfeminine, unhealthy, and 'white'. Education is considered a means to an end – a way to become a doctor or a lawyer or 'an Indian chief' – as though it was somehow also completely ridiculous.

RAINBOW COALITION OF THE MIND

But now I know an Indian chief – Wilma Mankiller, the first female chief of the Cherokee Nation in Oklahoma – whose struggle is also a struggle with language and representation. The Cherokee are also invisible to most Americans, even to most Oklahomans, even to most blacks. I've become fascinated by the unwillingness of 'American history' to include Oklahoma in its big picture. It's like one of those nuclear dump sites, some place nobody wants to know anything about.

Perhaps it remains this frightening unknown quantity because its population didn't whiten until the 1920s. Years after all the unwanted Native Americans in the Southeast were rounded up and herded to the 'Indian Territory', most notably in the Trail of Tears – ex-slaves began to rally there as well because of the rumors that black men were prosperous in the territory – the possibility of Oklahoma entering the union as an Indian or black state was seriously considered.

Native Americans wanted to call the Indian state Sequoyah, after the man who had invented the Cherokee alphabet. He thought the one great advantage whites had over his people was writing. So he set about improving the odds. I don't want to romanticize Cherokee development – the alphabet didn't save them from the hypocrisy of whites. But what strikes me as important about the Cherokees, and all Native American groups, is that they have a different historical relationship to the question of race, and demonstrate another paradigm of assimilation without success. The useful thing might be to make comparisons, to dislodge the phantom fears, to find out what's really there. The one thing both American Studies at Yale and at SUNY–Buffalo have in common is a total lack of interest in such questions.

Of course, we all contribute to the dichotomizing of black and white that allows the media to trivialize the Jackson campaign, and that erases again and again American cultural diversity. But I feel as though Sequoyah is a state of mind, the predisposition to regard the United States as a function of American pluralism, a rainbow coalition of great expectations, impossible to meet solely with classical solutions.

(1988)

11

Spike Lee and Black Women

In *The Crisis of the Negro Intellectual*, Harold Cruse defined and described the impossibility for Afro-Americans of ever isolating a pure separatist or integrationist agenda. Yet in his rush to supply prescriptions, Cruse missed the implications of his own scholarship: 'Integration', he warned, 'is ... leading to cultural negation.' As Cruse saw it, integration-minded intellectuals like James Baldwin and Lorraine Hansberry were infected with a lethal dose of false consciousness – a severe case of neither knowing nor caring what was *really* black. Thus Cruse called for profound changes in black self-perception: black intellectuals needed to toughen up, think more collectively and, above all, black up their political, economic and cultural projects, which they promptly did in the context of Black Power.

Almost twenty years after Cruse's initial call, black critic Greg Tate surveyed the results for high and low culture in a list-heavy celebration titled 'The Return of The Black Aesthetic: Cult-Nats Meet Freaky-Deke' (*Village Voice Literary Supplement*, December 1986). Tate proposed postmodernism as a way to heal the apparent schism between assimilation and cultural nationalism. 'Black artists', he wrote, 'have opened up the entire "text of blackness" for fun and games', which meant that it was no longer necessary to insist on African origins or the absence of European influences as the basis of black identity.

Tate's most encouraging sign of the new age was *She's Gotta Have It*, a low-budget feature made by a young black filmmaker named Spike Lee, which Tate described as 'a populist black poststructuralist dream'. Not only had Lee formulated 'an uncompromisingly black vision', he had 'shot [the film] for jackshit with a collectivist cast and crew', thus demolishing 'Hollywood's megabudget mystique'. This was consistent with Tate's notion of a cultural resistance that 'doesn't aim for transcendence of corporate culture's limits into some mystical liberated zone, but for critical intervention in the process by which capitalism is rationalized through mass culture and modernism.' Cultural assimilation and even accommodation were now OK, provided they were in a separatist framework. Yet Tate also applauded Lee's 'raceman' views on 'Whoopi's blue contacts, Michael's nose' and *The Color Purple*: not black enough.

When it came to apparent transgressions in the field of sexuality, the charge of racial inauthenticity was brought out, brushed off and presented as though it were brand-new. Issues of sexual difference were the special blind spot of Tate's theoretical formulations: women emerged only as also-rans in his numerous lists of who's getting it right, from Miles Davis to Amiri Baraka to Nona Hendryx. Nor did it appear relevant to mention that *She's Gotta Have It*, the showpiece of the new black aesthetic, was about a black woman who couldn't get enough of the old phallus, and who therefore had to be raped. Tate's obsession with the prison-house of historical narrative (blacks have only walk-on parts in Western Civilization's version) and the groovy way it could be replaced by filmic spectacle, or 'fun and games', rendered superfluous the mundane observation that in such spectacles, women almost always occupy a different status.

Since Tate's 1986 declarations, Spike Lee has provided further proof of some kind of major continental drift. His books, *Spike Lee's Gotta Have It* and *Uplift the Race: The Construction of School Daze* (the latter co-authored by Lisa Jones, both published by Simon & Schuster), as well as his new movie, *School Daze*, all participate in Tate's ambiguous vision of 'blackness'. This spring, Lee made a black-and-white, *vérité* campaign commercial for Jesse Jackson, and another movie is in the works. Melvin Van Peebles, whom this movement embraces as spiritual father, is also making a movie this summer. So is Robert Townsend, a West Coast actor who tired of the film industry's racism and decided to make his own vehicle. There are reported spinoffs from both the Lee and the Townsend projects as well. Perhaps film's indeterminacy and power make it seem the likely place for black American culture to emerge from disadvantage and invisibility. But there's a problem here, too, with which the 'blaxploitation' films of the 1960s and 1970s thoroughly acquainted us. Black films are obviously untenable without popular success in somebody's marketplace. I hope Lee, Townsend and Van Peebles et al. are not intending to demonstrate that black filmmakers can reclaim blaxploitation without revising its use of female humiliation as an inevitable by-product of plot resolution.

The only way to avoid a renaissance of filmic black sexism – while this is still a movement and not yet a full-blown industry – would be to take on the field of sexual difference deliberately and oppositionally. At first, it seemed that Spike Lee had done exactly that with *She's Gotta Have It*. 'It always amazed me,' Lee wrote in the journal he kept while making the film, 'how men can go out and bone any and everything between fifteen and eighty and it's OK. They are encouraged to have and enjoy sex, while it's not so for women. If they do what men do they're labeled whore, prostitute, freaks, nympho, etc. Why this double standard? Why not explore this?'

Lee thus invents a sex-loving female character named Nola Darling, who has three male lovers: Greer Childs, a narcissistic Buppie actor who likes being seen with Nola because she's attractive; Jamie Overstreet, a solid, average guy who wants to marry her; and Mars Blackmon, played by Lee himself, a B-boy on a bicycle who always makes Nola laugh. Nola, her male lovers and her female friends all address the camera to supply competing versions of who she really is. The structure of the film thus subverts whatever masculine authority Lee, as director, writer and producer, intermittently imposes.

But this film's fun has its limits. Significantly, *She's Gotta Have It* begins with an epigraph from the beginning of *Their Eyes Were Watching God*, in which Zora Neale Hurston romanticizes the irreconcilability of men and women. Nola's three lovers also remind me of Janie's three husbands in Hurston's novel. Jamie seems most like Logan Killicks, who offers Janie the lackluster security of forty acres and a mule and wants to degrade her when she fails to appreciate it. Greer Childs resembles Joe Starks, who becomes the mayor of an all-black town and wants to put Jamie on a pedestal. Tea Cake, who offers Janie pleasure and companionship 'on the muck' among the 'folk farthest down', seems a dead ringer for Mars Blackmon, whose love of fun emerges as a critique of conventional masculinity.

Although it is Jamie who finally rapes Nola into submission when she refuses to marry him, Lee's journal clearly suggests that he views Jamie as the best man among her lovers. For instance, Lee often remarks that while Nola has sex with all three men, she has orgasms only with Jamie. He has to caution himself against writing too many scenes in which Nola is crying. He doesn't know how Nola should react to Jamie's rape. Should she enjoy it? He settles for having Jamie reluctantly admit that *he* enjoyed it. Perhaps most important, Lee never calls it a rape. These matters work out considerably better in the film than in the notebooks – on screen, Lee resists the obvious conclusion, in which the best man marries Nola, the prize. But the film's mistrust of female sexuality is disturbingly obvious in Lee's handling of Nola's relationship with her lesbian friend, Opal Gilstrap, who comes on like the original serpent in the Garden of Eden. In many ways, especially in the scene where Lee's puckered lips traverse her flesh, Nola seems less a character than a dark continent to be explored and conquered. Although she addresses the camera directly, her language seems inane and self-canceling, as if she were selling something in a TV commercial. Still, *She's Gotta Have It* left me eager to see what Lee would do next.

School Daze takes on a scene that is already familiar to readers of the canon of Afro-American literature. It's the black college campus of Booker T. Washington's *Up From Slavery*, W.E.B. Du Bois' *The Souls of Black Folk*, Jean Toomer's *Cane*, Ralph Ellison's *Invisible Man*, Amiri Baraka's *Tales*. But such literary allusions cannot hope to compete with the film's animated pastiche of classic homecoming-football-game movies, slapstick humor and sight gags, Motown and Busby Berkeley production numbers, jazz, R & B and funk performance, black English, style and dance. To the perennial question of the classic Afro-American literary text – 'What kind of education can a black man expect, even at a black college, except a lesson in how to heel to a white master?' – Lee replies 'not much', in a film pointedly devoid of classrooms, professors and all the appurtenances of study. My question then becomes, reluctantly, what kind of education can a black woman expect to receive as audience for this film?

School Daze is a postmodern film version of Harold Cruse's *The Crisis of the Negro Intellectual*, with the dichotomies of Pan-Africanism versus accommodationist economics and black pride versus assimilation transposed into the madcap goings-on of pop cult's *Animal House* and the neocultural nationalism of Ishmael Reed's playful *Mumbo Jumbo*. But the accompanying political issues of separatism and integration are all but silenced by the film's all-black universe. Also prominently displayed is postmodernism's vision of women as monster kewpie dolls, whose wayward desires require on-screen punishment in movies such as *Half Moon Street*, *Blue Velvet*, *Mona Lisa*, *The House of Games* and *Ironweed*. While the film halfheartedly focuses on a conflict between students and administration over whether black Mission College should divest from South Africa, its obsession is with gender and sexuality: the viewer is invited to witness entirely distinct male and female versions of a contest between light-skinned, affluent Wannabees and dark-skinned, nappy-haired, lower-class Jigaboos.

The film's opening scene provides us with an introduction to the major male contingents, who generally devote their attention to global issues of cultural leadership or political responsibility (although a lot of what they do appears to be very silly). Dap, the story's protonationalist hero, and da Fellas, or male Jigaboos, are participating in a rally to protest South African apartheid and the failure of Mission College to divest. The president of the college, and the president of the board of trustees, either or both of whom participated in the civil rights demonstrations of the 1960s, are watching from an administration building window. Trouble promptly arrives in the form of the stylishly dressed Gamma Phi Gammas, the principal contingent of the Wannabees, led by a proto-Nazi Big Brother Almighty and flanked by the glamorous Gamma Rays. They don't give a damn about divestment or the plight of South African blacks. As Julian, Big Brother Almighty, so succinctly puts it, 'I'm from Detroit! Motown!'

The particular cause of conflict is the display the Gammas are making of breaking in eight baldheaded, sycophantic, slavelike pledgees, who are being led along, chain-gang style, on leashes. 'It take a real man to be a Gamma man!' the Gammites chant at the top of their lungs, 'Because only a Gamma man is a real man!' Among these Gammites, occupying a uniquely liminal status in the text (in that he is the only character we see communicating effectively with both groups) is none other than the big-eyed auteur Spike Lee, as Half-Pint, Dap's cousin, who is director, producer and writer of this film as well.

The women, both Jigaboos and Wannabees, take no apparent interest in either politics or culture except as passive consumers. The Gamma Rays wear expensive clothes, elaborate Farrah Fawcett hairdos and lots of makeup. The film's preoccupation is with their falseness, which reflects both their 'wanna be whiteness' and their femininity – as though they were black women in white women's drag. Jigaboo women, on the other hand, are natural women with natural hair; the film focuses on them primarily as objects of ridicule, humor and negation. Rachel, Dap's girlfriend, 'the darkest thing on campus' in her own words, seems the leader of the Jigaboo women by default. She doesn't really do anything except march alongside Dap, have sex with him and argue with him about whether she should finally, in her senior year, pledge a sorority, which seems a puzzling contradiction of the Jigaboo stance.

Women's affairs are epitomized by the film's largest musical number, 'Straight and Nappy'. Suddenly, Wannabee and Jigaboo women are transported to a mod-colored Madame Res-Res's Hair Salon to have it out. The Cotton Club music and the Josephine Baker dancing have all the heat and none of the dignity of the confrontation between white and Puerto Rican boys in West Side Story. Although a comically fat Jigaboo dancer weighs in against the nappy-headed side, otherwise slender female dancers, black and tan, battle early in the film for this ambiguous turf. At one point, Jigaboos don masks of Vivien Leigh playing Scarlett O'Hara to present a mirror image to Wannabee women. The Wannabees respond by donning masks of Hattie McDaniels playing her Mammy. Which would you rather be? For black women, either/or is really neither/nor.

On an even lower scale in the film's visual economy are the local yokels, or street bloods. Their confrontation with the Fellas at Church's Fried Chicken begins when one local, feigning femininity, asks, 'Is it true what they say about Mission men?' It ends with one of the Fellas saying that a yokel looks 'just like a bitch' because he uses Jerri Curl on his hair and wears a shower cap in the street. Thus, at the only moment when the film takes on the plight of poor black men, it simultaneously refuses even to consider black homosexual legitimacy.

I saw School Daze for the second time in Brooklyn's Fulton Mall, not far from where Jamie's first meeting with Nola in She's Gotta Have It was filmed. It was a Friday afternoon and the audience was packed with black women, teenagers and children. Every time the Jigaboo women came on the screen, perhaps because of their dark skin and their free-form, unstraightened hair, there was the uncomfortable laughter of disapproval. When the Gamma Rays appeared, there was more often the silence of complete immersion, or the cat-calls of men, or the involuntary 'oohing' of admiration. After all, the Gamma Rays look more like the women we're all used to seeing on movie screens. They also have their own musical number.

At the coronation of the Homecoming Queen, Gamma queen Jane Toussaint, who has long blond (dyed?) hair and blue eyes (contact lenses?), and the Gamma Rays, svelte and glamorous, sing 'Be Alone Tonight' in a slick imitation of a Motown girl group. The four women perform in slinky silver-and-black gowns with bows and ruffles from their knees to their ankles. They wear black patent leather high heels and sparkles in their long, cascading hair, t&a emphasized by dress cut and pelvis-gyrating choreography. They look like the ultimate Virginia Slims advertisement.

Light-skinned Jane Toussaint – who whispers softly à la both white and black girl groups in the 1960s, 'Boy, you know I love you' – is set up by this resplendent presentation of her wares for the anachronistic rape that will be the film's climax. While the dastardly deed is technically done by Half-Pint, he is commanded to do it by Julian, Big Brother Almighty, while fellow Gammas wait in the hall. That Jane is also tricked into agreeing to it by her boyfriend only makes this act seem more like the collective will of the text: figurative gang rape as filmic imperative. Dap, presumably the representative of this film's utopianism – just as Jamie was the ideal image of masculinity in She's Gotta Have It – is moved to take the drastic action of waking everybody up at dawn, because he sees Half-Pint's act as going too far. But where does Lee stand in all of this, with Dap or with Half-Pint, whom he plays? And dare we interpret his progress from playing 'the man who makes her laugh' to playing the rapist by popular demand?

I sat through *School Daze* twice that day in Brooklyn, wondering about my own increasing willingness to luxuriate in the film's youthful images and its seductive, playful musical score. I stopped in the theatre's bathroom before I left. Two women were humming and singing 'Do the Butt', one of the film's big musical performances, which has since become a hit on black radio. But there was a third woman who wasn't humming anything. She was standing in front of the mirror trying to comb her hair. Full-figured with dark brown skin, her short hair dyed traffic-light blond and covered with a long blond fall attached to a cloth headband, she was no 'wannabee' in any sense that *School Daze* could articulate. She kept trying to comb the fall, which had grown stiff and artificial looking, into a shape that might approximate the one it had been in when she'd purchased it. On her young, pretty face, she had that worried look black women often assume in public places when they look in the mirror.

I couldn't figure out how this woman could fail to see a relationship between her dilemma and the film she'd just seen. Did she resent Jane, identify with her, or perhaps a little bit of both? Moreover, I had the uneasy suspicion that the blond hairpiece and the blond dye had something to do with that curious process by which black female frustration becomes black female fashion. Which leads me to wonder: can black women survive another dose of 'Black Pride'?

(1988)

12

Doing the Right Thing

Am I advocating violence? No, but goddamn, the days of twenty-five million blacks being silent while our fellow brothers and sisters are exploited, oppressed, and murdered, have to come to an end. Racial persecution, not only in the United States, but all over the world, is not gonna go away; it seems it's getting worse (four years of Bush won't help). And if Crazy Eddie Koch gets re-elected for a fourth term as mayor of New York, what you see in *Do the Right Thing* will be light stuff. Yep, we have a choice, Malcolm or King. I know who I'm down with.
Spike Lee (with Lisa Jones), *Do the Right Thing: A Spike Lee Joint*,
Fireside Books: Simon & Schuster, 1989

In these dog days of right-wing suppression of the arts in Congress and reactionary intolerance on the Supreme Court, it seems wrong, in good conscience, to write about the problems of 'women' in Spike Lee's new film *Do the Right Thing*. Rather, the only valid progressive response would appear to be to celebrate Lee's courage in making a film about 'racism' that, unlike *Betrayed* and *Mississippi Burning* and *Places in the Heart*, is really about black people, and that doesn't end with whites and blacks linking arms to sing 'We Shall Overcome' as though Martin Luther King, Jr, had never been shot.

First, because we are surely headed for race riots much worse than the one depicted in the film if there aren't some drastic changes made in our present economic and political policies, in our representations of 'race', and in our individual attitudes about race. Second, because the film's story about the hottest day of the summer on a block in the heart of New York's Bed-Stuy focuses upon the hopelessness and despair of a poor, disenfranchised urban black male population which is increasingly regarded as the 'abject', not only by the white status quo but also by the black middle class. Third, because the film was made by a young black independent filmmaker whose mission is to demystify and reclaim the process of filmmaking for blacks, in particular those who are genuinely concerned about exploring its avant-garde political and aesthetic potential. And fourth, because no one in her right mind would want to be associated with the negative criticism that has been made of the film by people like Joe Klein at *New York* magazine, who asks why the police aren't more sympathetically portrayed, as if every other film or TV show weren't about how wonderful white cops are, or by the *Seven Days* writer who said the film might cause riots. Rather, I suspect this film may have acted as a symbolic substitute for a riot this summer.

In *Do the Right Thing*, it would be a mistake to focus on the specific details of female characterization. For whatever it's worth, Mother Sister (Ruby Dee), the neighborhood conscience and busybody; Tina (Rosie Perez), a Puerto Rican/black unmarried mother of Mookie's child; and Jade (Joie Lee), Mookie's sister, present much more 'positive images' than Mookie (Spike Lee), a money-hungry young pizza deliverer for Sal's Famous; Da Mayor (Ossie Davis), an elderly drunk who likes to give advice and arbitrate disputes; Radio Raheem (Bill Nunn), who carries a big ghetto blaster turned up to maximum volume; Smiley (Roger Guenveur Smith), who is mentally retarded and sells copies of the only photograph of Malcolm X and Martin Luther King, Jr, together; and Buggin Out (Giancarlo Esposito), a contentious protonationalist whose most prized possessions are his Air Jordan sneakers. Lee is not offering these characters as role models, nor does he portray them in depth. Like the characterizations of the males, the female characters are funny reversals of black stereotypes, foils for such white characters as Sol (Danny Aiello) and his sons Vito (Richard Edson) and Pino (John Turturro), Italians who own and run the neighborhood pizzeria, or the Korean couple (Steve Park and Ginny Yang) who run the grocery store across the street. Insignificant in themselves, each is completely instrumental to the larger purpose of the film, which is to set up a scenario in which the worst aspects of urban apartheid become explosive and intolerable. But one image of a female stands out in this arrangement because it so clearly transgresses the skeletal linear narrative that propels this film forward.

The film's opening sequence hits us with the jarring visualization of Tina in boxer shorts b-boy dancing to Public Enemy's 'Fight The Power', her large 'Negroid' lips emphasized in red lipstick as though she were a latter-day Josephine Baker, a younger Grace Jones. Without a glimmer of narrative explanation, we accept with perverse fascination this woman of color gyrating and grimacing in a series of titillating moves coded as androgynous resistance but without the power of an explicit feminist political critique. The reification here reminds one of an MTV video.

That this cinematic event is not meaningful but mythic and signals a gap in the text that will follow is confirmed when Tina is confined to a two-dimensional role in which she can only bitch mindlessly at Mookie about his failure to live up to his 'responsibilities' as father and lover.

In fact, everybody in this film bitches all the time. Indeed, the most surprising and effective thing about the movie is in its use of 'negative images'. But the shortcoming of the film remains that 'racism' is artificially purified of sexual difference, except in that brief moment when Mookie insists that his sister Jade should not return to the pizzeria where he works because Sal is coming on to her. It is almost as if Lee/Mookie were warning Jade (played by Lee's sister in real life), as a representative of black women in general, to stay out of the focus of his film.

Despite my conviction that films about racism, like this one, are infinitely preferable to all the films that simply pretend that nonwhite people don't exist, I am forced to raise an objection. I believe that they entirely miss their mark, that they reinscribe the very thing they aim to dislocate, when they trivialize or deny the importance of women's oppression in general, and the problems of black women in particular. Moreover, to do so makes no sense in terms of the material reality of representations of 'race' in American culture, which has always been profoundly entangled with issues of gender, sexuality, and the female body.

Although we are geared to focus on the careers of great men, in fact the history of black liberation struggles invoked by the photograph of King and Malcolm X together is unimaginable without the input of women. The present poverty and deprivation of the black community that the setting of the film in Bed-Stuy invokes is impossible to conceptualize accurately without thinking about women, as well as men, and their relationship to such issues as homelessness, teenage pregnancy, abortion, AIDS, drugs, illiteracy, Aid to Families with Dependent Children, unemployment, poverty, and police brutality. Yet the very dilemma that Mookie and his cohorts Radio Raheem, Smiley, and Buggin Out face and fail to surmount – how do blacks respond to racism – seems forged in a longstanding disinclination within black circles to consider women as subjects and objects of analysis in black formulations of social policy and political philosophy.

In the film, Buggin Out becomes infuriated to discover that Sal will not consider adding a photograph of a famous black person to his Wall of Fame, which features photographs of famous (white) Italian-Americans like Frank Sinatra, Al Pacino, and Robert De Niro. Near the end of the film, Radio Raheem and Smiley unite with Buggin Out to force the issue. The police inadvertently kill Radio Raheem in an attempt to subdue and arrest him. The racial violence of Howard Beach and the police brutality against such celebrated victims as Eleanor Bumpurs and Michael Stewart are explicitly invoked as a riot begins.

As Harold Cruse so provocatively suggested in *The Crisis of the Negro Intellectual* (1967), black political philosophy has always seesawed between an integrationist/assimilationist agenda and a cultural national-ist agenda. Each approach has had its own insurmountable difficulties. Integrationism always ends up being an embarrassment to its black supporters because of the almost inevitable racism and bad faith of its white supporters; they are willing to 'integrate' with a small portion of upper-class blacks only if the masses of poor blacks are willing to remain invisible and powerless. Cultural nationalism, on the other hand, has conventionally taken refuge in a fantasy of economic and political autonomy that far too often compounds its sins by falling into precisely the trap of bigotry and racism (against gays, women, Jews, 'honkies', and others) it was designed to escape. The problem with this is not just the danger it poses to whites, which has so far been mostly insignificant, but also the danger it poses to the black community internally in the form of intrasocial violence, brutality, and self-hatred.

By ending with a quote in support of nonviolent resistance from Martin Luther King, Jr, who is the hero of the integrationist/assimilation-ist position, and a quote in support of self-defense from Malcolm X, who is the hero of the cultural nationalist position, Lee squarely places his film in the vanguard of contemporary experiments to reinterpret the two approaches. But, beneath the surface, the entire debate spells 'history' as great men have made and written it, not as so many women and the poor have lived it. If the life-giving processes of the female body and the 'family' are not figured into the calculation, what remains is the lifeless, inhuman abstraction of war games.

(1989)

13

Entertainment Tomorrow

What follows will be both a defense of and a critique of what is usually called 'entertainment'. My main concern is not the production of mass culture because I cannot defend its production, given its roots in a heartless capitalist economy of global exploitation. Besides, critiques of this institution are plentiful enough. But from the point of view of the pleasure we get from participating in mass culture, a great deal more remains to be said. As the least altruistic and most self-indulgent aspect of culture, our tastes in entertainment may be the truest indication of our collective potential for tolerance and our political limits, our likelihood of doing better the next time. Particularly when entertainment utilizes multicultural strategies, it expands our cultural and political horizons, and stretches our intellectual and creative muscles.

More important than whether it teaches us something or not is that it can show us new ways to feel. Having fun is one way to begin to subvert the deadly authority that runs our country and plagues our lives because it's a way to remember what the body really feels and what we want freedom to be when we finally get there. I learned this first from my artist mother and my musician father. There was always music and black was always beautiful in our house. Moreover, growing up in a Harlem where 'entertainment' was the chief export confirmed this lesson. In the 60s, the white New Left cut its teeth not only on the serious doings of the Civil Rights Movement but also on Afro-American country and urban blues, and its rhythm & blues/rock 'n' roll offspring. And unlike the political leadership, the music always told the truth.

At its worst, however, mass culture can cajole us into buying what we've already got too much of: racism, sexism, American chauvinism, loving the rich and hating the poor. Just think of a television show like *Dallas*, which trivializes white supremacist greed. Other low points

111

include *The Morton Downey Show*. Fairly serious political issues become goofy cartoon characters, as in a recent show on *Who Speaks for Black America?* at Harlem's Apollo Theatre during which Roy Innis called the black audience 'ignorant' and knocked to the floor scandal-plagued Reverend Al Sharpton. How that must have played in Peoria. Or a movie like *Betrayed*, where racism becomes this mysterious and rare disease unrelated to historical agency, class conflict or cultural difference. As the plot unfolds, we discover that racism is not only genetic in Midwestern farmers but also macho and irresistible to women. Deborah Winger, an FBI agent who is fighting racism (not my sense of that organization's historical record), falls hopelessly in love with Tom Beringer, whose agrarian roots and working-class background seem to make inevitable his little spare-time hobby of murdering blacks and Jews. Or there's Geraldo Rivera and Oprah Winfrey and the whole morning and afternoon TV line-up. They offer a flood of misinformation, nationalistic propaganda, melodramatic distortion and hyperbolic hogwash. Worst of all, once I tune them in, I can't seem to bring myself to tune them out.

But the best of what I mean by mass entertainment involves the spontaneous and usually unchoreographed conjunction of one or more forms of 'popular culture' and the technological apparatus of the mass cultural. By 'popular culture' I mean that culture which still comes from 'the people', from the bottom up, although it can no longer claim to be uncontaminated by the poison of consumerism and the self-loathing it is ostensibly designed to ameliorate. In fact, popular culture is now deeply influenced by mass cultural appropriations of its formal qualities, which it may then reappropriate and revise in increasingly innovative gestures of autonomy. While the intricacy of this process makes popular culture virtually indistinguishable from mass culture, we can, nevertheless, identify the occurrence of the popular cultural by the ruptures it creates: not only its various ways of breaking with capitalist production – which becomes more and more difficult to do – but also by its ability to superimpose, upon the commercialism of one of the mass cultural forms, another agenda concerning 'the people'.

The prime recent example is Jesse Jackson's speech at the 1988 Democratic National Convention in Atlanta, during which the televisual intersected with Afro-American popular cultural traditions of the black church and black political speechmaking. As the time for the speech approached, I wondered how Jackson would handle the failure of the Rainbow Coalition to capture or dominate the ticket. The lifeless frame provided by the convention and the network coverage seemed impossible to salvage. The hollowness of the pseudo-event was palpable. In his speech, would Jackson manufacture an advantage, as every other pronouncement at this convention seemed manufactured (Randolph's

folksy 'That old dog won't hunt' to describe Republican policies; Teddy
Kennedy's 'Where was George?'; Barbara Jordan's defense of Bensten),
or would Jackson level? And how would he handle the potential for
widespread disillusionment among his supporters?

Although the media persistently claimed the opposite, Jackson's
support had never been a cult of personality. That's why it called itself a
coalition. Diverse groups who have had little understanding of each
other's priorities in the past were banding together to advance the
collective interests of the marginalized. I don't feel especially confident
about my ability to evaluate mainstream political events, mostly because
it seems impossible to know what is really going on. But when it comes to
mass art, like everybody else, I'm a bit of a connoisseur, and Jackson's
speech was mass art with a vengeance.

A consummate act of entertainment, it transcended all previous
standards in my television viewing history for staged, nonviolent,
televisual excitement. It was off the scale in terms of the energy it
generated and, interestingly enough, in defense of the electronic forms,
television and radio really scooped the story because the newspapers were
virtually powerless to do it justice. It was representation, not substantive
political change, that scored the victory here – by no means a trivial
matter when it comes to dealing with why most Americans find it
impossible to imagine a black president. Could this failure of imagination
(in which commercial television and radio are usually only too happy to
assist) have anything to do with the general aversion among registered
voters to necessary economic reforms like feeding and housing the poor,
or more humane foreign policies like dumping US political loyalties to
the white supremacist regime of South Africa? I think so.

Jackson's was ostensibly a concession speech, a throw-in-the-towel-in-
the-race-for-the-White House speech, and yet it seemed, alternatively, a
radical Baptist sermon on despair and the dignity of 'unwed' mothers, a
history lesson on the Civil Rights Movement and the integration of the
Democratic Party, a confession, a sharp denunciation of the global
politics of drugs, a strong defense of AIDS victims and the rights of the
gay community, and much more. The concrete visions of the various
trajectories of the speech, the branches of the various constituencies of
the Rainbow Coalition, would (and did), no doubt, conflict – especially
when it came to that part when he briefly, and dutifully, proposed
tolerance for the Democratic Party right.

Yet the sheer daring and dazzling style in revitalizing once again the
form of the political sermon – à la Martin Luther King, Jr, Adam
Clayton Powell, Jr, Malcolm X, Reverend Daughtry (and there have
been women, as well, such as Fannie Lou Hamer) – in the direction of
the improvisational blues statement, told the Afro-American audience,

at least, a lot about what could *not* be said. Remember, the form, as King, Malcolm X and Hamer employed it, was always about telling people things they didn't want to hear. It was about the necessarily innovative exercise of subverting boundaries and limitations still believed to be insurmountable. In other words, it was about the long haul.

Jackson did the key thing that a public speaker can do in order to subvert his own authority and engage the issue of 'the people' while himself in the untenable position of speaking to an audience of millions through the unfriendly medium of a network television camera. He identified himself with the silenced and powerless black woman who was his mother. He invoked his mother's teenage, 'unwed' difficulty in raising him. He proposed his mother's patchwork quilting as a standard by which to measure his political effectiveness. This use of the female figure was a critical aspect of his performance. It began when he went out into the audience to fetch Rosa Parks – the woman who was arrested for violating bus segregation in Montgomery, Alabama in the 1950s – as the 'mother' of the Civil Rights Movement. On the one hand, he was presenting himself as a conventional symbol of Democratic power politics. Even the introductions of his children, who were uniformly clean cut, articulate and well dressed, followed that format. On the other hand, Jackson's speech also seemed to be saying, 'Their grandma, and my mother, was a powerless black woman and so am I. Her powerlessness then is still my powerlessness now at this convention.'

Yet by this defense of Jackson's speech, I do not mean that it is the same as 'the real thing', the victory of concrete political transformation and growth. Still, Jackson's speech was designed to do the very important work of helping us to imagine change, on the theory that what we can imagine, we can make happen. In the process, there was strong insinuation of battles far from won, the Civil Rights Movement chief among them. The difficulty we have as a culture in acknowledging such levels of accomplishment, particularly on the part of blacks, is a major part of what's wrong with how we do things. If Ted Kennedy or Lloyd Bensten or anybody white had made such an extraordinary speech, it would have been lauded immediately and repeatedly, as an absolutely unforgettable event, to be endlessly interpreted and analyzed by left and liberal commentators.

On the other hand, I wouldn't try to offer any defense whatsoever for why Jackson would want to make peace with the despicable Mayor Koch of New York. Not only was Koch racist and unhelpful when Jackson was campaigning in the New York primaries, Koch seems, generally, to be advancing a program of urban fascism, the paramount aim of which is to disappear people of color, the homeless, street people, and anybody with a punk haircut.

Koch's long-term strategy became evident in the recent police riots in Tompkins Square Park on the Lower Eastside. Community demonstrators were protesting the city's attempt to close the park at midnight, thereby denying the homeless a place to sleep, and the restless a place to congregate and party. The police responded with surprising force and violence very late at night. Afraid to venture into the area (the rumor was that blacks were particular targets), I got most of my information from WBAI (which supplied the best coverage), as well as newspapers and television (which lagged several days behind). This was early August. While Lower Eastsiders, a fairly upwardly mobile and politically astute group, seem to have won the media battle (the closing of the park has been temporarily suspended), cool weather promises a re-escalation of Koch's cleanup efforts.

As for the Jackson strategy in all of this, it worked differently in practice than in theory. Jackson appeared none too pleased with Koch in the flesh, as a photo in *The New York Times* showing the concerned faces of Manhattan Borough President David Dinkins, Rep. Charles Rangel, Stanley Hill, the executive director of the Municipal Workers' Union, and Jackson himself, would indicate. To dissociate himself from Koch's policies even further, Jackson addressed an ongoing homelessness protest and demonstration at City Hall Park.

John Jiler recaps the group's history in the September 13 issue of *The Village Voice*: 'In June he [Koch] told the Parks people to get rid of them, but the move backfired. As a sanitation team began to devour the little village of cardboard and plastic, the press got wind of it and covered the event like a blanket. "Kochville", they began calling the settlement. As the homeless dug in, the mayor sizzled.'

That the Rainbow Coalition must lie down with Dukakis and Bensten is not my idea of fun either. Such are the all-too-familiar limitations of form: a dance is still just a dance no matter how 'black' it is. Form is not enough. Mass culture has made its millions by offering a substitute for substance – in automobiles and televisions, political parties and constitutional amendments – as everybody knows but keeps forgetting. So runs the critique.

WHAT'S COOKIN' IN HELL'S KITCHEN

Of course, the issue on the Lower Eastside and all over New York, except on Park Avenue, is labeled 'gentrification' by the press, which seems to pose the question of whether or not starving, homeless people can live

side by side in peace with Wall Street lawyers (everybody's favorite image
of the Yuppie). But the real issues are cultural tolerance – the kind of
thing the city of Yonkers is willing to blow its entire municipal budget in
order to avoid – and the potential for wholesale reform in housing the
poor, and not-so-poor, the welfare system, the Board of Education, the
prisons, drug programs, the police department, hospitals and health care,
not to mention the management of public spaces. Most of us are not
Wall Street lawyers. Most of us are not sleeping in the park, either. Yet.
So why don't the media talk more about the Rainbow?

Last summer, my first in New York in three years, I lived in a small
one-room apartment (about the size of many kitchens in 'middle
America') with my spouse equivalent Gene in an area known as Hell's
Kitchen. The uproar of dissonant musical tastes, the bellow and clamor
of domestic violence at all hours, the crack vials in the hallway, the large
numbers of homeless people sleeping in the streets, and the aggressiveness of the drug trade just down the block made it seem like 'hell'
after the last three and a half years of comparative bliss in an under-
populated Norman, Oklahoma and a beach-ridden San Diego, California. And yet, like everything else having to do with culture, I was of
two minds about it. On the one hand, the poverty, the violence, the
corruption, and the rampant economic exploitation were scary and
awful, and it was as clear in New York City as it must be in many of the
cities of the Third World that existing notions of 'government', 'law and
order', 'profit' and the economic needed immediate revision. People
were sleeping on the hard, nasty sidewalk. Children could barely get out
of the schoolyard for the drug pushers. And sooner or later, the white
man (a drug dealer) and the black woman (paying the rent, or so she
claimed in their loud arguments) in the first floor front were going to
succeed in killing one another and the police would finally have to come.

On the other hand, there was wisdom in those streets about culture-
in-the-making and culture-on-the-run – the choices people make, and
don't make, about how they will live despite too little space, not enough
money, and the nearly insurmountable difficulties of communication and
intimacy under the circumstances. I was moved and fascinated by the
extraordinary struggles for survival and pleasure that were constantly
going on around me, the mutual flow of black school children, Latino
shopkeepers, white building supers, Chinese restaurateurs, Korean
fruitstand owners, African vendors, addicts, winos, the regularly or
sporadically unemployed and under-employed, the elderly, the disabled,
the gay, the married, the lonely.

I don't mean we were all in the streets singing 'We Shall Overcome'
with linked arms. Like kept to like and ignored everything and everybody
else in a fairly heartless way. You could probably walk around with that

fried egg on your head that Bette Midler used to sing about and nobody would say anything. But my suspicion was that beneath the veneer of imperturbability everybody wore for self-protection, there was a different kind of paying attention: the first stage of tolerance, the last stage of apathy, or both.

In my leisure time, I didn't go to the movies much. Instead I jogged around and around in circles in De Witt Clinton Park on Eleventh Avenue, a place that Curtis Slewa of the Guardian Angels now says, one year later, is too drug-infested for the homeless, much less a jogging writer. But when I then ran in the mornings – besides the hotdog vendor, the short woman with eight dogs and the classful of young retarded adults playing ball – I often found homeless people still asleep on the benches or on the grass, people I came to recognize as individuals. There was a guy who used to build a cage over himself out of cardboard boxes, as he lay on a park bench under the trees. There was a young white male, who did not look homeless, who used to pace up and down chain-smoking and arguing with himself. There was a white female/black male couple that I used to see regularly enough to wonder about their domestic arrangements. How long had they been together? Had they met while homeless? Did they have sex on the grass? What did they talk about? I always wondered about the couples especially.

About midsummer I began to fantasize about making a movie about a character I would call C. Wright. She was a homeless black woman, twenty years old, addicted to crack, an 'unwed' mother whose child was being raised in a foster home, and who occasionally slept in De Witt Clinton park during the summer of 1988. She had become homeless not too long ago while still living at home when her father was laid off. In my imaginary movie, this information would be provided in a flashback in which an alcoholic mother and an abusive father first demand that she give up her baby, then drive her into the streets because of their own poverty.

One morning C. Wright wakes up in the park and sees a handsome young black man jogging in her direction. A former high school track star herself, she manages to pull herself together enough to start running again. To make a long story short, she subsequently marries the handsome young man, reclaims her child from the foster home, and goes on to win the New York Marathon. I used to see an American Express ad in the black magazines in which a young black family is shown having a day in the park. The young attractive 'mother' is jogging in the front. Behind her follows the young attractive 'husband' and 'father' on a bicycle with a small child strapped into a safety seat on the back. The black father has that bemused look, as though he isn't sure he will be able to keep up with the mother, who is commodification's version of a

black feminist. This was the sort of future I tried to construct for C.
Wright, and yet the plot presented certain large gaps in plausibility.

How would she obtain her running shoes? Where would she shower?
How would she get enough clean water to drink? Enough fresh fruit and
vegetables and fish to eat? How would she ever manage to 'just say no' to
crack, cheap wine, and chicken McNuggets? Where would the money
come from for an apartment so that she could get a decent night's sleep?
Finally, the logistics overwhelmed me, and I gave up thinking about C.
Wright's movie.

THE GREAT WHITE WAY

Of course, movies are known for proposing all sorts of improbable
scenarios and sustaining our belief in their basic presuppositions. What
being entertained is all about, in most cases, is imagining the impossible
or unlikely and making it appear painless. I happen to think that one of
the impending dangers in this country is that most of the time we are
called upon to imagine a world in which people of color will be invisible
again – unlike the streets outside New York City movie theatres. The
movies have always been an easy target in regard to this agenda,
although that's been changing with considerable black male casting in
movies like *Die Hard*, *Midnight Run*, and *Platoon*.

More disturbing to me are the photo fashion ads for Ralph Lauren's
Polo. When I look at Aryan faces with blond hair dressed in Waspy prep-
school uniforms, I start thinking about what imperialism must have
been like in 'the good old days'. The ads appear to be selling old-
fashioned family values, the lifestyle of old money, property, and estate
living. Among the white and Waspy this has always meant the exploitation and impoverishment of people of color and in the Third World.
Moreover, I think of the exorbitant prices that New World 'Yuppies' are
willing to pay for Polo's Old World look, and I fear that the equation
adds up to a fascist imagination. Or are they merely getting their
nostalgia out of their system in a harmless and profitable (dress-for-
success) fantasy? I don't think so: weren't these the same people who
voted for Reagan?

This summer, we moved to a much more spacious apartment in the
Cobble Hill section of Brooklyn. I felt less like a person with a fried egg
on my head, more like the 'cultural critic'. I couldn't help but notice that
entertainment seems to be New York's most crucial and frantic
commodity. In Cobble Hill, besides the stores and restaurants selling a

vast variety of ethnic foods as entertainment, there are all the other stores crammed with music tapes, record albums, VCR cassettes, 27-inch color TVs, radios with quadrophonic stereo, futuristic video games, slick magazines, I-Love-NY T-shirts, baby dolls that cry, wet, and sing, stuffed animals, plastic guns and warships, the New York State Lottery, *The National Inquirer*, *The Star*, and *TV Guide*, at every supermarket checkout counter, as well as the occasional sidewalk game of cards, dominoes, or checkers.

Surely, nowhere do people spend more time playing than here. In this part Latino, part Yemenite, part Italian, part Arab, part Yuppie and part Puppie (poor urban professional – that's me and Gene) neighborhood, just two blocks from a city housing project (lots of poor, unruly blacks and Puerto Ricans), there is almost constant public music. Besides the usual hand-held boom boxes and lingering car radios blaring rap, there are those civic-minded adults who like to put their stereo speakers in their windows to play the latest Latin jams.

Down the block, or downtown, or across the bridge in Manhattan, the entertainment multiplies with each mile. In Brooklyn, there's Fulton's Mall – the black shopper's answer to the 'miracle' on 34th Street – with its huge discount centers where everything is dirt cheap and worthless, its tall black East African street vendors selling everything from Duracell batteries to yapping mechanical dogs. The mall also has a few large movie theatres, many of which are playing Eddie Murphy's *Coming To America* at the moment, and none of which could pass a health or safety inspection.

There's Brooklyn Heights, with the better movie theatres, where Yuppies stroll with briefcases, in Adidas sneakers and loosened ties after a day on Wall Street. The Heights looks like a better entertainment center than it actually is. The only bookstore is a B. Dalton which promotes the usual commercial, bestselling crap.

As you cross the Manhattan Bridge, you enter Chinatown, teeming with twenty-four-hour restaurants, barbecue duck, the sidewalk commerce of Chinese vegetables, fireworks, and shrimps with the heads still on. There's the Bowery and Little Italy. Then the Lower Eastside, the West Village, Chelsea, and Union Square, all of it desperately trying to be entertaining over the distracting murmurs of the homeless and the crazed. Then there are the movies, the theatres, the concerts, and clubs, as well – Lincoln Center, Broadway, Off Broadway, Carnegie Hall. No mere mortal can do or see it all unless it's your full-time job. Even then you can't see it all. I guess that's why the professional critics rarely go below SoHo or above 57th Street.

In trying to see and hear what professional critics never see and hear, I felt as though I was attending one endless block party. In New York City,

Benjamin's mechanical reproduction has clearly become Baudrillard's cybernetic apocalyptic ecstasy of communication, in which everything is repeated to the point of meaninglessness. Or is it rather that the massive proliferation of entertainment as compensation, as escape, as the conspicuous consumption of the flattening of history and political consequence, is what urban existence is all about? It sometimes seems as though the city had at last identified a level which could accommodate and encompass us all, or so the I-Love-NY campaign would encourage us to believe.

But that's not the case at all. The fate of the Rainbow Coalition, the highly orchestrated television spectacles of Democratic and Republican Conventions and the police riots in and around Tompkins Square Park (spreading to Washington Square Park) allegedly around the issue of late-night noise (invariably somebody's idea of music), serve to illustrate the fact that one person's entertainment is another person's heartburn; we aren't all entertained by the same things. Our sense of what is entertaining is shaped as much by where we came from as where we see ourselves going, by the gut and by the wallet. Moreover, there's good reason to suspect that while entertainment can encourage an expansive imagination and cultural tolerance, it can also act as a substitute for, even an endless delay of concrete action, political change, the sharpening of critical consciousness.

Those of us who are more educated bide our time, waiting for things to improve, of their own volition apparently, go to the movies, watch TV (news and documentaries preferably), read our favorite books and magazines (journals for the academics), becoming more and more satisfied, presumably, with our 'freedoms', resigning ourselves to the impossibility of the real thing. Those of us who are less educated seem to prefer our entertainment in the streets, perhaps because the streets are the coolest place in the summer, perhaps because the streets are still rent-free. Meanwhile, it should have escaped no one's notice that while the two-party system doesn't work very well, televisions are working better and better.

This summer, I went to the theatre a lot because Gene is an actor. Off-Broadway and on-Broadway tickets are much more affordable if you know how the ticket wars work. Even the biggest Broadway show – especially if it isn't a musical – will sell standing room just before curtain time. And standing room doesn't involve milling around in the aisles – as I can recall having done at concerts in the 60s and 70s. Rather, you are assigned a spot designated by a brass plate with a number on it right behind the orchestra, where you may rest your elbows on a velvet cushion and no one can block your view because you are standing. Such tickets go for about ten dollars or so, and you are not all crushed in between the perfumes and furs and the people who want to kill you if you make any noise at all, even to whisper 'Isn't that Frank Rich?' Any other kind of ticket can be had for under ten dollars usually, if you're willing to stand in lines, come early, or subscribe to various agencies offering discount tickets.

Once I got in, I found New York theatre both fascinating and appalling. To begin with, it was much more racist and elitist and upper-class than I thought it could dare be, but perhaps it simply mirrors the values of the audience (extremely homogeneous in terms of age, dress and skin color) who support it with their (full price) ticket purchases. The fight for nontraditional casting of people of color in roles other than New Age spear carriers is waging a losing battle. As for race as an issue, it doesn't exist On Broadway or Off, except as a Yuppie nightmare.

Even in the plays of hip playwrights, you can count on the cast being lily-white, not for any particular reason that has to do with the plot or with verisimilitude, but just because it would be very startling to do anything else. Audiences do not want to have their values contested – if they don't want you in their living room, they don't want to watch you on a stage – or so runs the overly patronizing concern of the theatre companies that make these decisions for them. So it shouldn't be surprising at all when plays like Lanford Wilson's *Burn This* and David Mamet's *Speed-the-Plow*, both Broadway hits, have lily-white casts. Even the content of such plays seems to be about reproducing their own conditions of production. Gene and I saw *Speed-the-Plow* on a Friday night, and the audience was full of young, well-dressed Yuppie couples who seemed to look and think, more or less, exactly like the people on the stage (Madonna and Ron Silver). This was, no doubt, Mamet's idea of an implicit irony.

But when we get to the work of South African playwright Athol Fugard, best known for such anti-apartheid masterpieces as *Master Harold and The Boys*, only to find that he, too, has fallen into the convention of all-white casting in *Road to Mecca*, in an Off-Broadway production with the intensely rich Amy Irving in the lead role, you can't help but wonder if anybody in these parts has heard of racism at all. Although the play was instructive and fun on ageing, creativity and religious intolerance (Fugard himself played a bigoted Afrikaaner clergyman), and I loved the little old lady who was an artist, where was the controversial black majority? Does this mean that life just goes on in white South Africa? Does this mean that the white audience who adored *The Road to Mecca* hopes that life does just go on there? Is this some sort of ritual exorcism of apartheid in which one employs a dose of the poison in order to cure the disease?

Green Card by Joanna Akalaitis, also Off-Broadway, was touted as

hipper on the immigration experience, but was even more disappointing.
The closest thing to African descent in the show was Jesse Borrego, the
Puerto Rican lead from the TV show *Fame*, doing a Michael Jackson
moonwalk. 'The first great wave of immigration to the United States
(1815–1860) brought 3.5 million people, mostly Irish and German,' the
program notes observe. Although the notes go on to track immigration
into the 1980s, the waves of black people who flowed here on slave ships,
as well as those who followed as immigrants from the Caribbean and from
the African states (including our East African sidewalk vendors in Fulton
mall) never came up, unless you want to count the way the show starts.
Borrego comes out and yells: 'Any niggers in the audience?' What he
should have then said was, 'Good, because there aren't any in the show.'

But there's almost always some kind of really big, really successful
black musical on Broadway at any given moment, in order to remind
everybody what blacks do best (sing and dance), to attract black
theatregoers and yet keep the issue of 'race' in theatre steadfastly
apolitical. One such show, you might be surprised to learn, was *Sarafina*.
Although its story was ostensibly anti-apartheid, and its music by Hugh
Maskela was superb, it not only confirmed the version of apartheid we
have here, it seemed to hark back to the bad old heyday of Negro
minstrelsy when Josephine Baker got negative reviews for coming on too
grand to be 'cullud' in the Ziegfeld Follies. Everything was straight
slapstick, including the trembling behinds of the 'little girls', who ranged
from thirteen to thirty-five, in their short short pleated skirts with their
loud-mouthed teacher, who did nothing but yell, stretch her eyes and
throw her legs up in the air. In the context of an otherwise lily-white
Broadway – even if it does include a completely black cast from South
Africa – a show like this one means now what it meant in the 20s, 30s
and 40s. We, as a nation, continue to believe, or act as though we
believe difference to be, on the whole, a very bad thing.

(1988)

14

Mississippi Burning and *Bird*

For all its repetitive valorization of the campy 50s and the glorious 60s in film and TV, Hollywood has yet to have its own Civil Rights Movement. This legacy means that viewers are unable to locate any substantive treatment of black agency even in those films and TV shows that ostensibly focus on black topics. Instead, what you'll find lately – which is, I suppose, much better than nothing – is black music.

During the 50s in Harlem, Charlie Parker's trickster alto sax provided the catalyst for bebop and for the counter-cultural scene that developed around it. By the time cultural nationalism and Black Power rolled around in the 60s, Bird had become a cultural icon among black intellectuals and artists, equaled in stature only by Billie Holiday and John Coltrane, not only for his art but for his political anger. Even when his music, his natty style in dressing, his existential alienation, and his troubling addiction to drugs seemed to fade into the margins as irrelevant to Black Power's affirmation, Bird's shadow lingered still to remind us of black creativity's crucial element, its profound deformation of white cultural hegemony.

The beauty of the movie *Bird*, directed by Clint Eastwood, is, of course, the music. The heresy of bebop in concert with fellow conspirators Dizzy Gillespie, Bud Powell, Thelonious Monk, Kenny Clarke, and Max Roach (other artists embellished the original recordings for the film) still rattles the corpses that customarily assail our ears in movie houses and elsewhere. The horror, which the film sublimely advances, is the notion that this tortured black artist, played by Forest Whitaker, could have sprung full grown from the head of a white Zeus, issuing, as he seems to, from no black community, no black family, no black woman that he wouldn't have been better off without.

If it is true, as Parker himself claimed, that he was addicted to heroin from the age of twelve, this is perhaps the most important fact we can know about him after we know that he was what's called in the West 'a musical genius'. Yet in *Bird*, no more substantial reason seems to emerge to explain Parker's precipitous decline and death from drug addiction at thirty-five than that he is a black man trapped in a white man's movie. Parker as rootless, alienated from the black community, family and bourgeois existence, which he undoubtedly was, might have made a fascinating film. It is not really these issues that are explored in *Bird*, however, but rather the parasitic concept that Parker's life is only significant to the degree that it illustrates the antithesis of what it means to be white, male, and privileged. (The same seems true of the Bud Powell/Dexter Gordon character in *'Round Midnight*.) On the other hand, because we view the film through the body of Parker's music — awesome, lush, and on an entirely different trajectory — our objections are silenced.

I was prepared not to like *Mississippi Burning* because of director Alan Parker's statement to the effect that only a movie that focused on whites in the Civil Rights Movement — in this case, the two FBI agents who investigated the deaths of civil rights workers James Chaney, Michael Schwerner, and Andrew Goodman in 1964 — would be viable in a Hollywood film. My problem with this statement was not that it wasn't true. Rather, what made me think I wouldn't like the movie was that Parker was still so certain that he would be able to rise above Hollywood's conceptual apartheid to make the politically correct film. So I knew what to expect: that familiar blend of racism, heterosexism, and passive-aggressive white male chauvinism without which, say, *The Color Purple* would have been impossible to make.

But what I didn't expect was to find myself submerged, almost from the outset, in the dense, rich voice of Mahalia Jackson, perhaps the greatest black gospel singer ever recorded, singing a classic of the black church, 'Precious Lord, Take My Hand'. Of all the issues this film evades, it is least of all concerned with the plight of black women, and yet black women's singing voices are pervasive throughout and remain a constant cue. Above all, the supremely passionate voice of Mahalia — whose synthesis of blues and gospel in the 40s and 50s was an innovation comparable to Bird's, but in the realm of black women's music — is designed to tear down your resistance to Parker's apartheid aesthetics before the film has properly begun. Never mind Martin Luther King's pragmatic brand of black Christianity, for instance, as exemplified in Nina Simone singing 'Mississippi Goddamn!'. Parker prefers to ground his film's authority in a much larger though politically regressive tradition in the black church of hopelessness and despair. When the film ends with

'Take a Walk With Jesus' as the final solution, the old and recurring representation of blacks as pious, silent, and monolithically 'good' is reconsolidated. Gospel music, then, particularly the extraordinarily sorrowful singing of black women, ends up confirming the suspicion that substantive change in racial politics doesn't have a prayer.

When their car is stopped by the KKK and various police, Schwerner or Goodman says to the other two, including the black Chaney sitting in the back, 'Don't say anything, let me talk', which is precisely Parker's formula for dealing with blacks in the Civil Rights Movement. A shot of Chaney's face begins the film's endless stream of silent black faces, all eyes, fear, and unknowable blackness. The murders and violence that follow have an ominous and chilling effect as one watches the dismal politics of the rural South in 1964 reconsolidated and reinscribed in the dismal global aesthetics of Hollywood in 1989. Blackness, or black flesh, becomes the end point of an intrusive, proprietary gaze. Black eyes, heads, legs, sexual organs (or t&a, as in Parker's *Angel Heart* and *Fame*) become artifacts or art objects, reified or literally detached (in the film's fascination with lynchings and mutilation) in order to facilitate their manipulation as units of entertainment, much the way Jean-Paul Goude photographed Grace Jones, or Leni Riefenstahl photographed the Nuba. In the globalization of American culture's most durable form of neo-imperialism, an unanalyzable visualization of black flesh thus indefinitely substitutes for a discussion of racism that is long overdue.

But when Gene Hackman, as Agent Anderson, tells Willem Dafoe, Agent Ward, a story about his father's racism and then offers this explanation: he was 'an old man just so full of hate that he didn't know being poor was what was killing him', we have finally located the problem with white left-liberal conceptualizations of the 50s, the 60s, and the Rainbow in art and politics. In these conceptualizations, racism is marginalized while the economic is privileged, and racism's psychological unconscious is erased. The problem is with the notion that, in a racist empire, whites who trivialize racism and sexism can, nevertheless, provide progressive intellectual and creative leadership. Meanwhile, in the field of representation, most black people, even Bill Cosby and Oprah Winfrey, are trapped in their roles as art objects who never really speak, by which I mean they have not yet fundamentally altered the exclusionary patterns that currently characterize the production of knowledge and the structure of global communications. That black people are able to become a dominant presence in the field of American music, especially that music used in television and film, is, as I've already said, better than nothing at all, but hardly *perestroika*.

(1989)

PART III

Culture/History

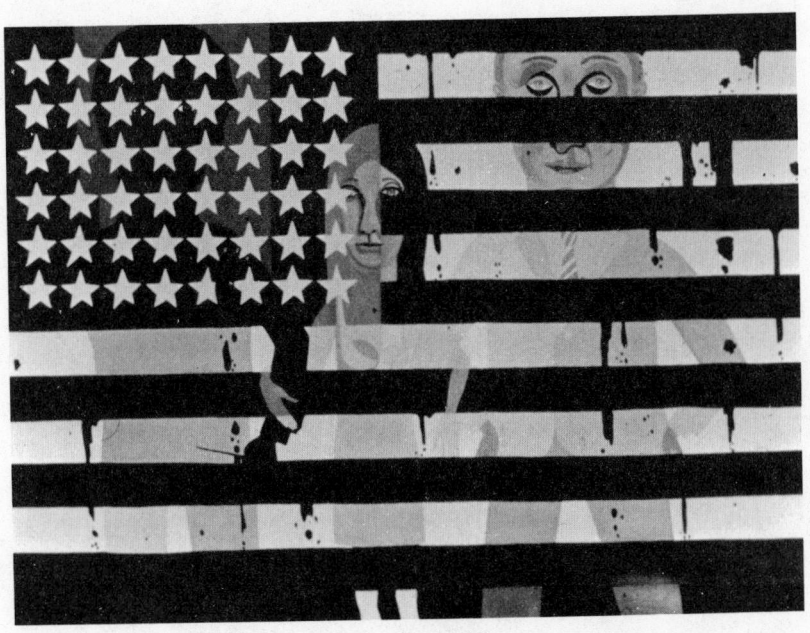

'The Flag Is Bleeding' by Faith Ringgold

15

For Colored Girls, the Rainbow
is Not Enough

At the New York Shakespeare Festival Anspacher Theatre, I am about to see *For Colored Girls Who Have Considered Suicide/When the Rainbow is Enuf*, a choreopoem by Ntozake Shange. As a black feminist, I usually feel cheated by black theatre, but this is the night I'll make up for all those other nights.

> dark phrases of womanhood/of never havin been a girl/half-notes scattered/ without rhythm no tune ... it's funny it's hysterical/the melody-lessness of her dance/don't tell nobody don't tell a soul/she's dancin' on beer cans & shingles.

Seven young black women — Shange is one of them — each in a plain cotton dress of a different color, barefoot and bareheaded. Everyone is good, but I see Trazana Beverley, in red, first — her sharp gestural wit, her flawless timing. Laurie Carlos has so much power I feel as though she is pushing me out of my seat.

> somebody/anybody/sing a black girl's song/bring her out/to know herself/to know you ... she's been dead so long/closed in silence so long she doesn't know the sound of her own voice

The subject is 'colored girls' — their growing up, their coming of age, their initiation into the horrors of dreams trampled underfoot, thwarted love, abortion, rape, and the verbal sidewalk assault. Men come up only as they are relevant to the black woman's discovery of her own life. I sit back to enjoy the explosion of details considered irrelevant to the main action in black plays from *Dutchman* by Amiri Baraka (LeRoi Jones) to *Ain't Supposed to Die a Natural Death* by Melvin Van Peebles.

Using a patchwork of vignettes, rhythm & blues lyrics, dance steps, and memories, Shange gets at almost every cheap stereotype of black women and tells a more likely story — the seductress who cries herself to sleep, the exotic quadroon of the nineteenth century who dances in rags, the 'evil' black woman who rolls her eyes at every man who speaks to her in the street because she's afraid.

We go from childhood street games, 'shake it to the east/shake it to the west/shake it to the one you like the best', to the night all of Mercer County graduated, 'i got drunk & cdnt figure out/whose hand waz on my thigh'; from the black girl who loves to latin and pretend she's Spanish, 'wit my colored new jersey self/ didn't know what anybody waz sayin/ cept if dancin waz proof of origin/i waz jibarita herself', to the woman who must see a masochistic affair through to the end, 'i want you to know this waz an experiment to see how selfish i cd be ... if i cd stand not bein wanted/when i wanted to be wanted'.

There's fantasy about the past, 'sechita/egyptian/goddess of creativity/ 2nd millennium', and there's the comedown, 'come over here bitch, can't you see this is $5?' There's revenge, 'she wanted to be unforgettable/she wanted to be a memory/a wound to every man/arrogant enough to want her/she waz the wrath/of women in windows/fingerin shades/ol lace curtains/camouflagin despair & stretch marks'.

Toward the end, the evening's most powerful statement is made: 'somebody almost run off wit alla my stuff/& i waz standin there/looking at myself/the whole time ... waz a man faster n my innocence/waz a lover/a nigga/i made too much room for ... did you know somebody almost got away with me. ...'

Then Beau Willi, a black man, a Vietnam veteran, an out-of-work gypsy cab driver, beats his pregnant wife and eventually drops their two children out of their tenement window. And finally, 'i waz missin somthin/a layin on of hands/the holiness of myself released ... i found god in myself/& i loved her/i loved her fiercely'. The cast goes off singing and hugging one another.

The ending immediately strikes me as abrupt and unsatisfying. Why has she followed such specific ethnic information about black women with a worn-out feminist cliché like, 'I found god in myself', to the tune of what sounded like a Lutheran hymn? I feel a little like a marathon runner, moving at a good speed, plenty of wind left and halfway there, who has been grabbed by the well-intentioned driver of a Jaguar XKE and dragged bodily across the finish line at 110 mph. In other words, I got there first, but I didn't win.

I do not want to be misunderstood. There is so much about black women that needs retelling; one has to start somewhere, and Shange's exploration of this aspect of our experience, admittedly the most primitive (but we were all there at some time and, if the truth be told, most of us still are), is as good a place as any. All I'm saying is that Shange's 'For Colored Girls' should not be viewed as the definitive statement on black women, just a very good beginning.

Very few have ever written with such clarity and honesty about the black woman's vulnerability, and no one has ever brought Shange's brand of tough humor and realism to it. Shange tells it like it really is: the black woman is not a superwoman. She wants to be loved and to be recognized just like anybody else. Pain hurts her just like it hurts anybody else. She is a victim of her own self-perpetuating despair – the love of her man is her only accepted means of defining herself; if he rejects her, she has nothing and is nothing. And so Shange offers the black woman a religious conversion to self-love as a solution to her problems.

But can self-love so rapidly follow rejection? Can a celebration of self really wipe out the powerful forces of a profound self-hatred and a hostile environment?

When I first heard of 'For Colored Girls', it was at the Henry Street Settlement's New Federal Theatre. It seemed as though no one black talked of anything else for weeks. 'Have you seen it? They. say the black man gets wasted.' Ticket lines were around the corner as much as an hour before show time. Then Joseph Papp moved 'For Colored Girls' to the Anspacher Theatre on June 1; it opened to packed audiences (anywhere from one-third to two-thirds black) and an ecstatic establishment press that hailed the 'choreopoem' as the most exciting thing to hit the theatre, off or on Broadway, this season.

'For Colored Girls' will move to Broadway September 15 at the Booth Theatre. Ntozake Shange, a light black woman, a playwright, a poet and fiction writer, has become an overnight star. Her four suicide attempts, her middle-class upbringing, and her 'feminist at eight' line are familiar now to an audience that just a year ago thought feminism and blackness, black middle-classness and pain were combinations as unthinkable as disco and Gregorian chant.

As for black people, the frenzied praise of the establishment critics seems to make them nervous. Many black women I know have told me that they loved 'Colored Girls', but my friends, mostly feminist, may not reflect the general climate in this case. My suspicion is that some black women are angry because 'For Colored Girls' exposes their fear of rejection as well as their anger at being rejected. They don't want to deal with that, so they talk about how Shange is persecuting the black man. For instance, an effort was made to organize black women to picket the theatre on the grounds that the play is 'unjust to black men'. Jacqueline Trescott, a black journalist, wrote in The Washington Post, 'Shange's men are beasts humiliated for the message of sisterly love. An uneasy question becomes: have the critics given 'Colored Girls' an extra measure of approval because it so clearly puts down black men?' And in the *SoHo Weekly News*, Zita Allen tells us 'most black men feel they are persecuted by "For Colored Girls" ... [and] insist it suggests lesbianism.'

Another black friend of mine, male, tells me a different story. He loved it, and, he insists, every black man he talked to loved it. 'I think black women think we feel guilty when we see how Ntozake has portrayed us. But we don't feel guilty. At least not that much. After all, she isn't talking about anything that doesn't happen. We've all done those things or something like them. It *is* the truth.'

Ntozake Shange was born Paulette Williams October 18, 1948, in Trenton, New Jersey. Her surgeon father and psychiatric social worker mother provided her with an environment that can best be described as the upper end of the black middle class; there were few blacks who had more. She was a Jack and Jiller (Jack and Jill is a social organization for middle-class black kids), a debutante twice, and while in college she partied with kids at Howard on the weekends. She lived in a big house in an integrated neighborhood, attended all-white schools, and had live-in maids. She graduated *cum laude* from Barnard College in 1970 and went directly on to earn her master's at the University of Southern California.

I was born (same name as the byline) January 4, 1952, in New York, New York. My musician father (parents were divorced when I was two) and my artist mother provided me with an environment which can best be described as slightly offbeat, a good deal leaner than Shange's but solidly black middle class. Mother forbade me membership in Jack and Jill or a coming-out party, but the first public school I ever attended was CCNY. I lived in a big apartment in a segregated neighborhood called Harlem, was attended by nurses in my early life, and we've usually had some kind of housekeeper. I worked my way through most of my college career and graduated, with little distinction, from City College.

Despite the rigorous demands of her schedule, Shange and I managed to meet for lunch one drizzling, uninspiring afternoon. Shange wears a nose ring, a set of two earrings in each ear, a print scarf topped with a patchwork denim cap, a yellow T-shirt, baggy painter's pants gathered at the ankle. I am dressed in my usual African gypsy get-up. I like her immediately. We both belonged to that stifling elite called the black middle class. We both had rejected its pretentiousness, its snobbishness, its bigoted, materialistic, mediocrity-loving view of the universe. I had had some advantages in the fight that Shange had not had: my parents were not rich, not black socialites, and they were artists. In many ways I am doing what I was raised to do, whereas Shange had gone against her destiny. I admire her for being a trailblazer.

Her first words could come from my own mouth: 'I had to write so that somebody would realize what my life is like. I was tired of being mistaken for the heroine. I was tired of being expected to be strong. I think that people say that black women are strong because it is a good way to make us feel alienated and hostile. Whatever happens, you must shut up and stand up again. We've been so busy being strong, we haven't had time to find out about ourselves.'

But how has Shange dealt with her past? 'A communist from an early age', Shange speaks of her bourgeois upbringing with a curious mixture of malice and pride. Her mother's people were 'high yellow Charlestonians' who were 'going to college in the early 1900s', and her father's father, a Garveyite and a follower of George Washington Carver, owned his own floor-waxing and window-cleaning business in Lakewood. New Jersey. She tells me about taking the train to Bedford Stuyvesant for rehearsals for the Brooklyn Girl Friends Cotillion ('the biggest and the best'), and about importing escorts: a freshman from Princeton, a freshman from Columbia, and a freshman from Rutgers, because local ones were not suitable.

'We were not a family in which everything had been sort of botched up,' she says, 'which is terribly significant, because if everything had been botched up, I wouldn't have been able to have the sort of tension I have about being proud of who I am, with anything to back it up.'

Yet Shange does not often write about her middle-classness. She writes in the dialect of the black ghetto and of black women in poverty. 'I found middle-class life terribly vacuous, incredibly boring. It just doesn't interest me, and I can't write about something that I'm not interested in.' The language of her poetry comes from the live-in maids who cared for her as a child. She seems defensive about it, but later on she admits quietly, 'I'm not avoiding writing about my middle-classness. There are just aspects of it that I haven't dealt with yet. When I understand them I'll probably write about them.'

In 1966 Shange went to Barnard, originally intending to get her PhD until she discovered what a small percentage of blacks had doctorates. 'I became terribly afraid that I would be isolating myself from all the other blacks in the country, either educationally or economically, and would be left, essentially, with nobody to play with.' She went out to California to work on her master's 'so I wouldn't have to teach public school'. She took her South African name, which means 'she who walks like a lion' and 'she who comes with her own things'. After class hours she kept away from the campus and lived in communal situations off and on with other writers, musicians, and dancers.

Shange also became a passionate feminist. She tells of a poetry reading at which a young man asked her why she never wrote about men. 'It irked me that someone would think that women were not an adequate subject. I really got much more involved with writing about women for that reason. I was determined that we were going to be viable and legitimate literary figures.'

Though Shange disagrees with the popular notion that black men are more oppressed than black women because of lynchings ('what about rape and wife beating?'), there were certain inconsistencies in her views of men that I found hard to figure out. In other interviews about 'For Colored Girls', she's said, 'That's my life out there'. But she tells me, 'I cannot say that black men have hurt me. I would say that I have been with Third World men in this country who have given me a lot of pain and a lot of pleasure, but I can't say they've hurt me. It is not biographically true.'

Shange has an interesting opinion on the importance of the black movement. 'It exorcised a lot of demons. It was a rite of passage. It told us we could do anything we wanted. But what it failed to do was give us the right to explore our own personal frustrations. Our personal lives need as much attention as the community.' Returning to the subject of black men, she says, 'They must learn to love without being a constricting force and they must be willing to deal with themselves. They haven't had much time to explore themselves. It becomes an insur-mountable task if you wait too long.'

Yet when I questioned her about the evidence of hostility between contemporary black men and black women, she said, 'I stay out of that entirely. That's for people who are into stress. See, I stay away from sexual goblins, because I can't be bothered. I have gender hostilities but they're truly gender hostilities. I'm not terribly concerned about whether a man is black or Indian or Filipino.'

The topic of pain brings us to her suicide attempts, and Shange traces her first try, not back to her marriage at nineteen as she has done in previous interviews, but to a lack of positive images to emulate when she was a child. 'I think I first tried to commit suicide because everybody kept telling me I couldn't do things. There was nothing to aspire to, no one to honor. Sojourner Truth wasn't a big enough role model for me. I couldn't go around abolishing slavery.'

As Shange explains what has happened to her when she has wanted to kill herself, her smile fades and she seems to go there. 'As soon as I get tired, I want to sleep forever. I'm not afraid of dying. I'm afraid of living. You see, I try not to forget anything. I remember experiences very clearly and when I do, I experience the pain again. I become totally unable to remember any good thing that ever happened to me.'

Yet she seems shocked and offended by the way her suicide attempts have been handled in the press. 'People took it some place I never took it. It was no more important to me at the time than the way I cook dinner. When I was there in that kind of pain, nobody was caring about it, and I really don't like the astounding response I'm getting. I mean what did they think I would do?' At this point I feel as though Shange is playing me like a yo-yo.

Middle class signifies ordinary to the general culture. But among blacks, middle class means special, since ordinary for us is dirt poor. Most of our middle-class parents advanced in this world by doing what everybody around them had told them couldn't be done – damn right they were special and their kids were going to be special, too. As a result, most middle-class black kids, and this is one facet of black life that I did not escape, were raised on daily lectures on how we had to be number one, how we should not follow what the other black kids did, or even the little white kids, because we had to be better than everybody. Never mind that a great many of us did just the opposite. The important thing is that after a while, if you survive, you begin to really think of yourself as special.

This affliction of specialness takes on even greater proportions if you are a black woman and if you actually manage to do something special, or even not so special – anything at all that sets you apart from a completely male-dominated, baby-having, uneducated, despondent welfare-receiving woman – making an income above the poverty level, graduating from college, getting married to a professional, absolutely anything. This is what makes me doubt that there will ever be an independent black middle-class women's movement. Black women seem to have very low expectations for themselves as a group. If a black woman has a few dollars in the bank and a Master Charge card, she's already thinking of herself as privileged, that she has no right to complain about anything, and that she has no connection whatsoever to that poor slob of a black woman on Lenox Avenue and 131st Street, or to any other black woman for that matter. Middle-class black women are slow to identify with each other's problems. We're all so special.

Shange is a very message-oriented writer. I've read the script of 'Colored Girls' several times, and in every poem there is a pointed feminist message. Shange is an extremely political person. But she told me, 'I'm not particularly for a black women's movement. If you're interested in black women, make something available to them, build something, then they'll have to come to you.' Perhaps, but does she really believe there can be such a thing as feminism for black women without a black feminist theory, and does she really think a black feminist can continue to exist, much less be effective, without a black women's movement?

If she does, I think she's politically naive. Ntozake has managed to conquer the disease of specialness more than many of us, enough to write a 'choreopoem' that has more than a little truth about *all* American black women, middle class, poor, or whatever, even if they do emphatically deny it. But she's not in deep enough yet.

(1976)

16

Slaves of History

The black woman slave inconveniently intersects three traditionally neglected topics in the field of history – blacks, women and the poor – which means that she is rarely the focus of inquiry. When she is not being ignored, her inner being remains shrouded in an impenetrable mystery – the kind that repels, not attracts, attention – because historians, like slaveholders, have been inclined to regard her life solely in terms of her service, or lack thereof, to her mate, her children, her master or mistress.

The odds against knowing anything about her life in the antebellum South seem insurmountable. History belongs to those who can speak for themselves, yet slaves were characteristically forbidden by law to read and write. In his famous *Narrative of the Life of Frederick Douglass, an American Slave, Written by Himself,* the celebrated abolitionist describes his escape from slavery as though it were the inevitable result of his achievement of literacy. Douglass learned to write while wandering the streets of Baltimore; but unlike him, few black female slaves were hired out in cities.

Moreover, few black women slaves were willing to abandon their children to risk freedom. Even those black women who did escape rarely acquired literacy, and they even more rarely, so far as we know, wrote books. The three best-known black women ex-slaves – Sojourner Truth, Harriet Tubman and Linda Brent – all three illiterate, communicate with us through the interventions of white female abolitionists.

Finally in Deborah Gray White's *Ar'n't I a Woman? Female Slaves in the Plantation South,*[1] we have a book-length effort to grapple with the enigma of the black woman slave. White looks at her longstanding neglect in the words of Sojourner Truth's evocative question to a Women's Rights Convention in Akron, Ohio in 1851:

... Look at me! Look at my arm! I have plowed, and planted, and gathered into barns, and no man could head me – and ar'n't I a woman? I could work as much and eat as much as a man (when I could get it), and bear de lash as well – and ar'n't I a woman?

(p. 14)

Once a slave in Ulster County, New York, Truth knew well the symbiotic relationship of sexism and racism. Her experience, and that of thousands of slave women, not only irreconcilably contradicted ante-bellum assumptions about the female's limited abilities, but also suggested those assumptions were intentionally hypocritical. But, White complains, 'so few scholars have dealt realistically with these questions' because of the nature of the slavery debate in our time.

White traces the problem back to Stanley Elkins' *Slavery, A Problem in American Institutional and Intellectual Life* (1959), which postulates a 'Sambo' personality – a kind of perpetual childishness and incompetence – as the inevitable outcome of the unmediated severity of the slave-master's power over the slave. White further observes that Elkins implicitly excluded black women slaves from his thesis: '... inasmuch as Samboism involves "feminine" traits,' White concludes, 'it is men of the race characterized as such who bear the burden of the insult'. Conse-quently, 'the emphasis of recent literature on slavery has been on negating Samboism,' White says. 'The male slave's "masculinity" was restored by putting black women in their proper "feminine" place.'

White finds fault even with Herbert Gutman's massive study, *The Black Family in Slavery and Freedom* (1976), which so thoroughly demolished the assumptions of E. Franklin Frazier, Daniel Patrick Moynihan and Elkins, that black women were the dominant figures in slave households:

Gutman made so much of the role of the slave men – in protecting slave women and children, in naming offspring, in the stabilizing effects of their presence in slave households – that women's roles were reduced to insignificance and largely ignored.

White sets out to redress the imbalance, although she duly notes the grave obstacles posed by the lack of relevant primary sources. 'Slave women were everywhere and yet nowhere,' she says. Relying heavily on WPA interviews with female ex-slaves from the 1930s, she readily admits to an element of conjecture in her conclusions. Nevertheless, her method is meticulous and restrained. Her best efforts go into unmasking some of the generalizations highly regarded in recent years.

For instance, in her chapter 'Jezebel and Mammy: the Mythology of

Female Slavery', White maintains that the two dominant myths slaveholding class produced about the black woman slave were actu private and public versions of the same conceptual problem. On the one hand, slaveholders conceived of the black woman slave as a Jezebel – aggressively carnal, Lilith turned animal. This conception explained her continued sexual exploitation by the master, her coerced breeding, the illegality of her marriage and the fragile bond between mother and child as a product of her own immorality – as well as justifying her half-naked torture by whipping and her labor in the fields.

On the other hand, particularly in the late antebellum period and in response to abolitionist criticism, pro-slavery propagandists pictured slavery as a school of moral instruction. Mammy, the black woman as asexual nurturer, competent, capable, more in charge of the Big House than either master or mistress, provided their principal proof. The myth of the plantation 'Mammy' seemed to contradict the allegations of the sexual exploitation of female house slaves, and exaggerate to the point of absurdity the maternal instincts of women who, ironically, could be separated from their children by sale at any time. The 'Mammy' was designed to convey the impression that all was well in the plantation South. Practicing what comparative sociologist Orlando Patterson described in *Slavery and Social Death* (1982) as the 'human technique of camouflaging a relation by defining it as the opposite of what it really is', slaveholders attempted to lull themselves and the nation asleep with the myth of the black woman's perennial power.

White explains that the Mammy image was a relatively late development in antebellum Southern self-perception. In *The Plantation Mistress* (1983), Catherine Clinton describes it as 'a figment of the combined romantic imaginations of the contemporary Southern ideologue and the modern Southern historian'. Despite the emphatic attention Eugene Genovese gave to the 'Mammy' in *Roll, Jordan, Roll: The World The Slaves Made*, and his claim that 'To understand her is to move toward understanding the tragedy of plantation paternalism', White believes that actual Mammies were probably relatively rare in the South, and exercised considerably less extensive powers over the larder, the kitchen and the domestic affairs of the Big House than the nostalgic memories of pro-slavery diaries, memoirs and novels would support.

White reads Southern patriarchal culture here as consolidating its symbolic power over both women and blacks in a single rhetorical move. 'As the personification of the ideal slave, and the ideal woman,' White tells us,

> Mammy was an ideal symbol of the patriarchal tradition. She was not just a
> product of the 'cultural uplift' theory, she was also a product of the forces

that in the South raised motherhood to sainthood. As part of the benign
slave tradition, and as part of the cult of domesticity, Mammy was the
centerpiece in the antebellum Southerner's perception of the perfectly
organized society.

(p. 58)

In general, White's approach is traditionally feminist, in the sense that
she explains the void more thoroughly than she fills it. She closes her
book with another occasion in the life of Sojourner Truth. In October,
1858, Sojourner Truth spoke in Silver Lake, Indiana. Men in the
audience challenged her to prove she was a woman. She responded by
baring her breasts.

Truth's experience serves as a metaphor for the slave woman's general
experience ... Slave women were the only women in America who were
sexually exploited with impunity, stripped and whipped with a lash, worked
like oxen. In the nineteenth century when the nation was preoccupied with
keeping women in the home and protecting them, only slave women were so
totally unprotected by men or by law. Only black women had their
womanhood so totally denied.

(p. 162)

More to the point, the men who questioned Truth's womanhood
probably went away dissatisfied with their glimpse of her breasts, for the
entire exchange was hopelessly mired in the kind of confusion that
inevitably accompanies the demystification of 'sexual politics'. Truth
herself used the occasion to present further evidence of her sexual labor
and exploitation; she told the audience that her breasts had fed many a
white infant.

What her experience as both slave and abolitionist lecturer had taught
her was that the condition known as 'womanhood' was man-made.
Although gender role definition has some consistent limitations,
variations in class and culture are partly designed to obfuscate the
uniform intentions of the patriarchy towards women. In fact, the
intentions of the patriarchy are always the same – to reinforce the upper-
class white male's seemingly unintentional monopoly over power and
influence, and to keep women of different classes and cultures from ever
recognizing their common predicament.

Gender definition is a provisional process. The light the condition of
the black woman slave sheds upon this process as it unfolded in the
United States – especially when it is compared to the 'cult of domesticity' that obscured the labor and exploitation of the upper-class white
woman – is probably the most illuminating story black feminist antebellum history yet may tell us. Black women slaves lived their lives on the

frontier of gender definition in a laboratory – the plantation South –⎞
that slaveholders tried to render invulnerable to critical scrutiny.   ⎠

Although White could have explored this line of inquiry, finally she
falls back on the ultimately mystifying posture of moral indignation, a
posture that has helped to keep many women scholars from revealing
the systemic logic of women's oppression. Ironically, she might have
avoided this trap if she had focused on other aspects of Elkins' argument
in *Slavery*. Elkins criticized the emotionalism of abolitionist arguments
against slavery as self-serving and ineffective, and suggested that guilt
feelings have corrupted historical scholarship on the antebellum South.

There are all sorts of reasons to be suspicious of Elkins' thesis, among
them his implicit appeal to a higher historical objectivity. But what is
useful is the reminder that historical scholarship is never a transparent
window on the past, revealing 'what really happened'. Just beneath the
surface there are the motives of the historian, and the society that
produced her or him, jumbling the communication. And just beneath
that there are the motives of the historical record itself, the politics of
who wrote letters and kept diaries and who didn't have time to, who
gave speeches and wrote books and who never got the chance to. Sifting
these sands may extricate more black women's history than dreamed of,
for it was in these processes that black women slaves were sifted out.

Speculation about 'what really happened' in the plantation South has
proven irresistible to American novelists and their readers. From *Uncle
Tom's Cabin* to *Gone With the Wind*, from *Mandingo* to *Roots* and *Beulah
Land*, the enduring fascination with the South as a hotbed of mis-
cegenation and an ethical embarrassment attests to the perennial
American anxiety about slavery as a field of sexual exploitation.

Yet little of this fiction has been written from the perspective of the
black woman slave. Her narrow access to the world, which effectively
erased her from the historical record, also impeded her conceptual-
ization in fiction; for how is the author to give the story in which she is
the center of intelligence a broad enough perspective to support the
omniscient tone so characteristic of the historical novel? Margaret
Walker in *Jubilee* begins the process of substitution by using Afro-
American folk culture – spirituals, work songs, folk medicine, Afro-
American Christianity – to provide the substance and insights of the
world of Vyry, her house-slave protagonist. But in *Dessa Rose*, a first
novel by the poet and playwright Sherley Anne Williams,[2] the problem
of point of view is turned to distinct narrative advantage by the
decentering of patriarchal authority. There is no omniscient tone here,
only the rhetorical play of relative perspective – or a rather specialized
lack of information – on the part of the main characters.

Dessa Rose, whose perspective is a product of her circumscribed experience as a black woman field slave, alternates the focus of point-of-view with Rufel, the plantation mistress whose perspective is a product of her 'femininity' as defined by antebellum Southern society, and Nehemiah, the pro-slavery writer whose perspective is a product of his racism and ambition. These three characters, each steeped in his or her peculiar provincialism, form three sides of a triangle that encompasses a key black male subject – Kaine, Dessa's slain lover – without including his thoughts, thus indicating his unique status in these proceedings as, I suspect, the unrealizable utopian vision of this work.

In the novel's immediate past, Dessa was an ordinary field hand, unremarkable in education, background or condition, precisely the Southern plantation's least fathomable and most mysterious figure. Despite her leadership in a slave uprising, Dessa never stops being ordinary, having no peculiar genius or compulsive ambivalence about freedom in the manner of William Styron's Dostoyevskian Nat Turner. The desire to be free, the novel makes clear, is as natural and inevitable to a slave as breathing; but most slaves, the novel implies, are willing to give up the chance for freedom to keep their families together.

This becomes impossible for Dessa when Kaine, the man she loves and a fellow slave on the Vaugham plantation in McAllen County, is killed for having hit the master. Pregnant with his child, Dessa hits the mistress in her grief, and is sold off the plantation where her family – most notably her 'Mammy' – remain, onto a slave coffle, a gang of slaves chained together for transport to market. She helps to lead an insurrection on the coffle in which five white men are killed. Although she is eventually caught, she is not executed right away as are the other captured slaves. When the book opens, she is being kept alive until the birth of her child because Wilson, the slavetrader who owned the coffle, and who has lost his arm and his sanity in the struggle (he refers to Dessa fearfully as a 'devil woman'), is obsessed with realizing the profit from the sale of her baby. During her imprisonment, she is interviewed by Nehemiah Adams, no slaveowner himself but the upwardly mobile son of a mechanic who is writing his second book of advice for slaveholders.

The progress of events in the novel is ruthlessly manipulated so that the action is rarely allowed to occur – as though the narrative were a transparent window upon the world – but rather reoccurs in someone's retrospective and biased account of it. Language dominates, rendering time and space two-dimensional and subjective. This technique emphasizes the ephemerality of antebellum record-keeping – echoing the problem of locating the 'true' history of black women slaves. And it parodies male expertise through the persona of Nehemiah Adams, whose knowledge of slavery is so strikingly a collection of prejudice and superstitions – such as that 'darkies' were 'subject to the same chills and sweats that overtake the veriest pack animal' and his fear that 'they fell asleep much as a cow would in the midst of a satisfying chew'.

Patriarchal authority is decentered; the world is seen from a profoundly limited and distinctly vulnerable perspective – as in the characteristically female point of view. Perhaps owing to Williams' skill as a poet – amply demonstrated in her tribute to Bessie Smith in her first book *Some One Angel Chile* (reissued by Morrow) – *how* something happens in the language of the book is as important as *what* happens. In the process, both Nehemiah and Kaine become 'female' subjects, hopelessly 'other' to the Southern antebellum world that really matters – Kaine because he's a slave, Nehemiah because he's slaveless.

Dessa Rose zeroes in on the dichotomous role of women in the antebellum South. Two survivors from the coffle, Dessa's co-conspirators, rescue her. They take her to a remote Alabama plantation where a young woman, Rufel Sutton, abandoned by her riverboat gambler husband, allows runaway slaves to live in exchange for helping out in the house and in the fields. At the center of the interaction between the white Rufel and the black Dessa lies the myth versus the reality of 'Mammy'. It had escaped my attention, until Alice Walker said so in an essay about *The Color Purple*, that blacks in the rural South had referred to their own mothers as 'Mammy'. Until then, I'd thought of Mammies in terms of Hattie McDaniels in *Gone With the Wind* – either a servant or a slave with a huge domestic responsibility. In *Dessa Rose*, both aspects of Mammy are explored as both Rufel and Dessa make proprietary claims on her.

When Dessa arrives at Rufel's house, she's just borne her child and she's delirious with fever. Rufel has no revolutionary or abolitionist intentions in providing a refuge for slave runaways – she has stumbled accidentally into the situation – but Dessa's condition arouses her sympathy, so Rufel puts her in her own bed, the only one in the house. And in a stunning reversal of white vs. black female roles in the antebellum South, Rufel breastfeeds Dessa's newborn child because Dessa has no milk:

> Rufel had taken the baby to her bosom almost without thought, to quiet his wailing while Ada and the other darkies settled the girl in the bedroom ... The sight of him so tiny and bloodied had pained her with an almost physical hurt and she had set about cleaning and clothing him with a single-minded intensity.
>
> (p. 101)

Born to a moderately prosperous family in Charleston, SC, Rufel married the wrong man – dashing Bertie Sutton, who boasted of a 'cotton plantation' in Northern Alabama, which turns out to be sparsely settled frontier land plainly inhospitable to the cultivation of cotton. Bertie has been gone for at least a year and a half when Dessa arrives at Sutton Glen. Meanwhile, Rufel's Mammy, a wedding gift from her father, has rallied a collection of runaway slaves to harvest the crops. Rufel has only the dimmest grasp of what has happened, can't cope with the fact that she hasn't heard from her family in four years, that Bertie may never return, that Mammy died the previous spring.

So Rufel spends the better part of the day sitting beside Dessa's bed, staring out of the window, sewing and daydreaming about her coming-out days in Charleston and her warm, talkative relationship with 'Mammy'. Occasionally, she speaks to herself aloud, and Dessa can't help but hear her. Rufel refers to Mammy more than once. Finally, Dessa interrupts her. 'You don't even know Mammy,' Dessa says.

> 'I do so,' the white woman said indignantly, 'Pappa give her –'
> 'Mammy live on the Vaugham plantation near Simeon on the Beauford River, McAllen County.' This was what they were taught to say if some white person asked them; their name and what place they belonged to . . .
> 'My, my – My Mammy –' the white woman sputtered.
> The words exploded inside Dessa . . . 'Your mammy!' . . . No white girl could ever have taken her place in mammy's bosom; no one.
> 'You ain't got no "mammy,"' she snapped.
>
> (p. 118)

By this time Dessa has realized that she and Rufel are talking about two different people, she about her own mother, Rufel about a servant named Dorcas, but she hangs upon this confusion over Mammy's identity the entire burden of her pent-up rage. She wins the argument with Rufel by pointing out that Rufel doesn't know her Mammy's name.

> 'You don't even not know mammy's name. Mammy have a name, have children.'
> 'She didn't.' The white woman, finger stabbing toward her own heart, finally rose. 'She just had me! I was like her child.'
> 'What was her name then?' Dessa taunted . . .
> 'Mammy,' the white woman yelled. 'That was her name.'
>
> (p. 119)

The confrontation starts a process of reflection in Rufel that leads her not only to remember Mammy's name, but also to wonder if she did have children of her own after all, and even to question the institution that had brought 'Mammy' – perhaps against her will – into Rufel's life. It is too late to correct her relation to Mammy/Dorcas, but she works out a relationship with Dessa. Its strength becomes clear when Rufel saves her from capture by Nehemiah, who has been combing the South looking for her:

> 'Ruth,' 'Dessa,' we said together; and 'Who was that white man –?' 'That was the white man –' and stopped. We couldn't hug each other, not on the streets, not in Arcopolis, not even after dark; we both had sense enough to know that. The town could even bar us from laughing; but that night we walked the boardwalk together and we didn't hide our grins.
>
> (p. 233)

As the story unfolds, both Dessa and Rufel learn more about the condition of the other in the antebellum South than either ever expected to know. Dessa is surprised to find out that 'White women wear some *clothes* under them dresses, child,' and that white women can also be raped by white men. Although Rufel 'thought that if white folks knew slaves as she knew us, wouldn't be no slavery,' still she must learn the precise bargaining power of 'femininity' in the Southern marketplace.

Dessa Rose reveals both the uniformities and the idiosyncrasies of 'woman's place', while making imaginative and unprecedented use of its male characters as well. Sherley Anne Williams' accomplishment is that she takes the reader some place she's not accustomed to going, some place historical scholarship may never take us – into the world that black and white women shared in the antebellum South. But what finally excites me the most about this novel is its definition of friendship as the collective struggle that ultimately transcends the stumbling-blocks of race and class. If the creative writer can't dream these dreams, who can?

(1986)

NOTES

1. New York: Norton, 1985.
2. New York: Morrow, 1986.

17

Ishmael Reed's Female Troubles

Ishmael Reed appeared on *Tony Brown's Journal* last summer to discuss the question of 'whether black feminist writers are victimizing black men'. The provocation was twofold: controversy over the movie of *The Color Purple*, based on Alice Walker's book, and the publication of Reed's novel *Reckless Eyeballing*, which explores the notion that black women writers are hapless pawns of manipulative white feminists. Although the television format implied that Reed was debating the possibility of black female disloyalty with the other guest on the show, literary critic Barbara Smith, they seemed to be articulating mutually exclusive perspectives from parallel worlds.

Smith edited a black feminist studies anthology called *All the Women Are White, All the Blacks Are Men, but Some of Us Are Brave*. Reed, seemingly unaware of the implications, paraphrased the title as 'All the women are good and all the men are bad'. In his world, such a substitution is as inevitable as the law of gravity, although Neo-Hoodoo, Reed's signature cosmology, is supposed to be repelled by binary oppositions. Neo-Hoodoo, as it occurs in Reed's poetry, fiction, and essays, rejects the stifling duality and reification of Western rationalism in order to question the automatic devaluation of black and other nonwhite males. But it does not confront the preeminent social instance of binary opposition: gender roles.

Last winter Ishmael Reed calmly explained to me that there was a media-wide conspiracy to blame black men for male chauvinism; mainstream feminists, consolidating a reconciliation with white men, needed a scapegoat – black men were it. (He might have added that he was doing everything in his power to assist this process.) Reed continued his obsessive ruminations on the Tony Brown show. A black male in the audience asked, 'Isn't feminism about that spoiled white woman in

Scarsdale?' Contending with a shouting Reed, Smith answered: 'What
black feminism is about is that black woman trying to raise her children
on welfare in Harlem. It's about our sisters who are in the SROs right
now surrounded by rats and drugs . . .'

To which Reed never responded. Instead, he cited FBI statistics for
July 1985, which he said attributed 80 per cent of sex offenses to white
males (in fact, according to the FBI, the annual figure for white males is
52 per cent). 'Black men have been chosen to take all of this heat . . .
we're not the only men who are male chauvinists,' Reed insisted. 'Why
don't they make movies about that?' Of course, they *do* make movies
about that. From priest to rapist, in *The Godfather* to *The Deerhunter* to
Blue Velvet, the white male is symbolic everyman of first and last choice.
So what is Reed really beefing about?

The problem appears to be that Reed doesn't relish the idea of black
women making public judgements about black men, although black men
in the know, from the ubiquitous Dr Poussaint (psych consultant for the
Cosby show) to Reed himself, insist on their right to define and describe
black women. Reed's inflexibility undoubtedly has something to do with
the 'double oppression' of black women; their double disqualification for
the exercise of power makes it all the more likely that black women
intellectuals will be hypercritical of black men (and white women as well,
but nobody seems much interested in this).

Reed fears that the double negative of being black and being a woman
in this society adds up to a positive advantage. In the grotesque world of
mass media, sometimes the double negatives appear to turn positive.
Consider the proliferation of black women fashion models, news broad-
casters, opera singers, and rock stars. Still, Janet Jackson's energetic
performance in 'Control' should be read as a cautionary tale: in our
culture, control doesn't proclaim itself. Here, the sign of the black
woman draws upon its own peculiar malleability: it is doubly divested of
meaning, and therefore particularly well suited to enigma without
content.

In the 'real' world of pressing economic, political, and social consequences, the double negatives don't cancel each other out. They line up,
one behind the other, like a combination punch, or the way black
women line up in downtown streets all across the country to sell or
display their bodies – extending interminably into the nether world of
what Ralph Ellison once called 'invisibility'.

When Alice Walker described herself as a 'womanist' in a 1984 essay,
I wondered about her obsessive need to dissociate herself from white
feminists. But the feminist baiting of Reed and his cohorts makes me
think Walker had the right idea after all. Black feminists are preoccupied
with basic issues of survival. Their writing tends to stress the precise

occasion of application, leaving the theorizing to somebody else – not because their engagement with feminist thought is less intense, but because black feminism is firmly grounded in a 'real life' preoccupation with a black female population that is disproportionately poor and voiceless.

The problem with feminist theory, in general, is its failure to be concerned with palpable alternatives to conventional living arrangements because of its fondness for generalizations that will encompass us all. The problem with black feminists is the tight space they are forced to occupy as the 'Other' of both black men and white women, who are 'Other' themselves. This means that alternative models are essential to black women writers; expressive acts are unthinkable without them. Walker makes these points when she compares Virginia Woolf to slave poet Phillis Wheatley, who lacked not only a room, but a *life* of her own.

Being the 'Other' of the 'Others' – and thus twice removed from power – also means that black women writers have to be careful not to offend. As they focus more and more on the patriarchy's decline, they become simultaneously frightening and provocative. On the one hand, people don't want to change; on the other hand, they know they have to.

Once upon a time, the black male was preeminent 'Other'. He seemed to epitomize free expression, profligate sexuality, organic society – all the opportunities lost under modern industrial capitalism. In Norman Mailer's 'The White Negro', for example, the white male becomes 'hip' in an attempt to appropriate the liberating essence of black maleness. Increasingly – with a leg up from Black Power and Civil Rights – black male writers have found ways to render their position an articulate and critical presence. Before Ishmael Reed, there was work by Richard Wright, Ralph Ellison, James Baldwin, John A. Williams, John Edgar Wideman, and Amiri Baraka in which the 'Other' spoke protest, and everybody seemed satisfied for a time.

Yet his preeminence as 'Other' was not secure. Just one of these writers, Ralph Ellison, achieved validation by the American literary establishment (and not only hasn't he written a second novel, but he's unpopular with blacks for his political conservatism). Lately, the situation seems more insecure than usual. Reed was next up for inclusion in the canon in the 70s, but his career appears to be in decline – precipitated, in no small part, by his perversely misogynistic views. Despite his popularity among black male critics, his novels receive less and less media attention, and all of his books except *Reckless Eyeballing* are now out of print, which doesn't bode well for canon inclusion.

Predictably, Reed sees himself as being in direct competition with white women. Part of his attack on black feminists is to claim that white feminists do their thinking for them ('Gloria Steinem has become some modern-day daughter of Dracula, claiming victim after victim, to carry out her orders,' Reed says). Among the many advantages of white male privilege is the occasional luxury of role reversal – think of the mock drag of white male rock stars. As a black male writer, Reed is saddled with a more limited vision. When the black woman, the 'Other' of the 'Other', insists on having a voice, his status quo is profoundly disrupted. For the upwardly mobile black male intellectual, role reversal is neither tenable nor entertaining.

If the articulate black male deals with the way white males have divided up the world in which communication between us occurs – and he has to deal with it to get ahead materially and/or intellectually – then he is bound to be highly skeptical of attempts to scale down male privilege, because it means that when he does finally 'get over', there's going to be less to get. I'm not saying that black men sit down and reason these things out. In fact, the black men who do think about them tend to come to different conclusions. With Reed, we're considering a kind of knee-jerk nonperceptiveness in which he mindlessly competes with white women for the number two spot, and will brook no interference from black women or anybody else. Even if it's to tell him the game has changed.

In Reed's work, characters and centuries come and go like color combinations in a kaleidoscope. Critics praise his narrative speed and abruptness. It's like watching Fellini, they say. It's like bebop. The man has his finger on the pulse of the times.

Unencumbered by the uptight strategies of mimesis, this 'cowboy in the boat of Ra' improvises plots that are perversely eventful parodies of the stodgy predictabilities of the Bildungsroman (*Free-Lance Pallbearers*, 1967), the Western (*Yellowback Radio Broke-Down*, 1969), the detective story (*Mumbo Jumbo*, 1972), Greek tragedy (*The Last Days of Louisiana Red*, 1974), the slave narrative (*Flight to Canada*, 1976), the Gothic mystery (*The Terrible Twos*, 1982), and the epic (*Reckless Eyeballing*, 1986). And yet Reed never quite parodies the most important foregone conclusion of the originals.

These genres have in common their validation of the white male center. Reed attempts to displace only the color of the center (like trying to peel the white off snow!), leaving intact, even confirming, the notion of centers and therefore peripheries. Parasitic relations are inherently unstable; if the same observation can be made about relations of domination in texts, then it may explain the frantic energy Reed brings to an increasingly elaborate mythology about the black female.

Reckless Eyeballing is the most extreme literary enactment so far of

Reed's female trouble. The novel is talky, bitter, complicated, accusatory
– the opposite of a charming text. It opens with protagonist Ian Ball's
dream that he is being tried as a witch in Salem. His judges, the Puritan
fathers, bear the face of Tremonisha Smarts, a black feminist whose
successful play, *Wrong-Headed Man*, transparently echoes *The Color
Purple*, and Becky French, a prominent and manipulative white New
York feminist. Ball's nightmare ends in metaphorical castration – 'a
snakeskinned hand was about to cut off a rattler's head with a large,
gleaming blade' – after he realizes that the guard who will lead him to the
gallows is his mother.

Here the Neo-Hoodooist falls back on a reassuring Neo-Freudian
geometry. The castrating female is so much an inevitability of this
narrative that a man must occupy that space if a woman won't. The
Salem witches condemned to death were almost all women. Ian Ball,
therefore, is cast in a female or 'feminine' role. The presence of the
mother as executioner evokes 'the suffocation of the mother' – a popular
name in the seventeenth century for the choking sensation considered a
common symptom of 'feminine' hysteria, used to confirm the diagnosis
of witchcraft. This painfully inarticulate text is a recurrence of that
symptom. The snake in the dream, it is worthwhile to remember, seems
to be chopping off his own head.

Ian Ball, clearly a stand-in for Reed, doesn't know his ass from his
elbow when it comes to American feminism – which, I suppose, makes
him yet another Afro-American trickster figure, like PaPa LaBas in
Mumbo Jumbo and *The Last Days of Louisiana Red*, like Raven Quickskill
in *Flight to Canada*, like Black Peter in *Terrible Twos*. In Afro-American
folklore, tricksters are characters steeped in motherwit who turn the
shortcomings of powerlessness to advantage. Reed has grafted on this
agenda the conflicting demands of an edenic triangle that owes most of
its inspiration to patriarchy. Consequently, his tricksters have been
undergoing a fierce process of degeneration and an identity crisis that
won't wait.

Ball – his arteries sluggish with gin and McDonald's burgers – is
plagued by the burden of a strong mother with second sight, whom he
suspects of watching his every move. The only candidate for an
influential father figure, Jake Brashford, is famous for a single play, *The
Man Who Was an Enigma*. Though unable to write another play,
Brashford keeps on receiving prizes, chairs, and grants.

Ball's first play puts him high on the 'theater feminists' sex list'
because its protagonist wants to be gang-raped; he attempts to clear his
name with black feminists by writing another play called *Reckless
Eyeballing*, which gives all the best roles to black female actors. In it, a
white woman named Cora Mae has caused the lynching of a black

Southern youth named Ham Hill. Twenty years later, Cora Mae, who has become a radical lesbian feminist (Reed's code for Totally Unreasonable Person), gets a court order to have Hill's body exhumed and tried for 'reckless eyeballing', which her white female attorney calls 'eye rape'.

At the heart of *Reckless Eyeballing* – coddled within concentric subplots about Nazism, anti-Semitism, rape, lynching – lies Reed's perception that American feminism says white women are not responsible for bigotry and racism.

From the last quarter of the nineteenth century until the middle of the twentieth, white Americans, mostly men, justified their lynching of black Americans, mostly men, by claiming that they were protecting white women from rape. Another early explanation of the lynchings was that white women were the cause of it all because of a deeply rooted psychological tendency to desire rape, which they communicated to their rope-toting men as an actuality. Reed, who cites Wilhelm Reich's *The Mass Psychology of Fascism* elsewhere and therefore ought to know better, is stuck at this stage of the dialogue.

He's not alone: the castrating woman (which is her tendency when she's not being castrated) has become a centerpiece in avant-garde Afro-American literature's attempt to personify the broken promises of America – from the red, white, and blue whore of Ellison's 'Battle Royal' to the bitch goddess of Amiri Baraka's *Dutchman*.

In the 'real' world, the black male has obviously had a hard time politically and economically, but he has repeatedly portrayed his difficulty as a ritual of castration. His humiliation in a phallocentric culture is his feminization. It was thus that the rape of the white woman became a key trope in the rhetorical strategy of compensation – which was part of what Reed was objecting to, presumably, in his caricature of Black Power in *The Last Days of Louisiana Red*. In his 1981 essay 'Black Macho, White Macho: The Stale Drama' (you said it!), Reed observes, 'While black male macho might be annoying, white male macho could be the death of us.' I thought he saw the connections as well.

Reed's determination to see feminism as a historical error reduces his black feminist characters to hand puppets mouthing his inane views. In *Reckless Eyeballing*, Tremonisha Smarts' opinions about Josephine Baker are particularly revealing (Baker, a potent symbol for Reed, is also on the cover of *Mumbo Jumbo*, in double images to evoke the two sides of the Haitian Voudoun goddess Erzulie). Here Smarts explains to Ball why Hitler slept with a picture of Baker over his bed the night of his Austrian campaign:

> He was getting even with his mother.... He had her picture on the wall of his bedroom, but the night that he's away from his room, sort of a shrine to

his mother, he fantasizes about sleeping with the demon princess, the wild temptress Lilith, Erzulie, the flapper who brought jazz dance to the Folies ... Jesus Christ had the same experience with a prostitute on the road, away from his prying mother, whom [sic] some say was the prostitute. A Lilith or Erzulie of her time. He had the same problem. Jesus, Hitler, both had weak fathers and strong, manipulative mothers.

How are we supposed to distinguish this 'suffocation of the mother' from garden variety Puritanism, which Reed once counted chief among sins?

Neo-Hoodoo harbors an intrinsic shortcoming. Borrowed in part from Zora Neale Hurston's anthropological investigations in the 30s, arguably literary in its intentions, Neo-Hoodoo is Reed's version of a syncretic creed based on New World adaptations of African religions. Manifestations of Neo-Hoodoo include the blues, bebop and the lindy, North American Hoodoo, Haitian Voudoun, and Mardi Gras – mostly occasions of dance, music, and religion in the New World.

The point is that Western rationalism and capitalist uptightness don't really bear imitation. Neither Afro-Americans nor other ethnic Americans (or any thinking Wasp for that matter) should be forced to live in these square holes. On the other hand, it doesn't make sense to look back nostalgically on an African/ethnic, primitive/rural past of greater simplicity and purer motives. Instead, Reed's Neo-Hoodoo suggests that the focus of speculation should be the improvisational nature of the diaspora – in other words, how it works when it works.

The fly in the buttermilk here, however, is Neo-Hoodoo's basis in religion, which has been laying its eggs of phallocentrism wherever it goes at least since Egyptians had a choice between the worship of Osiris and Isis. Feminist anthropologists warn us that even the worship of female gods was a reflection of the rising social need to set women apart as unfathomable, threatening, and 'Other'.

The potential appeal of Neo-Hoodoo is that it offers the possibility of intellectual alternatives for nonwhites committed to aggressive adaptation rather than passive assimilation or blending in. The religious syncreticism of New World nonwhite populations, Reed intends, will serve as a guide to completing the process of East meets West which was aborted by racism – not by slathering everything down into an innocuous paste, but by making it into gumbo.

Or has Neo-Hoodoo already entered another stage? The myopic philosophy Reed is currently bandying about is structurally unable to acknowledge the rise of sexism as an essential chapter in the story of all religious development in the West, in Africa, in the New World. Precisely because of Reed's inflexibility in these matters, the demoralization of the patriarchy seems an inevitable consequence in his world.

In *Mumbo Jumbo* and *The Last Days of Louisiana Red* PaPa LaBas (also the name of the loa of US Hoodoo) seems surefooted and persuasive as representative of the transcendent powers of Neo-Hoodoo – part Old World patriarch, part New World hougan. In *Mumbo Jumbo*, there's only a minor problem with one of LaBas' devotees being possessed by Erzulie. Hurston mentions Erzulie as having two incarnations in Voodoo – one as a love goddess, one as the 'terrible Erzulie' of Sect Rouge. Reed has become obsessed with the latter.

In *The Last Days of Louisiana Red*, an Erzulie-possessed Minnie, queen of the counterproductive Moochers, occupies the focal point of the text. Minnie the Moocher, after the Cab Calloway original, parodies Angela Davis' involvement in the Black Power Movement; she's a whiny, self-indulgent Afro-American version of Antigone. She was ruined by an ersatz Aunt Jemima called 'Nanny', who made her flapjacks, sang blues 'depicting negro men as brutish wayfaring louts', and told her 'Louisiana Red' stories in which black women outsmart black men. *Louisiana Red* and *Reckless Eyeballing* are the only Reed novels with women as a primary subject. Yet there is a definite tendency in all his books, beginning with *The Free-Lance Pallbearers*, to blame women characters for every evil that comes into the world.

With each book, Reed's tricksters become more schizophrenic, comfortable in the role of neither father nor son. In *Flight to Canada*, the able leadership of PaPa LaBas is nowhere in evidence. Instead, there's Uncle Robin – Uncle Tom reconceived as a crafty, literate old slave who rewrites his Master's will – and Raven Quickskill, whose subversive trickery goes no further than a poem that announces his escape and that prompts his Master to continue trying to recapture him even after the Emancipation. A woman, as usual, is on the wrong side; Mammy Barracuda, who as a kind of Sapphire/Lilith demonstrates a perverse loyalty to the slavemaster by bogarting the proto-feminist plantation mistress into wifely submission. In the underrated *Terrible Twos*, Black Peter is a more quixotic figure still – perhaps the secret ingredient behind the subversive mythology of St Nicholas, that suspiciously Dionysian rival to Christ. We are left in the not-so-capable hands of Nance Saturday – no relation to Black Peter, and never more than one clue ahead of the reader.

Reed's tricksters seem to flip-flop back and forth like fish out of water, reflecting increasing ambivalence about their relation to power. In the process, women become the only reliable scapegoat, and this obtuseness radically undermines the strategic basis of his whole oeuvre, which denounces reductivism and yet embraces it. In *Reckless Eyeballing*, male authority degenerates into unreconstituted hysteria. Jake Brashford explodes in a drunken rage of denunciation upon seeing Ball's new play, in which the skeleton of Ham Hill occupies the only male role: 'I'm your literary father, you shit,' he screams at Ball, whereupon he launches into a raucous rendition of Hambone – perhaps to shame Ball into memory of a time when black men didn't publish – slapping his thighs, singing grotesquely in dialect, until he is ejected by black male security guards.

What has become of the noble trickster? Mother Nature has overwhelmed him. In *Reckless*, black feminists are manipulated by white feminists. White feminists are slaves to the racism of white men. And white men are hamstrung by their ambivalent attachment to the Great Mother. Is Reed proposing a game of the dozens as the final solution to the Woman's Question? Is he terror-struck by his relative proximity as a black male to the castration complex of femaleness? Is he smarting over black feminist appropriation of the life and work of Zora Neale Hurston? Or is he sleepwalking? If any or all of these are the case, I suggest that a brief hibernation might not be totally unwarranted.

(1986)

18

Wilma Mankiller: Profile

A history of disastrous federal policies and a national mind-set that still presumes it's better to be a cowboy than an Indian mean that Native Americans remain invisible to most of us. But for the Cherokee Nation that situation began to change forever in July 1987, when Wilma Mankiller became the first woman elected Principal Chief.

A short, portly woman of forty-two who is elegantly and conventionally dressed, Wilma Mankiller doesn't look like anybody's idea of an Indian Chief – or a Mankiller. Serious and quiet, she smiles occasionally but rarely laughs, the first sign she isn't easy to know. 'People always ask me about my name,' she offers. A fairly common name among the Cherokee – there are Sixkillers, Whitekillers, and a Tenkiller Lake – she explains that 'Mankiller' was once a high Cherokee military rank that a male ancestor who lived in the Smokey Mountains liked so much he adopted it permanently. Her office is decorated in deep earth colors. Behind her on the wall there is a large, round mahogany plate, the Official Seal of the Cherokee Nation.

It came as no surprise to anyone in Tahlequah, Oklahoma, the capital of the Cherokee Nation, that Mankiller was triumphant. In 1983, after six years of spearheading an innovative program of community development constructing water systems and rehabilitating housing among poor, rural Cherokee in northeastern Oklahoma, Mankiller, a progressive Democrat, was elected Deputy Chief on a ticket with Ross Swimmer, a conservative Republican banker, as Principal Chief. When Swimmer was called away to Washington in 1985 to become director of the Bureau of Indian Affairs, Mankiller rose to the position of Principal Chief but, as she is quick to point out, without a mandate from the people.

'Because I have a somewhat radical political background, I thought people accepted me in the '83 election because I was paired with a

155

conservative,' Mankiller remembers. 'I felt a lack of personal power. I felt I had all the responsibility with none of the authority. So mostly during that period I just coped.'

When she ran for the top spot in 1987, against a former mayor (and former Deputy Chief) whose family owned a popular local newspaper, she mounted an intense and protracted election campaign. It included an unprecedented use of television, radio, and billboards, as though she were running for Congress. But the greatest strength of the campaign was a tireless Mankiller. Despite a recent bout with a rare form of muscular dystrophy and a severe kidney infection that put her in the hospital for two weeks, she made endless personal appearances in the fourteen counties of northeastern Oklahoma that make up the Cherokee Nation.

Her husband, Charlie Soap, who also worked doing rural development for the tribe, speaks fluent Cherokee and was instrumental in persuading male Cherokee that it was safe to have a female Chief. Despite the diversity and vastness of the Cherokee population – there are 78,000 members – Mankiller says she had no trouble keeping in touch with her constituency. 'Because I did rural development for a long time, I am well connected with all the rural communities and so I had enough people in all these outlying areas that I trusted.'

One of the few women mentioned in Cherokee history books is Nancy Ward, called 'The Last Beloved Woman' because when her husband was killed in an eighteenth-century battle, she fought and won the battle in his place. But Mankiller says her election reflects widely held and more deeply rooted values among the Cherokee.

Like many Native American tribes, the Cherokee were once matrilineal in descent and had clan mothers who shared political power with men. 'In fact,' Mankiller says, 'early historians referred to our tribal government as a petticoat government because of the strong role of the women in the tribe. Then we adopted a lot of ugly things that were part of the non-Indian world and one of those things was sexism. This whole system of tribal government was designed by men. So in 1687 women enjoyed a prominent role, but in 1987 we found people questioning whether women should be in leadership positions anywhere in the tribe. So my election was a step forward and step backward at the same time.'

The Cherokee Nation is the second largest Native American tribe in the United States, after the Navajo. They are the largest of the Five Civilized Tribes, who once occupied a large portion of the Southeast, and cooperated early and extensively with white settlers. In 1838, under policies initiated by an Indian-hating Andrew Jackson, they were forcibly removed to the Indian Territory of Oklahoma, in a diaspora known as 'The Trail of Tears'.

Having survived the dismantling of their tribal government in 1907, the redistribution of their lands in individual allotments, and the relocation programs of the 1950s, today the Cherokee Nation is a unique official entity, neither a reservation nor an entirely autonomous government, which administers a series of social welfare programs and tribal business enterprises.

'There are so many forces working against Indian tribes,' Mankiller says. 'There are people in Tulsa and Oklahoma City who don't realize our communities exist as they do today, that we have a language that is alive, that we have a tribal government that is thriving. Most people like to deal with us as though we were in a museum or a history book.'

Mankiller lives on Mankiller Flats, a 160-acre tract of land that was given to her grandfather by the federal government when Oklahoma became a state. When she was eleven years old, she and her father, who was full-blood Cherokee, her mother, who was white, and her six brothers and four sisters were forced to leave Oklahoma for San Francisco by two consecutive years of drought that devastated the family farm. 'Relocation was yet another answer from the federal government to the continuing dilemma of what to do with us,' Mankiller says of such Bureau of Indian Affairs measures. 'We are a people with many, many social indicators of decline and an awful lot of problems, so in the fifties they decided to mainstream us, to try to take us away from the tribal landbase and the tribal culture, get us into the cities. It was supposed to be a better life.'

This harrowing experience, which took her from a remote rural community without electricity or running water to a big city ghetto overnight, helped prompt Mankiller to become a social worker and an activist in the Native American rights movement in the 1960s. Since her return to Oklahoma in 1975, Mankiller's experience with mainstreaming has been crucial in shaping her determination to promulgate traditional Cherokee values and culture while at the same time working for progressive economic development. Mankiller brings her expertise with grass-roots economic development, as well as the particular needs and concerns of her community, to the board of the Ms Foundation for Women, which she joined in 1987.

'I'd like to see whole, healthy communities again,' Mankiller says of the future, 'communities in which tribe members would have access to adequate health care, higher education if they want it, a decent place to live and a decent place to work, and a strong commitment to tribal language and culture.'

The Institute for Cherokee Literacy is one part of Mankiller's plan. Knowledge of the Cherokee language is already fairly widespread among tribal members, although Mankiller herself is not fluent. Students of the

summer institute take intensive courses in reading and writing Cherokee
and then go back to their communities to teach what they've learned.
The programs to develop rural water systems and rehab houses, which
Mankiller began as Director of Community Development in 1979,
continue with their emphasis on self-help as a source of self-esteem. And
Mankiller has recently created a Department of Commerce that
combines all the tribe's business enterprises – motel, restaurant, two gift
shops, and Cherokee Gardens – with a project to spur the 'innovative
land use' of the rocky, difficult-to-manage tribal lands. Profit, as in the
projected plan to build a hydroelectric plant, must be balanced against
the needs of tribal members, as in the case of a wood-bundling enterprise
that provides much needed employment but that isn't making any
money.

Mankiller sees a future for the tribe in which the sense of 'collaboration' that she feels characterizes feminist thinking will contribute to tribal
progress and revitalization. 'I think I represent a different kind of Cherokee feminism,' she says. 'What I consider to be women's work – by that
I mean work that promotes the role of women in society – is done within
the context of the community. I have a strong feeling that if I bring
women and men together, that is just as much a part of my role as to
educate sexist men.'

(1988)

19

Twenty Years Later

On the day that Martin Luther King, Jr, was shot – April 4, 1968 – you couldn't get a dial tone in Harlem. Only sixteen then, I ran to the drugstore across the street to place a call to my grandmother on the theory that the problem was in our building alone. Although I didn't find a dial tone, I will never forget the peculiar sense of panic in the streets. There were lines at all the phone booths. When the sun set, there would be riots.

Only my grandmother had been a staunch supporter of King in my family. Like many black urban Northerners, the rest of us preferred the reformed Malcolm X. And there were, I dare say, considerable numbers of blacks North and South who passed through the 60s, going back and forth to work and taking a rest on holidays without any unusual sense of political conviction. Of course, the rioters would later strike the unmistakeable chord, but those of us who were out in the streets making phone calls were not doing so because we had finally reached some collective agreement about what should be done, but because we needed to touch base with one another in the face of the ultimate horror: white America had finally done the unspeakable. They had murdered the Prince of Peace.

Twenty years later on the anniversary of King's death it no longer seems half so clarifying to blame 'whites', not because every white person wasn't to blame in some sense but because blaming white people collectively hasn't moved us any closer to resolving the problem of a land which is, in fact, multicultural in composition and yet vehemently ethnocentric in public policy and rhetoric. The key mistake lies in viewing racism as a simple and straightforward matter of conscious and clearly mistaken beliefs about race, which are then acted upon in a violent and primitive way. Obviously, 'good' people are incapable of such warped thinking and behavior, and the 'bad' people are hopeless. While such observations may hold true for overt racism, most contemporary racism involves a much more complex and insidious cultural process. Given that Americans have almost entirely neglected to recognize that racism's work takes place first in the unconscious, collective processes of the family and the culture, together with the fact that the most optimistic of the neoconservatives have been announcing racism's demise for a while now, it should come as no surprise that we are witnessing a revival in this country – from Poughkeepsie to Howard Beach to Forsythe County – of classic, advanced-stage racism, overt and demonstrative.

As King's proverbial 'white men and black men, Jew and Gentile' join together to pretend that the Civil Rights Revolution is nearly accomplished and to mask the fact that King's dream hasn't really included enough of us, I am moved to reflect anew that freedom and equality were never intended to be real to most Americans, certainly not the six million blacks who were slaves on the eve of the Civil War.

As Orlando Patterson suggests in *Slavery and Social Death*, slavery's impact on its human fodder was pernicious. Perennial dishonor, natal alienation (not knowing who your people were) and social death were the psychic lot of the slave everywhere. In terms more relevant to the present, we may suggest that slavery's most lasting abuse of power was its tendency to annihilate the slave's potential for historical and political consciousness. Certainly the ongoing laughter and forgetting that has accompanied the Afro-American's chronic 'invisibility' – more the norm than Civil Rights Acts – from the time of the Emancipation Proclamation until now, would suggest that the psychic lot of the slave describes the current existential predicament of far too many black people. Afro-Americans, middle-class and poor, male and female, adult and child, continue to maintain an uncomfortable suspicion, which is all too often confirmed, that we are not seen for who we really are, that our needs are not considered by American business or government, that an aura of perennial dishonor lingers around the endeavors of our race.

King probably understood the problem better than many were willing to give him credit for. In *Where Do We Go From Here: Chaos or Community?* (1967), King envisioned the Civil Rights Movement as a chance to define and make real the United States' fundamentally utopian ideas of equality and freedom. 'Ever since the birth of the nation,' he wrote,

white America has had a schizophrenic personality on the question of race. She has been torn between selves – a self in which she proudly professed the great principles of democracy and a self in which she sadly practiced the antithesis of democracy. This tragic duality produced a strange indecisiveness and ambivalence toward the negro, causing America to take a step backward simultaneously with every step forward on the question of racial justice . . .

On the other hand, Patterson and other historians of slavery have remarked the irony that freedom and equality were ideas invented by those who were slaves. In the conclusion to his book, Patterson writes of

the unsettling discovery that an ideal cherished in the West beyond all others emerged as a necessary consequence of the degradation of slavery and the effort to negate it. The first men and women to struggle for freedom, the first to think of themselves as free in the only meaningful sense of the term, were freedmen . . . And so it was that freedom came into the world. Before slavery people simply could not have conceived of the thing we call freedom.

Almost ten years ago, and ten years after King's death, in 1978, I was the author of a new and controversial book, *Black Macho and the Myth of the Superwoman*, in which I criticized King's idealism and the tendency of the Civil Rights Movement to exclude women from public leadership (no women spoke at King's March on Washington, for instance) as the source of a misguided racial/sexual politics that ultimately helped to destroy the political effectiveness of the Black Power Movement. Specifically, what troubled readers was that I wrote about interracial sexual contact as a psychological center of gravity for what otherwise might be expected to be mutually antagonistic political agendas of racism, black (male) liberation and (white) feminism. By this I meant that not only did a racist South have a perverse focus on interracial sexual relations, but the same focus (perhaps as a corrective measure) seemed to intrude upon Civil Rights Movement activities in the South. Given their historical context, these interracial sexual relations form not only the insignificant material of the Civil Rights workers' private lives, they can also be viewed as the nascent scene of a power struggle between an emergent white feminist movement and an emergent male-dominated Black Power Movement. Of course, I was particularly interested in the role black women played in all of this.

As a black feminist, I was most concerned about the equality and freedom of black women, less in regard to our political and economic lives in a white-dominated society than in regard to the quality of our psychological and emotional lives in interaction with black men. It was my goal to articulate the complex manifestations of sexism in the black community's evolving conception of itself in struggle. In the process, I discounted the importance of white racism's role in dismantling and disfiguring the pluralistic and egalitarian impulses of not only Black

Power, but of Women's Liberation and the New Left as well. I now think
what made me so willing to emphasize sexism over racism – to put it
crudely – was the fact that I myself was a product of the Civil Rights
Revolution, so much so that I could not see (or did not want to see) its
otherness, its newness, or look upon it as anything but inevitable.

My commitment to feminism, then as now, involved, as well, a
commitment to the notion that, first, the so-called personal needed to be
examined politically if all our political, economic and civil rights as black
women were ever going to be fulfilled. But I failed to comprehend the full
range of the personal, as I included the myriad encounters with
humiliation that 'women' experienced in a sexist society, and discounted
the personal agony and anguish that racial segregation entails. It seems
to me the mistake I made is actually quite common. It involves the
tendency, which I have often remarked, on the part of advocates of
either a Black Liberationist position or a Women's Liberationist position
automatically to discount or ignore the terms of the other discourse. It is
clear to me now that the mistake is somehow intrinsic to the rhetoric of
liberation movements as we currently conceive of them, because the core
idea of liberation in Western culture invariably trivializes both racial and
sexual issues.

Those who make the mistake don't just make it because they are black
and not female, or because they are women and not black, or because
they are neither black nor female (as in the case of white men who may
disregard all 'other' perspectives despite otherwise 'good intentions').
This peculiar brand of solipsism occurs because the discussion of
liberation, or empowerment, when directly opposed to the condition of
powerlessness or enslavement as though the two were mutually exclusive,
seems to demand simple arguments that ultimately neutralize the ability
to describe or ameliorate the problem the argument was initially designed
to address.

As a black woman, I wasn't supposed to make the same mistake, and
yet the scholarship and analysis in book form that seems able to
comprehend the problem of race and the problem of gender with a single
idea or concept is perhaps nonexistent. Yes, black women grow up
living the reality in their bodies of how sexism and racism intersect,
coincide and collaborate, but the representation of that correspondence
has barely been written by them except in literature and poetry in which
it is heavily coded. Among those black women who have attempted such
a discussion in nonfiction book form – Bell Hooks, Audre Lorde, June
Jordan, Alice Walker, Paula Giddings, Hortense Spillers and myself –
the results have been difficult and problematic.

While I can't defend my thoughts in writing *Black Macho* – one of the
first of these books – I can remember being afraid to imagine what it

must have been like to suffer the indignity of having to sit in the back of a streetcar or being told you couldn't eat in a restaurant because you were black. On a barely conscious level, I felt contempt for Sojourner Truth's, Charlotte Forten's and James Baldwin's descriptions of such encounters precisely because of the degree to which I intuitively recognized that segregation made implicit the violation of the spirit and the body that lynching, castration, and mass violence made explicit. Under the circumstances, women's issues defined as feminist such as rape, domestic violence, and sexual harassment seemed comfortingly remote and raceless. That white people had once chosen to express their dislike for black people in the form of segregation, the institutionalization of which was the focus of the principal battles in King's career (I am excepting his fight against the war in Vietnam, which was probably his single most important political decision), engaged an aspect of material reality that I considered to be unfortunate but basically insignificant, a relic of an obsolete and already distant past. In other words, I found it quite literally beneath discussion.

Clearly, I chose to ignore how closely entwined segregation and its aura of violence actually were. I myself grew up in the segregated community of Harlem in New York. But I failed to consider the deformation of the power relation between the state and the individual that segregation forcefully implied. By the time a society has gotten around to legislating where a person can sit on a public conveyance, relations between such persons and the state are virtually unsalvageable. The state, as well as local government, private business and the individual citizens that support it, have gone out of their way to flout economic, common and political sense to render special insult and degradation to one class of American citizen, to, in fact, delegitimize and deny his or her citizenship by virtue of such acts of public separation and humiliation. Such acts would be impossible to imagine apart from the context of a history of slavery, of a Reconstruction effort demolished, of blacks robbed on a massive scale of their land, of decent health care and education, of life, liberty, and the pursuit of happiness.

Whereas the segregation and subjugation of the black South African majority seems an almost absurd resistance to the inevitable on the part of the dominant white South African minority regime, in the US segregation seemed gratuitous, one final unnecessary and redundant consolidation of the powerlessness of blacks. But segregation was not only political, it was provocatively personal and intimate, a way of white racism's reaching out its long arm to touch every black person in a private place.

Perhaps because it represents the unfathomable intersection of racial and sexual difference, the Civil Rights Movement's emerging official history discusses the subject of segregated bathrooms almost as infrequently as it discusses interracial sexual relationships. Nevertheless, segregated bathrooms provide a perfect illustration of segregation's implicit invasion of privacy. As in the case of much in black life that is rarely discussed explicitly and publicly, it is necessary to turn to black women fiction writers to fill the gap. Toni Morrison first wrote about the signs that distinguished segregated public facilities in 'What the Black Woman Thinks About Women's Lib' (*NYT* magazine, August 22, 1971): 'these signs were not just arrogant, they were malevolent: "Whites Only", "Colored Only", or perhaps just "Colored", permanently carved into the granite over a drinking fountain.'

Then she suggests that the bathrooms were a special case:

> But there was one set of signs that were not malevolent: in fact, rather reassuring in its accuracy and fine distinctions: the pair that said 'White Ladies' and 'Colored Women'. The difference between white and black females seemed to me an eminently satisfactory one.

But what a difference in her almost playful treatment of the subject here and her treatment in her second novel *Sula* (1973), in which the comparatively neat duality of bathrooms for colored women and white ladies gives way to a more complicated arrangement as Nel's mother Helene journeys to the South on segregated trains: 'When they changed trains in Birmingham for the last leg of the trip, they discovered what luxury they had been in through Kentucky and Tennessee, where the rest stops all had colored toilets. After Birmingham there were none.'

Morrison then tells us in some detail how poor, rural Southern black women accustomed to the situation helped middle-class Helene adjust so that,

> by the time they reached Slidell, not too far from Lake Pontchartrain, Helene could not only fold leaves as well as the fat woman, she never felt a stir as she passed the muddy eyes of the men who stood like wrecked Dorics under the station roof of those towns.

I could make a significant mistake in my assessment of the private and public weight of segregation, and the unmanageable, unspeakable feelings behind it from both sides of the line because I hadn't lived it, because I was born in 1952 in the North to a lower-middle-class family that became progressively more middle-class as I got older. The famous Supreme Court decision, Brown vs. Topeka Board of Education, desegregating the public schools was only two years away. My parents made it their economic priority to send me to private schools that

embraced Drs Mamie and Kenneth Clark's views regarding the delete-
rious effects of the segregated education on the delicate psyches of black
and white children. These were schools that followed the career of
Martin Luther King and the development of the Civil Rights Movement
with great interest and sympathy, as they made integration a part of their
agenda. In fact, the New Lincoln School, which I attended from 7th to
12th grade, shared a building with Harlem's Northside Center, where
Mamie and Kenneth Clark pursued their groundbreaking experiments
and research. As for the residential segregation in New York and the
segregation of our private lives, such arrangements were, we told
ourselves, expressions of free will and personal preference.

Consequently, my focus was upon the pain of integration, the
frustration of constantly being misunderstood by white teachers and
fellow students who expected you to be exactly like them or silent. To
imagine that the white power structure – from teachers to television –
which seemed to have nothing better to do than to make me feel small,
also hated me was too horrible to imagine. Despite the ease with which
we bandy the concept about, racial hatred was and is difficult to
comprehend except when the object of its tyranny is living under its
paralyzing gaze. It is even more difficult to calculate or describe.

Even as the legislative, political and economic burden of this hatred is
systematically reduced and reformulated, however, the personal, private,
unacknowledged experiences of racism accumulate to form the wound of
individual personality, to disastrous effect in the urban 'underclass'.
Ordinarily we retrieve King's legacy by pointing to his focus on economic
issues late in his career. But we should recognize, as well, the part of
King's message warning us that as long as racial hatred continues to exist
– regardless of how little it seems to be confirmed by legislative and
political structures – it will find a way to reconsolidate, to disrupt the
precarious national equilibrium, to poison the economic, political and
social lives of black citizens, starting with those who can least afford the
disadvantage – the poor.

What would I have thought when I was twenty-six, or even sixteen, if
someone had told me that I'd be teaching in the English Department at
the University of Oklahoma the year that Martin Luther King's birthday
finally became an official holiday? As far as I was concerned, it was
somebody else's job to remember King's birthday in 1984, especially now
that it was officially ordained that we would do so. After all, King was the
patriarchal head of a Civil Rights Movement that rarely rewarded with
public attention the full contribution of its female participants. Philo-
sophically, King stood for integration, peace, and love, but without
sexuality, an absence I considered absurd. But the University of Okla-

homa opened my unbelieving eyes to King's words about this nation taking 'a step back simultaneously with every step forward on the question of racial justice'. Surely no one could undo the Civil Rights Revolution.

On the official holiday to commemorate the birthday of Dr Martin Luther King, I found the campus enthralled in a massive and ritualistic celebration to change the numbers on a large board confirming their victory in the National Football Championship. I watched the students – mostly white but some black – streaming across campus on this unusually warm day in January with no sign that King had ever lived or died, except that they probably wouldn't be attending school together if he hadn't. Later that evening I watched the proceedings on a local television station, in which coach Barry Switzer and numerous members of a mostly black football team congratulated themselves on their win. There was no mention of King, while on another channel, via a national network, Stevie Wonder, Harry Belafonte, Elizabeth Taylor, and a long list of celebrities were insisting that the dream lived on in innumerable ways. There were no other public recognitions of King on his official holiday in the town of Norman, Oklahoma. There was a parade and a tribute to him in Oklahoma City but that was twenty miles away.

So I found myself quite suddenly moved to devote my two classes to the memory of King in order to express solidarity with my black students, to confirm that we were there, and to respond to the white female student in my composition class who told me, quite emphatically, 'King never did anything for us', as though she would be doing something for him by recognizing the day. Certainly my position as Assistant Professor in an all-white English Department at a university facing the advanced stages of EEOC (Equal Employment Opportunity Commission) pressure was silent tribute as well. But what a painful day this must have been all across the country for isolated black college students who had the misfortune to attend school in a place where King's holiday was being municipally ignored, who had to suffer his and their new and peculiar invisibility on this special day, special in that it was worse, not better, than the rest.

No doubt Martin Luther King was a great man. No doubt passive resistance and civil disobedience against segregation were the only way the Movement for Black Liberation could be certain of advancing in 1955. No doubt, as well, integration has still been a bitter cup for those of us who have lived to see both the great step forward and the great step backward. King, who did not, nevertheless knew that we had a long way to go.

Again, in 'Where Do We Go From Here' in 1967, King recalls the events leading up to the split in the Civil Rights Movement that occurred on the James Meridith Mississippi Freedom March in 1966, how Stokely

Carmichael of SNCC and Floyd McKissick of CORE were insistent on a break with previous Civil Rights policies of nonviolence, integration and chanting 'Freedom Now' in favor of a policy of self-defense, separatism and chanting 'Black Power'. King describes Black Power as a cry of anguish and despair, a desperate attempt to compensate, at a single blow, for centuries of powerlessness. 'It is no accident that the birth of this slogan in the Civil Rights Movement took place in Mississippi,' King writes, 'the state symbolizing the most blatant abuse of white power.' He also writes:

> Power properly understood is the ability to achieve purpose. It is the strength required to bring about social, political or economic changes. In this sense power is not only desirable but necessary in order to implement the demands of love and justice. One of the greatest problems of history is that the concepts of love and power are usually contrasted as polar opposites. Love is identified with a resignation of power and power with a denial of love ... What is needed is a realization that power without love is reckless and abusive and that love without power is sentimental and anemic. Power at its best is love implementing the demands of justice. Justice at its best is love correcting everything that stands against love.

But the commonsense argument that defeated King's analysis, and is still allowed to defeat it so far as I can tell, is that 'You can't legislate feelings'. Indeed, if you can't legislate feelings, if you cannot collectively and publicly address the problem of racial hatred and animosity, how will anything ever really change? It is precisely those unlegislatable feelings that reassert themselves as ever more ingenious evasions of existing Civil Rights legislation, as an increasingly thoughtless, inconsiderate and criminally negligent Supreme Court, Congress and Executive Branch, as unfair hiring, firing and under-education, as a cloak of invisibility pervasive throughout the sphere of cultural representation that projects the burden of guilt for racism, time and time again, onto the victim him- or herself.

Even the most progressive and sympathetic whites understand so little about how racism functions in their own lives, embedded in their belief structures, as to boggle the imagination. Blacks and other people of color are not automatically experts on racism either. Moreover, by viewing racism as the great unimaginable abyss into which only the uneducated and 'lower'-class white can fall, we make its transformation and elimination virtually impossible. The overt, explicit, fascistic racism that the Civil Rights Movement tackled in the South was, and is, the tip of the iceberg. Ninety per cent of what blacks experience as racism is what whites refuse to call racism until it bubbles and boils in such an unmistakeable manner, in Howard Beach for example, that no one, as the judge said, can any longer deny it. But, of course, by that time it is psychologically too late for everybody involved. It's the racism that lies around looking relatively harmless that can benefit most from our prompt attention. Unfortunately, it has grown dialectical and wily in its resistance to change since buses were finally desegregated in Montgomery.

For instance, there seems to be a conspiracy to keep black students from learning how to write, at least at the State University of New York at Buffalo where I've been teaching since fall 1987. The University of Oklahoma featured nearly all-black football and basketball teams, nearly all-white cheerleading squads, fraternities and sororities (annually the school newspaper insisted that both races prefer 'separate but equal'), as well as a host of other manifestations of racism and residual segregation. Yet both black and white students (I've heard the Native American students got the worst of this deal) all seemed to have received comparable writing instruction, perhaps because the student body was fairly homogeneous in terms of class. But in Buffalo, although I've hardly made a study of the subject, it would appear that black students are routinely passed from grade school to high school to college, and even occasionally graduate school, without having achieved even minimal writing skills. I have personally encountered such black female students and am told, quietly, by fellow white professors that the problem is statewide.

I have no doubt that the situation is further compounded by the unconscious racism of these and other white teachers who assume that it is impossible to reverse the inexorable process of under-education. Perhaps they're right, but it's not as though not being able to write (or read) was a handicap that black America can continue to absorb. It robs the black student of her ability to protest by any means but dropping out. The difficulties she's having with writing invariably reflect her lack of public confidence (her voice may be virtually inaudible in classroom discussion), her conviction that she is incapable of coherently representing her own oppositional impulses and anger, and communicating them in speech. Despite the scope of the problem – which I am beginning to see as the silencing of a 'race' – there seems to be no comprehensive effort to address the dilemma of the under-educated adult who, in segregated or desegregated grade schools and high schools, has been shortchanged at vital points in her educational life.

Extraordinarily, I find some correlation with the education I received in a private school and at a public college, the City College of New York. In both cases, almost all of my teachers were white; most of my classmates were white, as well. I was repeatedly told from 1st grade to 12th that I had a problem with writing. My 11th grade teacher even went so far as to tell my mother that I would never be able to finish college because of that writing problem. In college I had three wonderful teachers who were renegades. They taught me how to teach myself, but most of my teachers told me virtually nothing (and I majored in writing) about my work. This is not to say that I was being deprived of some superb instruction that the white students were getting. Rather, I was being ignored, although I didn't understand it at the time. I came to understand this when I began to teach, only to hear my black students complain, again and again, that their previous teachers, mostly white, had said nothing whatsoever about their writing.

It is impossible to contend with the intractable body of collective racism that condemns many of us to relive the 'social death' of slavery without facing the fact that blacks are female as well as male, that slavery often involved a specifically sexual persecution that trampled on definable gender roles, that black leadership has too often viewed itself as automatically male, that blacks have too often considered freedom the equivalent of manhood.

Lately I've begun to wonder whether my blindness to racism and segregation when I was younger and my black female students' difficulties in communicating aren't branch and leaf of the same dilemma: that Afro-American women have tended to code their most profound statements about sexuality and race relations in allegory and metaphor. Once there were blues singers like Ma Rainey, Bessie Smith and Billie Holiday. Now we have novelists and poets. Perhaps that is precisely the dilemma we face, that the problem of racism becomes complex and intractable, unspeakable except to the artist, when you add to it the problem of sex. Might this also be, from grade school to graduate school, the problem we have in representing ourselves in terms comprehensible to the dominant discourse? We are always trying to speak simultaneously of the experience inside the wrong race and the wrong gender in a culture that persists in seeing the problem of each as mutually exclusive.

The most bitter arguments I've had in my life have been with black people, especially black women, over the meaning of the Civil Rights Movement. When I was an adolescent and was living the Civil Rights Revolution of integrated schools, lunch counters, playgrounds and swimming pools, and was watching the major tragic events of the Civil Rights struggle on television, and later, when I was twenty-one and beginning to write about sexual politics in black America, it never occurred to me that the Civil Rights Movement was any less a part of my experience because I lived in the North. But, over and over again, black women have instructed me that those who directly participated in the Civil Rights struggle in the South, especially the black men and women of CORE, SNCC and SCLC, had a right to be possessive about that experience, fearful of misinterpretation, certain that anyone who hadn't been there couldn't understand. Like soldiers returning from the battlefield, like the Jews and the Palestinians who now trade blows on the West Bank, perhaps they're not so wrong as I once thought in believing that you had to have been there, you had to have lived it to have known what it was. But, in that case, I can't help but ask, what shall we do now as we watch the Civil Rights Revolution being undone?

In this regard, I recall Richard Kluger's account of Kenneth Clark's research in *Simple Justice*, a history of the Supreme Court decision desegregating the schools. Employing a doll test in which black children showed 'an unmistakable preference for the white doll and a rejection of the brown doll', Clark encountered virtually the same results when testing children who were educated in the 'integrated' North as he encountered in testing children in the South and, therefore, he refused to explicitly pinpoint segregation as the overriding factor in a larger cultural process of institutional racism that rendered the black child's self-hatred almost inevitable. But also, Kluger gives the following account of a black girl Clark tested in segregated Clarendon County, South Carolina:

> Clark asked one dark brown girl of seven – 'so dark that she was almost black' – to take the coloring test that he generally gave along with the doll test. 'When she was asked to color herself,' Clark would testify in court the following week, 'she was one of the few children who picked a flesh color, pink, to color herself. When asked to color a little boy the color she liked little boys to be, she looked all around the twenty-four crayons and picked up a white crayon and looked up at me with a shy smile and began to color. She said, "This doesn't show." So she pressed a little harder ... in order to get the white crayon to show.'

Can a racial analysis, or even a class analysis, that does not take into account the issue of sexuality and the problem of gender in a cultural framework ever begin to fully describe what was going on in this seven-year-old black girl's mind? Moreover, will she ever be able to describe it? Black women writers – Toni Morrison, Toni Cade Bambara, Alice Walker, Ntozake Shange, Gloria Naylor, Jamaica Kincaid, Michele Cliff – do her justice, but when will she be able to do herself justice?

There is no question in my mind that both Women's Liberation and Black Power were born of the struggle over issues of gender and sexuality within the Civil Rights Movement. Black women – Rosa Parks, Ella Baker, Fannie Lou Hamer, Doris Ruby Smith, just to mention the most obvious (there were hundreds, probably thousands) – provided crucial, although often anonymous, leadership in the Civil Rights Movement. Those years from 1966 to 1970 during which Black Power and Women's Liberation flowered were also the years in which the political and philosophical weight of the black woman was either erased or divided between black men and white women, who then proceeded to go their separate ways, pulling her apart in the process. Or as literary critic Barbara Johnson paraphrases the black feminist insight of Bell Hooks: 'The black woman is both invisible and ubiquitous: never seen in her own right but forever appropriated by the other for their own ends.'

It wasn't the first time this had happened. It had happened in the struggle between black male abolitionists and white suffragists over whether the 15th Amendment's extension of the franchise to ex-slaves would include women. Only Sojourner Truth, the record tells us, dared to argue that black women needed the vote as much as black men. It has happened in our discussions of black female singers like Ma Rainey, Bessie Smith, and Billie Holiday who are written about as either the 'Dark Divas' in a black, male-dominated tradition of Afro-American music, or the 'Mean Mothers' of a feminist aesthetic looking for a critical edge. And it is happening again in discussions of Zora Neale Hurston, Alice Walker and Toni Morrison, whose works are now currently being divided up, like turf, and appropriated by male Afro-Americanists and white feminist literary critics. But what concerns me even more is the peculiar reluctance of everybody – especially black women – to talk or write about such issues in a forthright manner. I grieve to witness, therefore, the willful under-education of potentially thoughtful and articulate young and middle-aged black women.

I have no answers for the questions I'm pondering here, no resolution except to go on writing about them. I only know it infuriates me to watch superbly educated white male lawyers from the ACLU advising Billy Boggs, or Joyce Brown, that it's her right as an American citizen to live on the streets, to defecate on herself and to tear up money. The latest I hear on TV news is that the ACLU has given her a part-time job, she's doing a speaking engagement at Harvard, and she's considering a book contract. Now that's more like it, although how many of us can get the television cameras to change our lives?

I strongly suspect that we need to consider old approaches, rethink what we've dismissed. I once thought King a romantic, idealistic visionary and, as such, not much use in terms of his contribution to political philosophy. But now I realize he had calmly figured out that official America had no conception of what equality might mean in its practical application, no intention whatsoever of making it happen. It would be up to all of its citizens, if they could ever rise – black and white; Jew, Gentile and Muslim; Native American, Cuban and Asian; male and female; gay, straight and transvestite; sick and well – to struggle with and through their feelings and ideas to give equality lasting and concrete significance.

(1988)

20

Who Owns Zora Neale Hurston?

Critics Carve Up the Legend

Habitually, Afro-American literary criticism has kept a strict lookout for backsliding to, say, the antebellum days when some free blacks wrote Southern state legislatures asking to be re-enslaved because their living conditions were so tenuous. The fear has been that because black writers had to please white audiences, editors, and publishers, a grotesque minstrelsy – discursively equivalent to Stepin Fetchit's shuffle – would surface in works of Afro-American literature, deadening the inevitable polemical sting. The prime exhibit for the prosecution was once Zora Neale Hurston, whose fiction and folklore collections have in the past been repeatedly dismissed by the black male literary establishment on the grounds that she was simply 'cutting the fool' for white folks' benefit.

But as a pioneer of the Harlem Renaissance's literary translation of the Afro-American oral tradition (blues and bebop, folklore, street language and black English, toasts, jive, and the dozens), Hurston dared to laugh at racist stereotypes – even to risk verifying them – in order to make a point on behalf of 'the folk farthest down'. At a time when the Ku Klux Klan was still lynching blacks en masse, and the tone of racial wisdom, à la W.E.B. Dubois and Richard Wright, was dignified and dramatic, Hurston rejected the racial uplift agenda of the Talented Tenth on the premise that ordinary bloods had something to say, too. As she wrote in her autobiography in 1942, among blacks 'there was a general acceptance of the monkey as kinfolks. Perhaps it was some distant memory of tribal monkey reverence from Africa. . . . Perhaps it was an acknowledgement of our talent for mimicry with the monkey as a symbol.' How black intellectuals must have cringed. Then.

Now Afro-Americanist extraordinaire Henry Louis Gates calls Hurston's rebellion 'signifying' or 'critical signification' and proposes the Signifying Monkey – preeminent trickster of the Afro-American oral tradition – as a figure to evoke the patterns of imitation and reversal that enable black narrative to respond to and defy an exclusionary white culture. Gates describes the way Hurston's figure works as 'the ironic reversal of a received racist image in the Western imagination of the black as simian, the Signifying Monkey – he who dwells at the margin of discourse, ever punning, ever troping, ever embodying the ambiguities of language.' Gates readily concedes that no writer before Ishmael Reed better demonstrated the range of signifying strategies than Zora Neale Hurston.

As folklorist, anthropologist, and novelist, she was vigilant in her quest to render the Afro-American oral tradition and its characteristic 'signifying' a permanent feature in the museum of American culture. And Gates suggests that in *Their Eyes Were Watching God*, Hurston was 'the first author of the tradition to represent signifying itself as a vehicle of liberation for an oppressed woman, and as a rhetorical strategy in the narration of fiction'. Which is why, despite the sexism that once clouded Afro-Americanists' view of Hurston's assets, Gates now leads a gang of black male Afro-Americanists who make pivotal use of Hurston's work in their most recent critical speculations.

They follow the lead of black feminist critics and novelists – Alice Walker, Sherley Anne Williams, Toni Cade Bambara, Mary Helen Washington, Barbara Christian – who first lionized Hurston, with the help of Robert Hemenway's biography. The change in her reputation is due in part to feminist enlightenment, but also to a general easing up: it's time to reassess Hurston's self-conscious manipulation of a kind of dialectical minstrelsy that may be the crucial mark of Afro-American cultural and artistic productivity.

Since slavery, Afro-Americans have produced culture in a peculiar limbo between languages, between nationalities. The integrity of the signifier (the Law of the Father or the Sacred Word) was always a scandal from the Afro-American point of view – as unobtainable as American justice. The resultant narrative funkiness, which can also look like political evasiveness, is what Ralph Ellison may have meant by 'invisibility' in 1952. Remember in the beginning of *Invisible Man*, the grandson is instructed to 'overcome'm with yeses, undermine'm with grins, agree'm to death and destruction ...' Afro-American literary criticism has finally drawn substantial insight into the subtleties of race business from the literature itself.

Still, that Afro-American critics should be interested in an Afro-American writer, though she is female, seems to require no backbreaking explanation, even if it's never happened before, which it *never* has. Yet how do we explain the interest of Yale's Harold Bloom, godfather of white, patriarchy-obsessed literary theory? Bloom, who is editing Chelsea

House's vast series of critical anthologies ominously entitled *Modern Critical Views*, has devoted one of the early volumes to Hurston. How do we explain the work of Marxist critic Susan Willis, who has written *Specifying*, a book on black women writers that takes its name from Hurston's use of the term in her autobiography, *Dust Tracks on a Road*? Or the two articles on Hurston in deconstructionist Barbara Johnson's new book, *A World of Difference*? Or even the emergence of a pseudo-black feminist criticism practiced by white feminists, the outstanding example of which is the introduction to *Conjuring: Black Women, Fiction and Literature*, where Marjorie Pryse appears to be attempting a codification of Alice Walker's 'womanist' method? Last year's annual meeting of the National Women's Studies Association, which focused on 'Women of Color', leads me to think that a host of other 'modern critical views' will soon follow.

All well and good, you may say. About time. Literature needs a rainbow coalition – black, white, male, female, artists and academics, historicists and deconstructionists joining together to insure the preservation of Hurston's work and reputation. Except that canon formation has little to do with such benign cultural practice. Rather, Hurston's extraordinary textual ambivalence about race, class, nationality, sex, religion, and family, her cryptic, inscrutable subjectivity, offers a crucial vantage point on the crisis in signification that fuels postmodernism and haunts Western self-esteem – and which, not coincidentally, lies at the core of the Afro-American experience. So, like groupies descending on Elvis Presley's estate, critics are engaged in a mostly ill-mannered stampede to have some memento of the black woman who could mock the 1954 Supreme Court decision desegregating the schools, who simultaneously insisted upon substantive racial difference and no difference at all, who epitomizes our inability to revise the text of American racism, or to acknowledge its sexism. For what is at stake is the integrity and vitality of language, literature, and American thought, from the bottom up.

Remember how this whole Zora Neale Hurston thing got off the ground. Not how it started, which was when Hurston made the best move of her literary career by dying of stroke, poverty, and a profound lack of literary appreciation in a welfare home in Saint Lucie County, Florida in 1960. Focus on Alice Walker's mystical attempt (documented in her essay 'Looking for Zora') to locate Hurston's body in an abandoned cemetery overgrown with weeds by calling out to her, 'Zora ... I'm here. Are you?' When Walker's foot sank into a hole, she took it as a sign. In that spot, she installed a granite stone reading, 'Zora Neale Hurston "A Genius of The South" [she borrowed Jean Toomer's poetic use of the phrase], 1901–1960, Novelist, Folklorist Anthropologist'. From 1960 to 1973, Hurston had been buried in an unmarked grave in a segregated cemetery in Fort Pierce, Florida, a place Hemenway calls 'symbolic of the black writer's historical fate in America'.

The current unceremonious exhuming of the Hurston corpse should be considered in the reflected glory of these two distinctly different memorials – the erasure, anonymity, and degradation of the unmarked pauper's grave, and the double-whammy of canonization as signified by the gravestone that may have missed the mark, and that employs the term *genius* ambivalently and in quotes. Not only may we be canonizing a Hurston who never existed, or the wrong corpse, but it may simply be intrinsic to the process of canonization (think mummification) to lay waste to the symbolic and intellectual urgency of this or any other cultural object of our affections.

The efforts of Washington, Walker, Williams, Bambara, and Hemenway to resurrect and republish Hurston have certainly been useful (although I privately wonder about so much reverential awe for a woman who scorned the stuff), but what if their unwillingness to submit Hurston's signifying to rigorous examination invites others, who are not of the faith, to misuse her to derail the future of black women in literature and literary criticism? The time to consider such questions is upon us, for Hurston's cultural use has clearly passed beyond the control of black feminists/womanists.

Even when the opportunity obviously exists to describe and define the black woman in her own terms, her own voice, white male and female and black male expertise may persist in silencing her by unwanted sexual/ textual acts. Take Harold Bloom's book on Hurston. Bloom means well, I suppose, but in an introduction almost too short to bother reading, he sweeps aside those critical challenges to the canon that first recovered Hurston's achievements from the dust heap of marginality: 'Her sense of power has nothing in common with politics of any persuasion, with contemporary modes of feminism, or even with those questers who search for a black aesthetic.'

Rather, he makes a case for Hurston's protagonist Janie, firmly locating her in the only tradition that matters to him – the one that began with Samuel Richardson's Clarissa and peaked with Dreiser's Carrie and Lawrence's Ursula and Gudrun. Predictably, he recasts *Their Eyes Were Watching God* as the story of a woman's struggle with repression. The blackness of virtually everybody in the book takes a backseat to the issue of Janie's beleaguered sexuality. Further, according to Bloom, it's another woman, the grandmother, who offers the largest obstacle to Janie's sexual fulfillment and self-articulation. Grandma's pretext, that she was raped in slavery and that her daughter, Janie's

mother, fared not much better, is utterly ignored in Bloom's elegant but
slapdash revision. He wraps it up by proposing that we see Hurston as the
Wife of Bath, that anti-feminist mouthpiece proposed in the fourteenth
century as a cure for priests who would choose marriage over celibacy.
Cute, huh?

What follows in the book, you might wonder. Precisely the Afro-
Americanist and feminist interpretations Bloom has just erased – the
prefaces, introductions, and articles by Darwin Turner, Larry Neale,
Hemenway, Walker, Williams, and Washington that have accompanied
Hurston's republication these past fourteen years.

The cumulative effect is of some kind of cosmic blunder: Bloom's
introduction doesn't introduce but rather supersedes the text that
follows. He morbidly objectifies Hurston in a sexually charged image of
Western culture's embedded anti-feminism. Hurston's silent black body
floats to the surface of a systemic dilemma. The irony is that Afro-
American studies and women's studies courses will constitute a captive
audience for this book.

It was in my first narrative writing class at the City College of New
York that I first encountered Hurston. In 1971, that twilight year of
Black Power, on a campus at the margins of open enrollment and my
native Harlem, I felt buried alive by the self-regard of black males and the
blindness of the faculty's typical white male, who could not imagine a
black feminist writer. Then my writing teacher, Mark Mirsky, pressed
upon me a hardcover copy of *Mules and Men*, Hurston's deceptively
simple presentation of black storytelling, the oral tradition, and voodoo
in the 30s in the rural South.

Her unequivocal presentation of 'rustic folk' as speaking subjects
whose race was not compromised but informed by their sexuality was
music to my ears. *Mules and Men* portrayed Afro-American oral tradition
in three settings. In Hurston's hometown, all-black Eatonville, old friends
treat her like long-lost family. Twice she makes extended visits to an
impoverished sawmill camp in Loughman, Florida. The women in
Loughman often engage in knife fights, and Hurston requires the constant
protection of the roughest of them all, Big Sweet, who is described admir-
ingly by one of Hurston's male informants as 'uh whole woman and half uh
man'. Finally, there's the quasi-European, quasi-African New Orleans,
where Hurston pursues several apprenticeships as a voodo priestess.

Her archly heretical tone about such sacred cows as racial pride, skin
color, slavery, the eating of watermelon, the singing of the blues and
conjure, her skillful narrative flow into and out of dialect, and the
multiple rhetorical strategies of her 'native' informants, were a revelation
to me. Not because I'd never heard such linguistic antics before – in

Harlem, the crossroads of the African diaspora, such a medley of voices was not unfamiliar – but I'd never seen the attempt to write it down.

Soon after that, I read *Their Eyes Were Watching God* in connection with a newly inaugurated women's studies program at CCNY and was thoroughly enchanted, although alarmed. On one hand, in a community deeply split over the appropriate use of black English, Hurston's confident handling of dialect gave this story the rigor and readability of a black *Alice in Wonderland*. On the other hand, I was disappointed that Janie didn't pursue intellectual curiosity, as Zora playing herself did in *Mules and Men*, barreling down the backroads of Florida in her Chevrolet in search of stories old and new, borrowed and blue. Instead of a career, Janie pursues the right kind of marriage and finally finds it with Tea Cake, who teaches her how to play checkers and beats her, then brags to his friends about how ladylike she is and how easily she scars.

Black feminists Alice Walker, Mary Helen Washington, and Sherley Anne Williams have suggested that it's wisest to see such moments in the plot as subsidiary to Janie's triumph of voice when she virtually loud-talks her second husband to death and achieves mastery in the telling of her own tale at the end of the book. It's true that concentrating on this symbolic resolution is more satisfying than dealing with how Hurston ultimately faced the conflict and left it unresolved. But Harold Bloom also defends the evolution of Janie in his ritual canonization of *Their Eyes*. In the process, he further consolidates the black female absence in a white male literary establishment – which suggests to me that other 'critical views' more subversive than 'modern' must be ventured.

The book I've read since 1971 that helped me to see both *Their Eyes Were Watching God* and Hurston's career in another light is *Dust Tracks on a Road*. Here is Hurston's recapitulation of the blues wisdom concerning black women, as opposed to 'brown' women like Janie:

They brought bad luck for a week if they came to your house of a Monday morning. They were evil. They slept with their fists balled up ready to fight and squabble even while they were asleep. They even had evil dreams. White, yellow and brown girls dreamed about roses and perfumes and kisses. Black gals dreamed about guns, razors, ice picks, hatchets and hot lye. I heard men swear they had seen women dreaming and knew these things to be true.

Here Hurston is at her signifying best. These remarks constitute a major transitional moment in a chapter called 'My People! My People!' that discusses, or rather juggles, competing notions of 'race'. In a seductively entertaining way that makes you first think you're reading fluff, Hurston repeatedly assaults the concept of racial essence, revealing its basis as absurd and fundamentally rhetorical. She does this by exploring a series of rhetorical relations – between blacks and whites, the black middle class and the black poor, males and females, blacks and tans – what each says about the other in the process of defining the superior self. Hurston gives the impression of a constantly shifting perspective (much like Virginia Woolf's in *A Room of One's Own*) until it becomes clear that race is a game played with mirrors called words. While she's at it, she gives W.E.B. Dubois' celebrated 'colorline', as in 'the problem of the twentieth century is a problem of the colorline', a good working over.

Although she draws the rather obvious conclusion that blacks, therefore, are individuals, what's more important is the polyvocal and multidirectional terms in which the argument is made. Here's how she ends this chapter in her autobiography:

> I maintain that I have been a Negro three times – a Negro baby, a Negro girl and a Negro woman. Still, if you have received no clear-cut impression of what *The Negro in America* is like, then you are in the same place with me. There is no *The Negro* here.

Politics is less the issue than the amazing audacity of this woman who dared to challenge the rhetoric and posturing of a race. Hurston's work – the nonfiction writing on oral tradition in *Tell My Horse*, *The Sanctified Church*, *Mules and Men*, and *Dust Tracks on a Road*, as well as the fiction of *Their Eyes Were Watching God*, *Jonah's Gourd Vine*, *Mose, Man of the Mountain*, and the short stories – forms an essential complement to the occasional tunnel vision of Booker T. Washington, Jean Toomer, James Weldon Johnson, Alain Locke, Langston Hughes, Sterling Brown, and Richard Wright. Dubois, Hughes, Brown, and Wright all expressed grave doubts about the viability of Hurston's writing – and that's precisely why we ought to read her and them in tandem. She provides a funky footbridge between the lofty pronouncements of a public racial self-consciousness and a private (ordinarily anonymous) collective black sensibility, a sense that somebody/women had another view of things.

How peculiar that Hurston should be taught, read, and written about as though the context of Afro-American cultural and intellectual history did not exist. For one thing, Hurston was always signifying. If you don't know the boys, how do you know what she was signifying on?

In *Specifying*, Susan Willis announces the intention of historicizing the literature of contemporary black women writers. But not unlike Bloom's crypto-deconstructionism, Willis' 'historicism' inserts 'Hurston' where one might expect to read history. Her analysis of Hurston's rhetoric suffers the consequences. For instance, Willis takes the title of her book from a passage in *Dust Tracks on a Road* in which Hurston describes her first encounter with Big Sweet, who was in the process of 'specifying' somebody:

Big Sweet broke the news to him, in one of her mildest bulletins that his pa
was a double humpted camel and his ma was a grass gut cow, but even so, he
tore her wide open in the act of getting born, and so on and so forth . . .

Bypassing more complex explanations of the use of figurative language
in the Afro-American oral tradition, some of which Hurston herself
helped to supply, Willis settles upon 'name-calling' to denote 'specifying', and concludes that it 'represents a form of narrative integrity.
Historically, it speaks for a noncommodified relationship to language, a
time when the slippage between words and meaning would not have
obtained or been tolerated.'

The translation of 'specifying' that Hurston offers within the text is
'putting your foot up' on somebody, which Big Sweet promptly does
when a troublemaker in camp threatens Hurston with a knife. 'Specifying', more like Gates' 'Signifying', is a fluid, relational process uncon-
cerned with original intent. If the slippage between signifier and signified
is the problem, the writing of Zora Neale Hurston is not the cure, except
to the degree that the cure is making the unconscious judgement
apparent, re-establishing the severed links between 'linguistic undecid-
ability' and economic and political fact. Hurston often did this in her
writing, not by forcing meaning to heel, but rather by tracking its
proliferation/demise.

Willis makes valid observations, but her interpretation bears the
unmistakeable stamp of the tourist because of her failure to read Hurston
in the context of Afro-American letters and her determination to cast
black women's writing in polar opposition to the alienation and reification of white middle-class culture.

I don't mean to imply that you have to be a black feminist to do Zora
Neale Hurston justice. A fine example of a way to tackle the territory is
provided by Barbara Johnson in A World of Difference. Her approach is
forthright from the beginning: 'It was not clear to me what I, a white
deconstructor, was doing talking about Zora Neale Hurston, a black
novelist and anthropologist, or to whom I was talking. . . . Was I talking
to white critics, black critics, or myself?' Johnson decides that the answer
is 'all of the above' and that her interest in Hurston's 'strategies and
structures of problematic address' does not have a single motivation. 'I
had a lot to learn then,' she writes, 'from Hurston's way of dealing with
multiple agendas and heterogeneous implied readers.'

Johnson recalls the double-voicing of the Afro-American literary
tradition in terms of Dubois' famous veil metaphor, which divides the
Afro-American citizen, automatically assumed to be male, between
contending allegiances to race and country. She illustrates Hurston's
location in that discourse by quoting from Richard Wright's review of

Their Eyes Were Watching God, in which he wrote that 'the sensory sweep of her novel carries no theme, no message, no thought'. Johnson says of this statement, 'the full range of questions and experiences of Janie's life are as invisible to a mind steeped in maleness as Ellison's *Invisible Man* is to minds steeped in whiteness'.

Following black feminist readings, Johnson suggests that Janie's display of rhetorical mastery in the male-dominated world of an all-black town constructs a symbolic resolution of the dilemma that plagued Hurston's career. But she proposes, as well, that discussions of race or gender invariably rely upon an oppositional or dualistic logic that forces the black woman writer into a virtually untenable position in critical discourse.

As Johnson finally puts it, 'The black woman is both invisible and ubiquitous; never seen in her own right but forever appropriated by the others for their own ends.' Yet even in Hurston's nonfiction writing, ultimate resolution of the dilemma is always displaced, for as Johnson insists, 'unification and simplification are fantasies of domination, not understanding' and 'the task of the writer' is 'to narrate both the appeal and the injustice of universalization, in a voice that assumes and articulates its own, ever-differing self-difference'.

In her nonfiction writing, Hurston insists that Afro-American oral tradition is unique and irreplaceable, thereby seeming to confirm the notion of an irreducible racial essence. At the same time, she makes the counterclaim that 'race' as a way of categorizing and limiting a writer's domain simply shouldn't and doesn't exist. Although generalizations about Hurston are probably useless, her life offers a possible explanation of this apparent contradiction.

While Hurston's anchor in New York was her scholarship with Franz Boas in anthropology at Columbia, the road was rocky still. Besides the criticism of her male peers, constant financial troubles, and the increasing inaccessibility of publication, Hurston had bad luck with husbands, didn't get along with her family, and couldn't keep a teaching job. Invariably, her response to 'worriation' was to go on another folklore hunting trip in the South, or South America or the Caribbean. Financial and professional security were strangers to her all her life, which may explain why she never seemed to recover from the shock of the headlines in the *Afro-American*, a black Baltimore paper, reporting a morals charge in 1948 that accused her of sodomizing the teenage son of her Harlem landlady while she was, in fact, out of the city. Though she soon fled the North for the South's 'heart of darkness', never to return, her writing became more politically conservative and color blind: she was clearly disillusioned with the racial politics of a Northern black bourgeoisie that had never offered her anything but torment anyway.

The biographical approach has its uses, but I like Johnson's take on Hurston's self-contradiction. For Hurston, she says, 'Difference is a misreading of sameness, but it must be represented in order to be erased. The resistance to finding out that the other is the same springs out of the reluctance to admit that the same is other.' The point here, it seems to me, is both political and literary: black and white, male and female exist in asymmetrical relation to one another; they are not neat little opposites to be drawn and quartered. We recognize the persistence of such measures in our narratives in order to dismantle them in our lives.

Forceful black female critical voices are needed to verify the crucial assault on the logic of binary oppositions of race, class, and sex already launched by contemporary black women novelists, poets, and playwrights. Scrutiny of Hurston's nonfiction writing could inspire us to take on this task. Instead, the thrust of black feminist writing on Hurston implicitly proposes her life and work as a role model for contemporary black female scholarship, intellectual curiosity, and literary production. The model is too narrow.

Black feminist criticism on Hurston may already be changing its tune, or so *Invented Lives: Narratives of Black Women 1860–1960*, edited and annotated by Mary Helen Washington, would seem to indicate. Washington's introduction to excerpts from Hurston's novels questions the viability of Janie as a heroic voice and suggests that Hurston's real sympathies lay with John Pearson, the protagonist of *Jonah's Gourd Vine*. Hurston depicts the oral tradition in the all-black town of *Their Eyes* as sex-segregated and male-dominated: Janie doesn't stand a chance. Is Washington's analysis a step in the right direction, or is it the inevitable swing of the pendulum back to a position dismissive of Hurston's work?

We need a re-evaluation of Hurston's re-evaluation, a running blow-by-blow commentary on the progress and health of the black female literary/critical voice and its relationship to the mainstream. As for role models, we might do ourselves greater service to choose among that school of black women writers flourishing now – Paule Marshall, Toni Morrison, Alice Walker, Audre Lorde, Toni Cade Bambara, Sonia Sanchez, June Jordan, Ntozake Shange, Gloria Naylor, Thulani Davis, Lucille Clifton, Sherley Anne Williams, Maya Angelou, critics Barbara Christian, Barbara Smith, Mary Helen Washington, Gloria Hull, Bell Hooks. It is now that black women are 'writing themselves into history', as black feminist critic Hortense Spillers aptly puts it in her afterword to *Conjuring*.

Yet there are those of us who fear the proliferation of continental theory. Audre Lorde and Barbara Christian have said as much, on the grounds that 'the master's tools cannot be used to dismantle the master's house', which makes me think the reluctance of black women writers to rise to the challenge of critical self-definition may not be only the fault of male and/or white intimidation. As Bell Hooks suggested recently, in an essay called 'Talking Back', critical writing may hold a special terror for black women as a result of an anti-intellectual bias that is automatic, unconscious, and defensive in our upbringing.

To be more specific, little black girls are not encouraged at home or at school to value their own thoughts. To articulate them is often labeled 'talking back' and even punished. The sense that black females should be either supportive or silent is carried over into adulthood. So, like Jane Austen hiding her novel-writing under blotting paper in the family room, black women, too, have been forced to conceal their best contemporary articulations of self under the cloak of fiction. Even our endless respectful tributes to our mothers' courage and endurance in the face of slavery and racial oppression may actually interfere with our intellectual growing up as daughters.

It's time to consider that the process of concealment, which was once essential to our collective survival, has outlived its usefulness. Although I'll grant you that talking back is a risky business, the alternative is for Afro-American women to continue to be objects, not subjects, in the global production of knowledge. So, hagiography is fine if you have the time, but more urgent matters call. It probably won't do any of us any good to make that childless trickster Zora Hurston into a madonna figure, whose arms we can lie in and be safe. Black women have written numerous autobiographies, among which *Dust Tracks on a Road* takes the prize for inscrutability. We do well to remember that when dust tracks blow away, they are impossible to follow.

MARKS OF ZORA

On the one hand, black and white, and male and female exist in asymmetrical relation. On the other hand, as Barbara Johnson proposes in *A World of Difference*, the following categories reflect the bitter facts of segregation.

Black Women/X (Radical Negation)

Conjuring: Black Women, Fiction and Literary Tradition. Edited by Marjorie Pryse and Hortense Spillers (Indiana University Press, 1985): A strange medley. The introduction suggests an anthology of black and white feminist literary criticism masquerading as black pre-feminist synthesis, or magic, or conjure. The collection itself has some solid historicist moments not to be scoffed at by those who would recollect (for the first time?) Pauline Hopkins, Jessie Fauset, Ann Petry's *The Street*, Margaret Walker's *Jubilee*, and sci-fi writer Octavia Butler. But the peak experience comes at the end in an afterword by the inimitable Hortense Spillers, who reads the 'tradition' of black women writers and a current unfolding 'black female writing community' of Pulitzers, MLAs, movies, and magazine covers as overlapping 'cross-currents' and 'discontinuities' of interpretation.

Color, Sex and Poetry: Three Women Writers of the Harlem Renaissance. By Gloria T. Hull (Indiana University Press, 1987): Useful though not wildly interesting despite the wonderful title. Alice Dunbar-Nelson, Angelina Grimke, and Georgia Douglas Johnson, three black women poets contemporary with Hurston, are re-examined amid a Harlem Renaissance that didn't think much of women artists. *Give Us Each Day: The Diary of Alice Dunbar-Nelson*, edited by Gloria T. Hull, is more interesting for the occasional grisly detail, the day-to-day record of a black woman writer in the 20s.

Black Women Writers (1950–1980): A Critical Evaluation. Edited by Mari Evans (Anchor/Doubleday, 1984): An invaluable reference for those who wish to know what devotees of the 'Black Aesthetic' make of contemporary black women writers. Indispensable for those who wonder about Sonia Sanchez, Mari Evans, Lucille Clifton, Nikki Giovanni, and others who haven't made the MLA circuit yet. The book's best feature is the statements the writers make about their own work, full of the surprise of their own voices.

Sturdy Black Bridges: Visions of Black Women in Literature. Edited by Roseann P. Bell, Bettye J. Parker, and Beverley Guy Sheftall (Anchor Books, 1979): A unique black feminist/nationalist anthology of criticism, interviews, photographs, bibliographies, fiction, and poetry. A collector's item. Black feminist sensibility in genesis. Aside from Hortense Spillers' criticism of James Baldwin's novels and Ellease Southerland on voodoo in Hurston's fiction, the interviews are the must-see. Toni Cade Bambara and Toni Morrison talk shop. George Kent, Addison Gayle, and C.L.R. James talk the spectre of black women writers.

All the Women Are White, All the Blacks Are Men, But Some of Us Are Brave: Black Women's Studies. Edited by Gloria T. Hull, Patricia

Bell Scott, and Barbara Smith (Feminist Press, 1981): A landmark occasion for black feminism. An abundance of riches, including Lorraine Bethel on Zora Neale, Barbara Smith on Toni Morrison, and Michele Russell on black women blues singers.

Black Women Novelists: The Development of a Tradition, 1892–1976. By Barbara Christian (Greenwood Press, 1980): Although this book is considered somewhat outmoded because of its painstaking, old-fashioned historical approach, it is still the Bible in the field of black feminist criticism as far as I'm concerned; essential and fascinating reading for anybody interested in black women novelists. Christian is particularly adept at providing the social, political, and intellectual context for evaluating Hurston's accomplishments. An invaluable teaching guide.

Invented Lives: Narratives of Black Women 1860–1960. Edited by Mary Helen Washington (Anchor/Doubleday, 1987): This book consists largely of excerpts from hard-to-find editions of novels by black women (many of which are coming back into print via an Oxford University Press series edited by Henry Louis Gates). Washington, the dean of black feminist critics, provides interpretations of Frances Harper, Nella Larsen, Zora Neale Hurston, and Gwendolyn Brooks, among others, which are generally perceptive and always provocative.

White Women/Complementarity

Specifying: Black Women Writing the American Experience. By Susan Willis (University of Wisconsin, 1987): An odd Marxist colonization (domestication? deflowering?) of black women writers Hurston, Paule Marshall, Toni Morrison, Alice Walker, and Toni Cade Bambara, arranged in ascending order of complexity, with the huge gap between Hurston and Marshall left virtually unexplained. Willis will only say no other black women writers are qualified to take on the big M of Modernism. While her basic assertions may be crucial – that black women are providing a materialist re-reading of Afro-American history, and displacing traditional urban–rural and Southern–Northern dichotomies – the way she goes about making her case is reductive. Fredric Jameson she ain't. In a word, it's prescriptive. You could have this one filled at the drugstore.

A World of Difference. By Barbara Johnson (Johns Hopkins University Press, 1987): For feminists who want an introduction to the world of Yale criticism and deconstruction, this is it. Dazzling and fun, from the memorial to the formidable (or should I say notorious?) Paul de Man, which introduces the possibility of feminist deconstruction, to the revisions and re-readings of motherhood as a nearly untenable discursive position. Mary Shelley's *Frankenstein*, Mallarmé with womb envy, and the childless Zora Neale are the prototypical literary mother figures here. The book ends with a tour de force on the rhetoric of abortion.

Black Men/The Other

Figures in Black: Words, Signs and The Racial Self. By Henry Louis Gates (Oxford University Press, 1987): Entertaining and dramatic. Harlequins (with African faces) borrowed from the commedia dell'arte become the black Sambo and the white Bones of American minstrel shows, thus signaling this book's preoccupation with binary opposition as the key to the conundrum of 'race' in American culture. Black women writers occupy key roles. In 1773, Phillis Wheatley's poetry falls on Thomas Jefferson's deaf ears. In 1859, *Our Nig* by Harriet Wilson subsumes black slave narratives and white plantation fiction in a book that defies genre. In the Harlem Renaissance and beyond, the unpopularity of black dialect (and its association with minstrelsy) worries the borders of race, class, and sex in the writings of Jean Toomer, Sterling Brown, and Zora Neale Hurston. A Signifying Monkey (Ishmael Reed) drives the point(s) home.

Modernism and the Harlem Renaissance. By Houston Baker (University of Chicago Press, 1987): Longish essay (short book) at a monstrous price. Kinda fun if you're looking for a neo-black nationalist revamping of 'modernism' (not rigorously defined), but not really worth it if you're looking for women, except Ma Rainey on the cover and the scant comments in her honor as the voice (the muse?) of 'black discursive modernism' via poet Sterling Brown's male gaze. Baker's obsession here is with a 'mastery of form' and a 'deformation of mastery' that is potentially intriguing, but doesn't go far enough to block the usual lineup – Booker T., W.E.B., Chesnutt, Dunbar, Alain Locke, et al. Topsy, Bessie Smith, and Zora only dance through frenetically. If you want to see Baker making much over 'women', check out his *Blues, Ideology and Afro-American Literature* (1985), in which his reading of

Linda Brent's slave narrative is intense; his re-reading of Hurston's *Their Eyes* only slightly less so.

The Sexual Mountain and Black Women Writers: Adventures in Sex, Literature and Real Life. By Calvin Hernton (Anchor/Doubleday, 1987): My evaluation of this book is probably skewed because I am mentioned in the title essay in a way that brings back painful memories of *Black Macho*-mania. Still, it seems to me that Hernton's chivalrous efforts to explain contemporary black women writers to detractors are not grounded in even a minimal acquaintance with contemporary theories of Afro-American and feminist literary criticism. Perhaps you'll say that here, finally, is a book about black women writers for the general reader, to which I can only reply that a book on black women writers which says as much about me as it does about Zora Neale Hurston makes you wonder who is appropriating whom.

White Men/Universality

Modern Critical Views: Zora Neale Hurston. Edited by Harold Bloom (Chelsea House, 1986): Most of the pieces anthologized here have already been seen by anyone who's been following Hurston's republication. And the introduction assaults the validity of both feminist and Afro-American literary criticism – in four brief pages. Buy Washington and Christian and even Willis instead. Failing that, xerox.

(1988)

21

Reading 1968: The Great American

Whitewash

After 1968, none of the 'other' groups in struggle – neither women nor racial 'minorities' nor sexual 'minorities' nor the handicapped nor the 'ecologists' (those who refused the acceptance, unquestioningly, of the imperatives of increased global production) – would ever again accept the legitimacy of 'waiting' upon some other revolution.

Immanuel Wallerstein, '1968, Revolution in the World System:
Theses and Queries', 1988

We must become more radically historical than is envisioned by the Marxist tradition. By becoming more 'radically historical' I mean confronting more candidly the myriad of effects and consequences (intended and unintended, conscious and unconscious) of power-laden and conflict-ridden social practice – e.g. the complex confluence of human bodies, traditions and institutions.

Cornel West, 'Race and Social Theory: Toward a Genealogical
Materialist Analysis', 1987

I recently participated in a conference called '1968 in Global Retrospective', which was built around a twenty-seven-page paper by Immanuel Wallerstein about 1968 as 'one of the great formative events in the history of our modern world-system, the kind we call watershed events'. My job was to talk about 'The Key Role of "Minority" Revolutions', and to chair a panel on 'Representations of 1968: Invention and Use of Symbols', which included 1968 historians Todd Gitlin, David Caute, Jim Hoberman and James Miller.

MINORITY REVOLUTIONS IN A MAJOR KEY

As I observe the emerging patterns of codification and interpretation of US and global 1960s history, I am beginning to understand how Afro-American intellectual history, despite the publication of Harold Cruse's *The Crisis of The Negro Intellectual* in 1967, and so many other books since then, continues not to exist for most white scholarship and commentary. Therefore, it continues to hold only marginal interest for those who would reflect upon the fate of 'minority revolutions'. Yet it is Afro-American intellectual reflection and analysis of itself, its relationship to the New Left, and other 'minority' revolutions that needs to be considered here. First, because it is precisely the ascendency of the 'minor' which most distinguishes the events of a global 1968 'world-historical movement'. Second, if one fails to consider the intellectual perspective of the 'minor' – in this case the Afro-American perspective, but it might just as well be (although this would not be the same) the Asian-American perspective or the gay perspective – then theory in conjunction with history helps to consolidate at the level of collective memory the very segregation 1960s youth were once so determined to undo.

Such Afro-Americanists as Cornel West, Manning Marable, Hortense Spillers, Henry Louis Gates, Houston Baker, Hazel Carby, Paula Giddings, and Bell Hooks have been instrumental in revealing an underlying coherence in Afro-American intellectual and cultural development. Collectively, such efforts begin to reveal the degree to which people of African descent in the US have demonstrated in writing and speaking a historical consciousness generally much more subtle and inclusive than mainstream, official versions, one that connects the world views of Phillis Wheatley, Frederick Douglass and Frances Harper to Ida B. Wells, W.E.B. Dubois and Zora Neale Hurston to C.L.R. James, James Baldwin and Lorraine Hansberry to Stuart Hall, Amiri Baraka and Toni Morrison.

In 1968, such political figures as Angela Davis, Stokely Carmichael, Martin Luther King, Malcolm X and Ron Karenga, and such writers as Langston Hughes, Sonia Sanchez, Amiri Baraka and Harold Cruse, and such performers as Harry Belafonte, Nina Simone, Odetta and James Brown were crucial to how politically engaged people in the period imagined their goals. Now, in retrospect, the impact and significance of these figures is made to seem light indeed, unless, of course, the project becomes to write a *black* history of 1968, but then that would still be 'minor' and 'minority' history, something I do not recommend as a solution.

My intention here is to point out the tendency for 'history' in the major sense to corroborate a racist, phallocentric hegemony by always marginalizing, trivializing, and decentering a black subject, even as its specific historical object may involve an apparent focus upon issues of ethnicity or racism or, as in this case, 'minority revolutions'. Yet that history which focuses upon the 'minor' or the 'minority' may help to corroborate the same apartheid, the same phallocentric center, while banishing to the margins the context that makes, and continues to make, black subjectivity a problem. If white mainstream historians of the New Left have a problem utilizing histories of the 'minor' by black authors, they should address that problem, first, as a crucial step to be taken prior to any meaningful examination of the phenomenon of 1968 and its consequences for the present.

To put it another way, somehow, ultimately, black subjectivity, particularly the subjectivity of black women, always seems irrelevant to any serious academic or political discussion of a 'black', 'ethnic', or 'minority' object. This problem is characteristic of how the production of knowledge is constantly employed in reinforcing intellectual racism. Moreover, this habit of leaving the black subject out always seems to coincide with a preference for global or synthetic or structural views. It should continue no longer.

My role here is to contest the notion of a 'world system' as yet another attempt to universalize white male intellectual authority over the 'voiceless'. However, I don't for a moment believe that high-minded collections of oral history, which allow 'the people to speak for themselves', or autonomous insular black intellectual debate will entirely fill the gap. So long as the paradigm employed is sufficiently oriented toward process rather than structure, I have no objection to the notion of 'world systems' in and of themselves, especially since I understand that in this case it carries the more practical purpose of addressing the problem of an increasingly global economic arrangement that stifles substantive change and resistance at the local or the national level, or at the level of a specific issue such as ethnicity, class, or sexuality.

For instance, if you look at the drug problem in black communities in big cities in the US, while it encompasses specific issues of ethnicity, class and sexuality at both the local and the national level, one can't properly understand the problem until it is considered in the context of a global political/economic arrangement in which the disadvantage to black citizens of the US is outweighed by the advantages in the global marketplace. I understand that most of the people of color in the world are getting screwed as a function of a world system, so it makes sense that amelioration would propose a global approach at some point.

Moreover, regarding the idea that there may be repetitions and parallels in events around the globe, particularly now that a global communications network, including television, film and wire services, hooks us all up to the same simultaneous stimulation, I am in complete agreement.

I have, for instance, noticed certain patterns, conscious and unconscious, in contemporary black cultural and intellectual reflections on the limits of 1960s black male political leadership 'style', in terms of its failure to recognize or accommodate the question of sexual difference. In black film and literature from the US, England and Africa, there has developed a conventional feminist critique of inequality within the Black Liberation Movement, a trend toward subverting the male/female gender duality in favor of multiple sexualities, including homosexuality and lesbianism, as well as an increasing focus on the inadequacies of a rigid and inflexible concept of masculinity. Besides the considerable literature that explores such issues (novels, plays and poetry by Ntozake Shange, Alice Walker, Toni Morrison, Toni Cade Bambara, Lucille Clifton, Audre Lorde, along with black male writers Ishmael Reed, Charles Johnson, John Edgar Wideman and David Bradley), I see Spike Lee's *School Daze* (1988), Isaac Julien and Maureen Blackwood's *The Passion of Remembrance* (1986), and Sarah Maldoror's *Sambizanga* (1972), about the struggle for liberation in Angola, all as films in which there is a related concern about the loss of a unitary concept of 'the black (male) leader'.

For instance, in *School Daze* (at a level that is perhaps unconscious to director Spike Lee), Dap's leadership, and thus his role as protagonist, is constantly questioned and challenged, not only by the college administration, but also by the 'women' and by his friends, as well as by the continuous flow of dance, song, style and sexual spectacle that fights with him for the focus of the film and seems to be saying that this film has more important business to attend to than telling his linear (phallic) narrative.

In *Passion of Remembrance*, which more candidly embraces a critique of sixties male leadership and its knee-jerk heterosexism, the combination of carnivalesque spectacle, political commentary and archival footage is, finally, much more satisfying than the English film most often lauded for these attributes, *Sammy and Rosie Get Laid* (1987). While I admire the films of Stephen Frears and Hanif Kureishi, especially *My Beautiful Laundrette*, their version of Third Worldism seems problematic. It becomes an opportunity for a fashionable kind of cynicism (much like liberalism) about the possibility for fundamental world change, coupled with an explicit but unanalyzed hierarchizing of a literate and prosperous 'Third World' (mostly Indian) and an illiterate and impoverished 'Third World' (mostly black) in England. From the first scene in *Sammy and Rosie*, it is blacks who are marginalized in that they occupy the film's most desperate and precarious social, sexual and economic positions.

That these positions are visualized usually in the absence of any verbal explanation only makes it more urgent that they be interrogated.

In *Sambizanga*, while the critique seems somewhat unconscious on the director's part, the black male 'leader' is both figuratively and literally slain from the beginning of the film. From the scene in which the crying of the men is not visualized, we gather that a point is being made about revolutions and sexual difference. Rather, it is the film's focus on the crying of the women and its relationship to cultural continuity that seems to indicate the means by which the struggle will continue.

In real life in the US – if you can call *The Morton Downey Show* real life – this critique of past black male leadership takes the form of Roy Innis and Al Sharpton's fistfight at Harlem's Apollo Theatre, ostensibly over the case of Tawana Brawley. Meanwhile, Brawley is a fifteen-year-old black teenager whose rape is somehow unimaginable and unspeakable to present black political discourse, as the debate rages over whether Sharpton is a 'fake'. Black male leadership seems no better prepared to fathom the black teenager's psychological, social, economic, and educational plight now than in 1968. And no better prepared to cast out the Sharptons.

At the same time, we should not dismiss too quickly the inherent dangers that even progressive 'world systems' present. This is the danger of neo-colonialism or neo-imperialism in intellectual form, and what makes it so is that mostly only white males are empowered to engage in that discourse. The problem is, as Trinh Minh-ha points out, 'they work toward your erasure while urging you to keep your life and ethnic values within the border of your homelands. This is called the policy of "separate development" in apartheid language.'

SOMEWHERE OVER THE RAINBOW

There has never existed heretofore international (that is, interzonal) solidarity of any significance. And this fact has given rise to much bitterness. One, the immediate day-to-day concerns of the populations of the three zones are today in many ways strikingly different. The movements that exist in these three zones reflect their differences. Secondly, many of the short-run objectives of movements in the three zones would, if achieved, have the effect of improving the situation for some persons in that zone at the expense of other persons in other zones. Thirdly, no desirable transformation of the capitalist world economy is possible in the absence of trans-zonal political cooperation by antisystemic movements.

This trans-zonal cooperation would have to be both strategic and tactical.

It might be easier (albeit still not easy) to establish the bases of tactical cooperation. But strategic? It is probable that strategic collaboration can only be on the basis of a profound radicalization of objectives. For the great impediment to trans-zonal strategic collaboration is the incredible socio-economic polarization of the existing world system. But is there an objective (and not merely a voluntaristic) basis for such a radicalization?

Immanuel Wallerstein, 1988

I am not concerned to question here the nature of this proposal. Rather, my focus is upon 'a profound radicalization of objectives' all but inaccessible through the theorizing of 'world systems'. This theorizing, after all, in no way subverts or transforms white male academic authority and, therefore, confirms our present unsatisfactory arrangements of cultural hegemony. The only door through which 'change' at a critical level can enter is by altering the composition of the community that considers the problems of 'objectives'. White men in positions of power have to stop thinking that it is their place alone to determine the course of our lives.

I am not proposing that if Wallerstein were black, everything would be fine. I am not a nationalist or a postnationalist, nor does 'racial pride' make a lot of sense to me as a political goal (although I guess I have my fair share). Rather, I am proposing that if the experiences of race, ethnicity, gender, and sexuality were made central to future consider-ations of 'world systems', the process would be a lot more convincing in terms of locating a 'profound radicalization of objectives'. Moreover, this blind spot on ethnicity and sexuality transcends the problem of 'minor-ities' as 'women and blacks', who are not, after all, global minorities, but who are simply minor in the sphere of knowledge production. Not only is there a failure to consider the question of world systems or global perspectives from the view of the racial or sexual 'other'. There is also a failure to consider the other that may ultimately be at the center of even a so-called majority white male existence, the other of ethnicity, religion, sexuality, rationality (which he repetitively banishes), the other of homelessness, both geographical and existential, which may be the driving force behind this compulsive white male Western insistence upon majority, authority and dominance.

So the question for me is not even whether or not Wallerstein is right or wrong. Such a question cannot be addressed until we have contended with the discrepancy in that perspective itself, the view from which the history of 1968 is first recollected that obliterates the possibility of black subjectivity, not only in the US but in the Caribbean and Africa as well. Perhaps the clearest occasion upon which this occurs is in Waller-stein's Thesis 4: 'Counterculture was part of the revolutionary euphoria,

but was not politically central to 1968'. The subsequent explanation of
this thesis goes on to define the 'counterculture' in a way that not only
precludes its historical relationship to Afro-American culture, but also
renders 1960s Afro-American social and political life, including the Civil
Rights Movement and Black Power, entirely invisible. Afro-American
cultural production then becomes an incidental and minor aspect of US
and European counterculture or, in this case, a nonentity. The historical
relationship is first reversed: counterculture no longer comes out of Afro-
American culture but rather the other way around. Rock 'n' roll's roots
in an Afro-American blues tradition are not acknowledged. The beat
aesthetic is no longer influenced by the lifestyles and performances of
black jazz musicians. And American youth culture bears no relationship
whatsoever to black street culture.

Then, in the most preemptive move, the one that makes history
irrecoverable by transforming it into myth, the counterculture is defined
as that which is gratuitous, that which belongs to no one, which is not
culture at all, but *counter-to-culture* or against culture. 'We generally
mean by counterculture', Wallerstein writes, 'behavior in daily life
(sexuality, drugs, dress) and in the arts that is unconventional, non-
"bourgeois", and Dionysiac.' There is never any doubt in this statement
that there is a more useful, mainstream, conventional, bourgeois, and
Apollonian culture that will counteract the countercultural. The countercultural is then perceived as entirely peripheral to profound change.
Still, I would like to claim this degraded form of culture as the true
location for a revolutionary potential in Afro-American social life.

Afro-American culture has long been the starting point for white self-
criticism in the US. Mid-twentieth-century white and black youths were
impressed by the resilience and versatility of Afro-American culture: its
working mothers employed as domestics with husbands or men who
could not find work; its poor elderly black men who had labored for a
pittance all their lives yet could invent songs of indescribable beauty in
which they accurately weighed the material and psychological complexity
of their world; its tradition of religious music, which seemed to turn the
hypocrisy of conventional white Protestantism inside out; its church-
going people who would lay their bodies down before waterhoses, dogs,
and white Southern racism and then get up and fight for the Mississippi
Freedom Party and against US military involvement in the Vietnam
War.

The realization that such people existed despite the efforts of a white,
racist ruling class to destroy their dignity and appropriate their vitality
was a crucial influence on the widespread conviction in 1968 that US
dominance and world hegemony were unconscionable and parasitic, and
that the 'Old Left' lacked the sensitivity to grapple with real people in a

real world of cultural diversity. Afro-American culture was instrumental
in forming the aspirations of the New Left, as well as minority revolutions – not so much by its considerable political activity, but precisely by
its counterculture. While this 'minor' culture may sometimes be difficult
to link directly to political protest, it was always clearly formed in the
spirit of subverting a majority culture that tried to choke it at the root.
Precisely in its sex, drugs, dance, music, and style, it kept the record of its
discontents accurately and well. Perhaps this counterculture is the site
where mainstream culture is still most forcefully challenged, even as
'revolutions' come and go.

Like everything else human, there are many countercultures, not just
one. For instance, today, black youth resist total white hegemonic
control over everyday life, often by means considered counter to culture,
by drug use and the life of the streets, by their unwillingness to go to
school and their inclination to have babies. While such developments are
largely the result of an economic and educational stagnation imposed
upon them from above, black teenagers respond to this situation partly in
the form of an interpretation (from drug use to pregnancy to rap) that is
connected, by influence and osmosis, to countercultural developments,
white, black and brown, in the 50s and 60s.

As for those decades, I am certain of a deliberate and self-conscious
black counterculture because my parents – my father, who was a jazz
musician, my mother, who was an artist, and my stepfather, who was their
close friend – were part of it in the 50s. In the 1960s, my father, divorced
from my mother and an unsuccessful musician, would die of a heroin
overdose. In 1965, the summer he died, my mother, my sister and I took
classes at Amiri Baraka's (then Leroi Jones) newly inaugurated School of
Black Arts in Harlem. A public high school teacher who was moon-
lighting as an artist, my mother Faith became a 1960s radical, taking an
active role in the black struggle against the United Federation of
Teachers over 'decentralization' of the public schools.

In those years, the hardest thing to figure out was culture, how our
everyday lives would bear the mark of our political commitment, for it
was immediately clear to everyone, once the Civil Rights and Voting
Rights bills had been settled, that US capitalist hegemony undermined
you most at the level of the everyday. In 1963, Faith began to produce a
series of paintings called 'American People', in which she tried to capture
the drama and the underlying structure of the racism that the Civil
Rights Movement confronted, as we then viewed it on our television
screens, as it affected race relations in the North, as it was written about
by James Baldwin in The Fire Next Time (1963) and Amiri Baraka in
Dutchman (1964). In 1970, when I became a student at the City College
of New York, I was already struck by how many politically active black

students were getting involved in heavy drug use, dying at a hospital across the street.

1968 REVISITED

'Where is tomorrow's avant-garde in art and entertainment to take on the racial bias of the snowblind, the sexual politics of the frigid, and the class anxieties of the perennially upper crust?' When I asked this question a few months ago, I was trying to make light of something that is not light at all. As ridiculous as it may seem, a white cultural avant-garde, here and abroad, has always believed it possible to make an oppositional art without fundamentally challenging hegemonic notions of race, sexuality, and even class.

Of course, when I was a kid, we didn't call it 'white cultural hegemony'. We called it the 'Great American Whitewash'. I had the great good fortune to be raised in a family of artists (my stepfather was not an artist but worked at General Motors to finance our creativity) in which resistance to the old truism, 'If you're white, you're all right; if you're brown stick around; and if you're black, stay back', was viewed not only as paramount to making art, but basic to one's psychological survival. I still find it astonishing when white people consistently conceptualize resistance in ways that minimize the importance of race, or the vital contribution black artists and intellectuals have made to the discussion of that issue.

But I was first struck by the true dimensions of this problem in 1970, when Faith and I attended a guerrilla art action protest against Art Strike, which was itself a protest against 'racism, war and repression'. A group of famous white male artists led by Robert Morris decided to withdraw their work from the Venice Biennale, a prestigious international exhibition, in order to protest US bombing of Cambodia and the murder of college students at Kent, Jackson and Augusta. Although the protest was supposed to be against 'Racism, War, and Repression' (sexism was not yet on their agenda), Art Strike then expected to mount a counter-Biennale in New York without altering the all-white male composition of the show. This seems to be the key to understanding the intrinsic limits of Western cultural avant-gardism: while it can no longer deny its own white male supremacist presuppositions, it cannot be rid of them either.

In the first years of our feminism, working through an organization that we founded called Women Students and Artists for Black Art

Liberation (WSABAL), Faith and others succeeded in opening this exhibition to women and people of color. WSABAL was also influential in the subsequent development of Ad Hoc Women Artists, led by Lucy Lippard. This group repeated WSABAL's 50 per cent women demand in their protest against the Whitney Biennial, which was in the habit of including white male artists almost exclusively. Specifically because of Faith's research and support of Ad Hoc, black women artists Barbara Chase Riboud and Bettye Saar were included in the next Whitney Biennial.

Of course, Faith's activism against the museums had not begun in 1970. It really began in 1968, the year of Martin Luther King's assassination, when every black artist and cultural worker in the country was galvanized into action. Only sixteen years old at the time, I accompanied Faith to the first demonstration of black artists against the Whitney Museum and then to a series of free-for-all (Art Workers' Coalition) demonstrations against the Museum of Modern Art. The museums were still reluctant to call in the police at that point. Yet, since the Civil Rights Movement, Black Power, and the riots, it was no longer tolerable simply to 'picket' in an orderly fashion. These demonstrations were increasingly unpredictable, full of street theatre and creative mayhem, very countercultural in the Wallerstein/Dionysiac sense.

In one case, I can remember museum administrators and security guards standing helplessly by as Faith led a walking tour through MoMA's first-floor galleries during which she lectured on the influence of African art and the art of the African Diaspora on the so-called modern art displayed there. The manner in which academic and critical expertise and the museum's curatorial staff conspired to render the importance of that influence either invisible, trivial, or merely instrumental shaped her remarks. When we finally came to a room in which the works of a black artist were displayed – perhaps two or three gouaches from Jacob Lawrence's 1930s 'Black Migration Series' – Faith designated it the location for the Martin Luther King Wing, which was then the principal demand of the Art Workers' Coalition demonstrations at MoMA. This wing was supposed to serve as an exhibition space that would revolve around a cultural education center and would train blacks, Puerto Ricans, and Native Americans in art history and museum administration. This cultural education center would lead to the canonization of some black artists and the hiring of a few nonwhite curators, but its main intention was to promote an increase in the number of young people of color who would be drawn to careers in art and art education, to foster a more meaningful relationship to museums and 'high culture' for the throngs of nonwhite public school children who were obliged to visit the museums every year.

For many, the Civil Rights Movement was their first exposure to the power of Rainbow Coalitions. My first experience came during those years of involvement with the Art Workers' Coalition. But the lessons were hard ones. Ultimately, there would be no Martin Luther King Wing, no cultural center, only retrospective exhibitions for black artists Romare Bearden and Richard Hunt, which made them (no doubt because they were men) even more famous than Barbara Chase Riboud and Bettye Saar.

The resulting tokenism of a few museum shows for a few black artists did not really change the embedded elitism of the art world. Visual art is still perceived by many as the exclusive entertainment of the rich, as though the rest of us didn't need something to look at. At the same time, the important thing seemed to be that my mother was an activist whose work as an artist was consistent with her politics, although I pointedly failed to mention any such thing in my own recollection of the 1960s in *Black Macho*. This was perhaps my greatest and most unfortunate oversight, since her politics were my politics in the 1960s and for much of the 1970s. If you are lucky enough to have a mother who has a forcefully autonomous political vision, it will be a while before you can be expected to come up with any idea of your own. Of course, I didn't realize this when I wrote *Black Macho* at the age of twenty-six. Moreover, it is not the style in commercial publishing to give credit where credit is due. Particularly when the credit is due to your mother who is just as black as you are!

Now, however, as recollections of the 1960s mount up – among others, Todd Gitlin's *The Sixties: Years of Hope, Days of Rage*, James Miller's *Democracy Is in the Streets: From Port Huron to the Siege of Chicago*, David Caute's *The Year of the Barricades: A Journey Through 1968*, Sara Evans' *Personal Politics: The Roots of Women's Liberation in the Civil Rights Movement and the New Left*, George Katsiaficas' *The Imagination of the New Left: A Global Analysis of 1968* and *Daring to Be Bad: Radical Feminism in America, 1967–1975* by Alice Echols – we are again facing the Great American Whitewash. Not only has the breadth of the Afro-American cultural presence and contribution almost ceased to exist, but also black, Latino, Asian, feminist and gay 'minorities' have become 'minor' again, as though the revisions of the 60s and the 70s in the way we conceptualize 'history' had never happened.

This is so despite institutions like the Studio Museum in Harlem, which mounted a 1960s show in 1985 called 'Tradition and Conflict: Images of a Turbulent Decade, 1963–1973' that included endless examples of politically engaged art by women and blacks in the 1960s. Besides Faith, the show included black artists who have long done political work like Bettye Saar, Charles White, Louis Mailou Jones, Benny Andrews, Elizabeth Catlett, Romare Bearden, Jacob Lawrence, Viviane Brown, Camille Billops, Dana Chandler, and David Hammonds, together with white political artists like May Stevens, Leon Golub, and Nancy Spiro. There were also black artists whose work tends to be less political in explicit content, but whose use of abstract form, design and medium challenges the conventions of Western art, the elitism of its hook-up with US capitalism, forging a link with African and other non-European visual traditions: such artists were Joe Overstreet (whose more political 'New Aunt Jemima' was included), Daniel LaRue Johnson, Vincent Smith, Barbara Chase Riboud, Howardina Pindell, Malcolm Bailey and Mel Edwards.

The catalogue, a landmark publication still on sale at the Studio Museum in Harlem, includes essays by Vincent Smith, Lucy Lippard and Mary Schmidt-Campbell. Schmidt-Campbell remarks upon the repeated use of images of the US flag and of Aunt Jemima in the art of Afro-American artists of the 1960s. By that time, Faith had used images of the flag in 'God Bless America' and the large mural, 'The Flag is Bleeding', which were both part of 'The American People' series. She had used the flag again in her 'America Black' series in a painting called 'Die Nigger Flag for The Moon', which was a parody of the flag that US astronauts planted on the moon in 1969.

In 1971, at the Judson Memorial Church in New York, we helped to organize, along with John Hendricks and Jon Tosh of Guerrilla Art Action, a flag exhibition to protest the Federal law against 'desecrating the flag'. Faith was arrested as one of the Judson Three for violating this law. Minimal artist Carl Andre taped a strip of flag stamps across the floor for people to walk on. Yvonne Rainier's troupe tied flags around their necks and danced naked without music. There were these and other wonderful gestures of white avant-garde humor, but what do you suppose would have happened if a black artist had taped a strip of flag stamps across the floor for people to walk on, or a black dance troupe had stripped their clothes off and danced nude with the American flag draped around their necks? Would they have been as readily recorded and applauded? No more than the many artists of color who participated in this exhibition were recorded and applauded. I think the reason for this is racism, knee-jerk, know-nothing, nativist racism among the avant-garde left, the counterculture, and among those who have hitherto written about them.

(1988)

22

Tim Rollins and KOS:

the *Amerika* Series

Critical pedagogy is a form of cultural politics.

Henry A. Giroux

For me, art and education are like two sides of the same sheet of paper, separate disciplines and yet indivisible.

Tim Rollins

In 1981, Tim Rollins was a twenty-six-year-old white artist from Maine who had studied with Joseph Kosuth at the School of Visual Arts, had co-founded Group Material, an alternative space and advocacy group for socially committed art, and who taught art as part of the special education program at I.S. 52 in South Bronx. At the time, he made the highly unconventional, radical decision that he would combine his own art-making with the teaching of art to black and Puerto Rican public school children. This decision led to the founding of KOS, Kids of Survival, and the Art & Knowledge Workshop.

Together with a small, evolving group of 'learning disabled' and 'emotionally handicapped' kids from the South Bronx, Rollins began a process of political art-making which had the dual purpose of educating kids in the South Bronx about the world outside and educating the world outside about the South Bronx. But the real breakthrough in method came when Carlito Rivera, one of the kids in the Workshop, drew on one of Tim Rollins' books. 'I wanted to kill him at first,' Rollins says, 'but boy, it looked great. And it was wild because here you have this dyslexic kid who couldn't read a word of the book, but in the drawing on the page – boom! there it was – all in an image. How did this kid know that this was the essence of the book?'

It was a breakthrough precisely because the heartbreaking struggle around literacy and reading was so central to the problem of critical and pedagogical resistance among radical teachers like Rollins and the counter-resistance it inevitably aroused among poor black and Puerto Rican kids in the South Bronx and other urban ghettos. At the heart of the difficulty were the so-called 'learning disabled' and 'emotionally handicapped' kids Rollins was working with, categories endlessly expanded by the Board of Education in order to accommodate the increasing numbers of children of color considered ineducable. Painting on text – moreover, the classical text of European art and literature – became a way of simultaneously staging a protest against the failure of our educational system as it is conceived by the dominant discourse, and de-territorializing the still-remaining instructive vitality of high modernism.

'The making of the work is the pedagogy,' Rollins explains. 'The art is a means to knowledge of the world. That's why our project is so different from regular school – the kids are immersed in production – cultural production.' The destruction and the construction of the text are held in a precarious balance as Rollins pays homage to his education (a BFA from the School of Visual Arts and an MA in Art Education from New York University) by taking the kids to museums, by reading to them from the 'classics', and by teaching them the mechanics of art-making; and the kids pay homage to their education in prison-like schools and in the streets of a crack and AIDS-ridden South Bronx by sharing with Rollins their emotional and aesthetic sensitivities. They join forces in their mutual instrumentalization of the text in the realm of the visual. Often the roots of their common understanding of images lie in the abject in popular culture, for example, in horror movies and monster comic books such as Marvel Comic's X-men. The X-Men, which began in the 60s, is about a group of teenage mutants whose deformities give them super-powers to fight evil in the world. Their spiritual and intellectual leader is a bald-headed professor who communicates with them by telepathy.

Although Rollins is nothing like the bald-headed professor in the comic book, the members of KOS like to think of themselves as the X-Men. X-Men comic books are listed first on a Workshop bibliography that 'may help you develop a deeper understanding of our work', which KOS distributes during its fairly frequent public appearances on panels. That bibliography also includes Paulo Freire's A Pedagogy of the Oppressed, Ralph Waldo Emerson's essay on 'Self-Reliance', Henry David Thoreau's Walden, Deleuze and Guattari's Kafka – Towards a Minor Literature, Robert Coles' Children of Crisis, Georges Bataille's Literature and Evil, Lionel Trilling's Beyond Culture, Dr Seuss' The Cat in the Hat, Tillie Olsen's Silences, and The Autobiography of Malcolm X.

It is doubtful whether any of the current members of the Workshop besides Rollins, such as Richard Cruz (19), Georges Garces (16), Carlito Rivera (17), Annette Rosado (16), Nelson Montes (17), and Jose Parissi (21), have read these works. Some of the members of KOS are dyslexic. Those who can read admit they find it boring. But the object of this exercise is more the critical pedagogical environment that the bibliography, the production of the work, and the process have created. That workshop participants should aspire to intellectual growth is implicit in all their work. If they haven't read the books, the books are there for them to read, and the encouragement is there as well. More to the point, Rollins says,

> The work is about survival – survival as individuals, as a group, as a people, a nation, a species. And it's about the survival of the books themselves, literature, language, culture. That's why knowledge is so important, because without knowledge about how the world works and where our ideas and hopes come from, there can be no freedom, there can be no democracy. Knowledge isn't power in itself – it's what you *do* with information that makes a difference. Our art works are teaching machines.

Rollins embraces the pedagogical philosophy of Paulo Freire, the renowned Brazilian educator, who maintains that progressive and liberatory education is necessarily dialogical, by which he means that the dominant model for education should not be a passive transfer of knowledge from teacher to student but rather the active dialogue of teacher and student. Of course, the problem here is that dialogue is the hallmark of the elite, private school education. In contrast, public school education de-emphasizes personal contact and exchange between teachers and students because small classes are too expensive. Also, the pedagogical ideal tends to be authoritarian, perhaps partly in order to make a preference out of a necessity. (A lot of teachers are simply concerned with maintaining 'control' in the classroom.) But the gravest obstacle of all to the dialogic, multicultural classroom confronting even the most radical and committed teacher today (even if that teacher is a person of color) is finding a common language in which dialogue and the production of knowledge can take place. 'I don't believe in self-liberation,' Freire says in A *Pedagogy for Liberation.*

> Liberation is a social act. Liberating education is a social process of illumination.... Even when you individually feel yourself most free, if this feeling is not a social feeling, if you are not able to use your recent freedom to help others to be free by transforming the totality of society, then you are exercising only an individualistic attitude towards empowerment or freedom.

Even if the revolutionary austerity of such a program is not entirely appealing, Freire still makes a crucial point about how one might teach critical literacy, not only to the children of the middle class and children who can already read, but also, more pressingly, to· the increasing numbers of children, particularly children of color, who are being trained and prepared only to linger on the margins of the status quo.

As for the common language in which a dialogue can take place between teacher and students, and not just any dialogue but one that moves the student towards critical engagement with the text of Western culture, Rollins has come up with a very special answer. 'We make art with books, and we turn books into art,' he says. In response, Richard Cruz, one of the Workshop members, says, 'I guess art is one of the only ways we show our point of view, about how we see the world.' 'Our paintings are us,' Annette Rosado adds, 'and we're showing ourselves to people like an open book.' Which seems at least a beginning.

Ironically, these 'teaching machines' have propelled KOS to the tangible art world success of having a dealer in SoHo (Jay Gorney) and having their work included in the collections of the Museum of Modern Art, Charles Saatchi, and the Chase Manhattan Bank. So far the income has gone right back into KOS's foundation, allowing the Workshop to become independent from the censorship-prone machinations of Federal funds for the arts and from the bureaucracy of the public school system, which would prefer that they emphasize quantity over quality. As is conventional in art education programs, the focus would then be on training good art consumers, not astute cultural producers. The foundation pays salaries and stipends and underwrites the trips that the Workshop has made around the country and around the world to see and to make art. In the future, Rollins plans to organize the South Bronx Academy of Fine Art – a free, fully accredited, private school for fourteen-to-eighteen-year-olds from the South Bronx. But the most impressive form of their success so far has been a critical pedagogical process that daily seeks to transform the lives of Workshop participants as well as the community around it. It is a model that might be adapted for use in a variety of educational settings.

The first *Amerika* painting I ever saw was 'Amerika – For The People Of Bathgate', 1988, which appears on the wall of Central Elementary School 4 on Bathgate Avenue in the South Bronx. I was in a taxicab with Tim Rollins on a cold Saturday morning in February, riding into a desolate neighborhood that is apparently abandoned on the weekends – no people, just that inexorable urban greyness – when we turned the corner of Bathgate Avenue, and there it was looming above us. Right away I had to smile. The painting made no pretense of being anything but paint; yet a series of golden horns as abstract and wild in variation as characters in Dr Seuss seemed to be flying about in space, raising a joyous, clattering, anarchic racket in the morning light. I could almost hear it. Moreover, I could not stop wanting to look at it.

The reproductions and transparencies I had seen of the *Amerika* series the week before in Dia's SoHo offices had scarcely prepared me for such pleasure. While they seemed both agreeable and amusing, I must admit that I am no longer easily impressed by paintings. For me, the way the paintings are made and what is to be made of the paintings has to be at least as important as any reading I might have of their intrinsic quality. For 'painting' does not merely signify my grandmother's Sunday painting for her own amusement, or even my mother's successful painting as a feminist artist, but rather the endless reproductions of Leonardo da Vinci's 'Mona Lisa' that toured the US when I was a child, or Vincent Van Gogh's 'Sunflowers', which was sold recently for millions of dollars.

It seems appropriate to include 'the painting' in what Walter Benjamin refers to as 'cultural treasures', which he advises us to view with 'cautious detachment'. His famous statement that 'There's no document of civilization which is not at the same time a document of barbarism' can also be interpreted to mean that European high culture not only reconsolidates white dominance of the political and economic spheres, but also repetitively restages the barbarism of the original conquests of imperialism and colonialism by excluding people of color, poor people, and Third World people from the production of 'cultural treasures'. In particular, the individual 'painting' executed by the individual 'artist' has become a symbol of the intense reification and alienation that plagues and deforms the utopian potential of cultural production in the West. The history of fine art in the West seems calculated to render the art of the 'other' as the exotic, primitive exception to their usual systematic exclusion. In the art world, white is still right, and the issues of race, class, and cultural diversity are eternally mystified behind the rhetoric of 'quality' and 'standards' and 'high culture'.

So, it was the process of Tim Rollins + KOS, the idea of a multicultural collaboration focusing as much on the political and cultural transformation of the people involved as on the vagaries of the art market, that attracted me. Accordingly, it was just as well that the first *Amerika* painting I saw was the Bathgate mural, for it is perhaps the consummate public work. So perfectly and subversively discontinuous with its lifeless public space, it gave me a chance to realize that, in fact, the collaborative and inclusive mode of production of Tim Rollins + KOS does make a difference in the end result of the work itself. Not only does the *Amerika* series find its perfect venue on the wall of a South

Bronx public school, it is also successful at transforming that space at the level of the visual. As in the live performances of New Music groups like Sun Ra, Ornette Coleman, or the New World Saxophone Quartet, the formal unity of vision we so deeply desire in art had somehow been seduced into a truce with the articulation of diverse 'visions' and 'voices'. I refer to 'voices' and 'visions' even as *Amerika*'s golden horns seem to be laughing at the possibility of mimesis. The visualization of musical instruments so bizarrely deformed raises the question of music and harmony even as it bypasses the literal response.

The most fascinating thing of all was that it was obvious more than one person had a hand in 'Amerika – For The People Of Bathgate'. An aura of improvisation associated with jazz and ordinarily inconceivable in the concrete and material terms of the visual sphere seemed present as well. 'Difference' is held 'in a state of balance', Jean Fisher has aptly said of the *Amerika* paintings, in a 'celebration of cultural heterogeneity'. I now like to think that just seeing the Bathgate mural would have also given me some inkling of the history of the extraordinary collaborative and pedagogical process employed by Tim Rollins + KOS in the making of the *Amerika* series.

But in addition to the important accomplishments growing out of this collaboration, I have some problems with the success story of Tim Rollins + KOS, the first and most obvious being their name and the fact that of the group only Rollins (because he's white, male, and educated?) has had an individual identity in the art world. The other two difficulties are actually two sides of the same dilemma. On the one hand, there is their critical and irreverent approach to 'modernism' and 'high culture'. This seems to be Rollins' choice stemming from his background in conceptual art, his admiration for the ideas of Joseph Beuys, and his role as co-founder of Group Material. On the other hand, there is their failure to be significantly engaged by multicultural texts or issues.

These are both part of the same problem because the preoccupation with demonstrating a critical approach to modernism tends to render superfluous and unsophisticated the exploration of different ethnic or sexual specificities. This conflict has always prevented a white, male, political avant-garde in the arts from becoming seriously and critically engaged by nonwhite or nonmale, political avant-gardes in the arts – especially since texts and art by people of color are not infrequently actively involved in constructing modernist aesthetic and philosophical criteria of their own.

Despite the widespread notion among white scholars and critics that modernism is exclusively high European and, therefore, lily white and, therefore, something that should pass like apartheid, there has emerged among black critics in literary criticism (and it seems to me relevant to discussions of black cultural production in music, dance, theatre, and the visual arts as well) a parallel notion of black modernism (or black modernisms). The term 'modernism' is used not in order to periodize but in order to describe sometimes ongoing aspects of cultural production in the Third World and what Gayatri Spivak refers to as 'internal colonization' in the so-called First World (which would appear to include almost all 'minority' cultural production).

I do not want to get into a discussion here about the distinctive features of modernism, except to say that they would obviously include some of the most widely held and thoroughly institutionalized values about what art is and ought to be in the present. By borrowing the term 'modernism' in order to describe some varieties of 'minority' art practice, I not only mean to choose this way to name those features that mark intense European or white American influence in black or 'minority' cultural production (such as the very concepts of the individual artist, the novel, the painting, or the symphony) but also to identify where black or minority cultural production has borrowed from 'white' modernism in order to reinvent, revise, reclaim, redefine those notions concerning the spiritual and ethical value and purpose of art.

I am thinking particularly of the idea of art as transcendent, as in Walter Pater, or the idea that art will cure what ails 'civilization', as in Matthew Arnold, even as such ideas are increasingly accompanied by their constant and incessant problematization in Kafka, T.S. Eliot, James Joyce, Gertrude Stein, and others. This is so much the case that much of modernism inadvertently memorializes the failure of art to transcend the material. But there is also the setting up of a dichotomy between the cynicism and demoralization of realizing art's failure to cure 'civilization' and the notion that something – the 'other', 'Nature', 'the unconscious' – lies beyond both 'civilization' and 'art' and can, therefore, offer salvation.

Most significantly in the case of modernists like Gauguin or Picasso, a 'primitive other' is made to signify the possibility of moving beyond. Of course, we've come to understand that such a dichotomy is the raw material of 'racism', 'neo-imperialism', 'neo-colonialism', and the passive-aggressive course of appropriation that has accompanied the rise of transglobal capital. It is perhaps necessary to recognize as well that as whites were using such ideology to turn their backs on the cultural production of people of color, artists of color were picking up the pieces, borrowing, re-appropriating that which had been appropriated, constructing a dialogue with white modernism (one-sided and unheeded by white modernists) and, significantly, a dialogue with a silent, inarticulate 'primitive other' whom they saw as their former or their undiscovered selves. The more educated and the more schooled artists of

color were in the precepts of European art, the more middle-class they
were – and they really needed to be both in order to survive – the more
likely they were to join white artists in conceptualizing a 'primitive other'
as unfathomable, even as they might refer to it as a better, wiser, truer
self. As black artists and artists of color whom I would describe as
modernists – Jean Toomer, Langston Hughes, Richard Wright, Ralph
Ellison, Zora Neale Hurston, Jacob Lawrence, Romare Bearden – tried
to close the gap between their educated 'white' selves and their primitive
'black' selves, they were nevertheless, involuntarily or voluntarily,
engaged in a relentless critique of such unities as the self, the primitive,
the natural through their enunciation of how these categories have been
used to render blacks 'invisible'. To return to my earlier point, if
modernism is viewed as a network of diverse, heterogeneous, and still
open-ended approaches to the problem of cultural progress, then it
becomes possible to talk not only about European modernism in the past,
but also the use of modernist strategies (among others) by emergent
cultural formations of the Third World, as well as minority cultures in
the 'First World'.

The relevance of all of this to Tim Rollins + KOS involves only
speculation on my part, since what they're doing doesn't really fit any of
the familiar categories. It seems to me quite clear that while Rollins' own
inclinations as an artist would generally place him among postmodern
strategists, he has often remarked that his relationship to KOS has been
pulling him towards a re-evaluation of modernism and modernist strategies such as abstract painting. My hypothesis is quite simply that aspects
of modernism – for instance, Picasso's 'Guernica' or Georgia O'Keeffe's
'Southwest' – make more sense to the young artists of color in KOS than
they do to Rollins, and as such, they are moving him towards their
practice. I want to emphasize that I do not mean they are coming up with
a rehash of obsolete, white modernist strategies, but rather that Rollins is
engaged with them, perhaps somewhat unknowingly, in the formulation
of yet another multicultural strain of modernism. It is more streetwise,
democratic, and inclusive than the old 'white' modernism; it is less naive
or 'ethnic' than the old 'black' modernisms; yet, at the same time, it is
more utopian and hopeful than any kind of postmodernism heretofore. It
is doing in art something like what you might get in dance if you
crossbred the Alvin Ailey Dance Company with Pina Bausch.

But the problem of the absence of multiculturalism at the level of
content remains. When asked why KOS doesn't read Toni Morrison's
Song of Solomon, Rollins is dismissive. 'We're too close to it,' he'll say, or,
'We prefer to work with dead art,' like Kafka and Flaubert. Novels and
paintings are dead forms, so what more fitting tribute to the failure of
modernism than painting on a novel? People of color and their deploy-

ment of novels and paintings simply don't enter into it.

While it is true that the examination of the work of a black female writer like Morrison does run counter to the critical purpose of the group as defined by Rollins, I can't help but wonder if *Song of Solomon* is really that much more readable to these mostly Puerto Rican teenage boys. My perception in teaching such novels at universities is that even young black girls don't have any special access to Morrison's language. They have to be taught to read her. In particular, they have to be taught to read her critically. But if Morrison is, however, more readable to KOS, then wouldn't that make it precisely the text to make reading less 'boring'?

Yet a further question remains whether or not there would be the same interest in the art market for a KOS that painted on the text of Toni Morrison or Toni Cade Bambara, or even *The Autobiography of Malcolm X*, as they did at an earlier stage. Which brings us back to the emphasis in a white art world on a white male, Tim Rollins, at the head of KOS. Isn't it also true that if Rollins were black and a woman and the texts were black or Puerto Rican, with the 'kids' being black or Puerto Rican as well, we would be talking about something much less marketable, something infinitely more obscure?

While the group began its existence in 1982, with a rapid turnover in the kids who made it up, the first real success came with the first 'Amerika' painting done during the school year of 1984–85. Rollins' classroom on the third floor of I.S. 52 was where all the difficult kids congregated when they had nothing else to do. The canvas covered with the pages from Franz Kafka's novel *Amerika* hung in the room for a year. Rollins told the evocative story of Karl and the Nature Theatre of Oklahoma, and perhaps forty kids, only one of whom is still in KOS, took a serious shot at designing golden horns. 'Shots' seems not an entirely metaphorical way of describing what was happening in a classroom in which throwing things was not uncommon. The result was 'Amerika I', first exhibited in 'The State of the Art: The New Social Commentary' at the Barbara Gladstone Gallery. It was subsequently sold to Chase Manhattan Bank, and undoubtedly was important in securing for them a National Endowment for the Arts grant. This money was used to pay for a studio of their own to go to after school, the first step towards independence, autonomy, and an art world identity for the Workshop.

Twelve other 'Amerikas' would follow. Among these were 'Amerika IX, 1987, a collaboration with kids in Charlotte, North Carolina, 'America XI', 1988, a collaboration with kids in Minneapolis, Minnesota, and 'Amerika for Thoreau', 1988, a collaboration with teenagers from the Dorchester and Roxbury areas in Boston, Massachusetts. The mural 'Amerika – For The People Of Bathgate', 1988, was made in collaboration with the faculty and students of Central Elementary School 4 in the South Bronx.

Kafka never finished the novel *Amerika*, and he never intended that it should be published, having left instructions with Max Brod, his best friend, to burn all of his manuscripts. Nor did he ever visit the US, although it is reported that he thought of Americans as 'healthy and optimistic'. Yet that isn't the picture Kafka actually paints of Amerika. In the book Karl, the protagonist, forced to leave his native land at sixteen because he had made a servant girl pregnant, comes to Amerika on a boat. A wealthy and powerful uncle appears at the boat to take Karl in. After a brief period of language instruction and horseback riding lessons, he is rather arbitrarily disinherited for disobeying the uncle's advice. Karl then embarks on a series of adventures during which he encounters a variety of unscrupulous characters, all of whom take advantage of his youth and his lack of family in order to exploit and abuse him. Nevertheless, the novel ends on an upbeat note with a gap in the text and then the final chapter called 'The Nature Theatre of Oklahoma'.

It is this chapter which concerns Tim Rollins + KOS. Rollins narrates the story:

'At the end of the year, he's ready to go home. He says to himself, "I can't handle it. I'm a failure. I can't make it in Amerika." And so just as he's about ready to get back on the boat and go home, he hears this sound. It sounds like a Salvation Army band. They're all carrying these placards. And the placards say, "Come join the Nature Theatre of Oklahoma! The Nature Theatre of Oklahoma where anyone can be an artist and everyone is welcome!" And Karl looks at this and thinks, "I have been lied to, I have been cheated, I have been robbed, and I am sure this is just another situation where I'm going to get ripped off. But then again, that one sign says 'Everyone is welcome'. Even if it is bullshit, I'm going to try it. I've never seen that in Amerika before." So he joins.

'Then they say, "Well, we're leaving for Clayton tonight on a train. We're all going to go at midnight so you've got to get registered at the race track. You have to register before midnight because that's when the train goes, and you lose your chance forever." So he goes to the racetrack, and as he approaches the racetrack, he hears this incredible sound of a traffic jam, and it's hundreds of horns like a jazz orchestra or something. And as he walks into the racetrack he sees an incredible scene of hundreds of people standing on pedestals, dressed up like angels blowing whatever they want to on these long golden horns. There's a big fat person who's making little noises, and a little skinny person making big noises, and it's this big kind of mess. All these sounds together.

'And Karl asks the old man who brings him in, "What is this?" and the guy says, "This is Amerika where everyone has a voice and everyone can say what they want." That's it. Then I say, "Now look, you all have your own taste and you have different voices. If you could be a golden instrument, if you could play a song of your freedom and dignity and your future and everything you feel about Amerika and this country, what would your horn look like?"'

The process for Tim Rollins + KOS is a lengthy one, sometimes a year and often much longer. When making an *Amerika* painting – or any of their other projects such as the *Temptations of St Anthony* series, or *The Red Badge of Courage* series in which they painted wounds, or *The Scarlet Letter* series in which they made elaborate calligraphic 'A's – KOS will select and study the relevant works of other artists in museums and in art books, and images from popular culture. They will do thousands of drawings, which they call 'jamming'. Then they'll begin to do painted studies on individual pages of the text itself. They sometimes do a large painting as a study. Only at the end of this process is the full-scale work made.

In the case of the *Amerika* series, the variety of horns that have emerged has been simply stupendous – from letters to body parts to animals to piles of shit, floating sperm, baseball bats, and animals – yet none of the images engages in direct representation. Everything looks a little like something but not quite enough to call it that. The group has drawn its inspiration from a wide variety of sources: Marcel Duchamp, Francisco Goya, Grünewald, Georgia O'Keeffe, Picasso, Miró, Paul Klee, William Morris, Uccello, African and Native American art, Dr Seuss, medical textbooks, comic books, and newspapers, just to name a few. Perhaps the most successful painting in the series, uniting their political concerns with the visual effect, has been 'Amerika V', which was done as a memorial to the racial incident at Howard Beach. All of the paintings share a compelling and sophisticated beauty.

For me, however, a bittersweet note in all of this is the idea of Oklahoma being the home of the Nature Theatre where anybody can be an artist. Kafka could have scarcely had any idea of what the real Oklahoma was like as the final destination to which the so-called 'Five Civilized Tribes' of the Southeast were driven in a series of forced marches called 'The Trail of Tears'. Yet his vision of the Nature Theatre seems to bear traces of foreboding as well as utopian hopefulness.

These traces of foreboding appear most graphically in two details of the story often overlooked. First, the hundreds of angels with horns are not just people but 'women' on pedestals; second, Karl calls himself 'Negro' when he signs up for work at the Nature Theatre in a typically Kafkaesque scene in which it is repeatedly insisted that 'Negro' could not be his real name, although no one says why. Few Americans have any idea of Oklahoma in history or in the present, except that it's the place they never want to go. Perhaps because of the fame of the musical *Oklahoma*, today's urban dwellers think of it as the home of rednecks and oilmen. But, in fact, after the Civil War blacks thought of it as the land of opportunity, and there was talk of it being designated a black state or a Native American state around the time that it entered the union. Now black and Puerto Rican kids in the South Bronx, who can read neither Kafka nor the history of Oklahoma (although they can imagine both), are painting golden horns on the pages of a German novel that invokes the name of Oklahoma in the spirit of hope, freedom, democracy, and art. Only, as the children of neo-imperialism, they know there isn't any physical frontier, so they'll have to invent their own.

(1989)

NOTES

The quotes from Tim Rollins + KOS are from an exhibition catalogue published by Riverside Studios, London, a forthcoming interview in *Flash Art*, October, 1989, by Joshua Deeter, as well as interviews I've conducted with them in their studio. The ideas on critical literacy and the dialogic classroom come from Ira Schor and Paulo Freire, *A Pedagogy for Liberation: Dialogues on Transforming Education*, South Hadley, Mass.: Bergin & Garvey, 1987; Henry A. Giroux, *Schooling And The Struggle For Public Life: Critical Pedagogy in The Modern Age*, Minneapolis: University of Minnesota Press, 1988; and Stanley Aronowitz and Henry A. Giroux, *Education Under Siege: The Conservative, Liberal and Radical Debate Over Schooling*, South Hadley, Mass.: Bergin & Garvey, 1985. The quotes from Walter Benjamin are from the essay 'Theses on the Philosophy of History' in *Illuminations*, New York: Schocken Books, 1968. The discussion of modernism in relationship to 'minority' and 'Third World' cultural production draws indirectly from Henry Louis Gates' notion of 'critical signification' described in *Figures in Black: Words, Signs, and the Racial Self*, New York: Oxford University Press, 1987; Houston Baker's attempt to describe black cultural production in terms of modernism without relying upon a notion of influence in *Modernism and The Harlem Renaissance*, Chicago: University of Chicago, 1987; and Gayatri Spivak's notion of the difficulty of subaltern speech in 'Can The Subaltern Speak?', *Wedge: The Imperialism of Representation/The Representation of Imperialism*, 7/8: Winter:Spring, 1985; and the problem of 'internal colonization' and a postcolonial elite in 'Who Claims Alterity?' in Barbara Kruger and Phil Mariani, eds, *Remaking History*, Dia Art Foundation, Seattle: Bay Press, 1989. Also, I must acknowledge some debt to Fredric Jameson's much maligned essay on the frequency of political allegory in Third World narratives, 'Third World Literature in the Era of Multinational Capitalism', *Social Text* 15: Fall 1986; as well as to the demystifying response of Aijaz Ahmad, 'Jameson's Rhetoric of Otherness and the "National Allegory"', *Social Text* 17: Fall 1987. Hal Foster's seminal essay 'The "Primitive" Unconscious of Modern Art, or White Skin Black Masks' remains a crucial text and is included in *Recodings: Art, Spectacle, Cultural Politics*, Seattle: Bay Press, 1985.

PART IV

Theory

2 3

Variations on Negation and the

Heresy of Black Feminist Creativity

In short, the image of black women writing in isolation, across time and space, is conduced toward radical revision. The room of one's own explodes its four walls to embrace the classroom, the library, and the various mechanisms of institutional and media life, including conferences, the lecture platform, the television talk show, the publishing house, the 'bestseller' and collections of critical essays.

Hortense Spillers, 'Cross-currents, Discontinuities:
Black Feminist Fiction', 1985

Difference is not difference to some ears, but awkwardness or incompleteness. Aphasia. Unable or unwilling? ... You who understand the dehumanization of forced removal-relocation-reeducation-redefinition, the humiliation of having to falsify your own reality, your voice – you know. And often cannot *say* it. You try and keep on trying to unsay it, for if you don't, they will not fail to fill in the blanks on your own behalf, and you will be said.

Trinh T. Minh-ha, 'Difference: "A Special Third World Women Issue"',
1986–87[1]

In the past nineteen years since the publication of Toni Morrison's *The Bluest Eye*, black women writers have begun to produce a literature that transcends its intrinsic political boundaries of 'invisibility' to address the world. Yet despite the ostentatious commercial success of a few books by black women writers, the creativity of most black women writers – especially if it doesn't fit the Book-of-the-Month Club/*New York Times* bestseller mold – continues to remain virtually unknown.

The underlying significance of this scenario is revealed by the fact that black feminist interpretation has been all but extinguished in mainstream and academic discourses, despite an overall cultural context in which the mechanical reproduction of interpretation and analysis through electronic media is profuse and omnipresent. Black women writers and critics are routinely kept from having an impact on how the fields of literature and literary criticism are defined and applied. Meanwhile, the highly visible success of a few black women writers serves to completely obscure the profound nature of the challenge black feminist creativity might pose to white male cultural hegemony.

Nobody in particular and everybody in general seems responsible for this situation. Even as universities, museums and publishing houses, what Ishmael Reed calls 'cultural detention centers' run by defenders of the status quo and their surrogates, are the unrelenting arbiters of cultural standards that exclude or erase the diverse creativity of nonelite populations, postmodernists, new historicists, deconstructionists, Marxists, Afro-Americanists and even some black female academics don't substantially challenge the exclusionary parlor games of canon formation and the production of knowledge. Moreover, black feminists themselves are inclined to agree that black women have no interest in criticism, interpretation and theoretical analysis, nor any capacity for it.

I can provide an example of how this works from my own experience as a journalist. Recently, I was asked to do a short profile essay/interview on Henry Louis Gates, for a new black magazine called *Emerge*. Generally, Afro-American literary criticism would be rarely mentioned in the black press. Two things work to make Gates the exception. First, Gates himself has been writing for *The New York Times*, which automatically gives him a great deal of credibility. Second, Gates' primary work is the consolidation of an Afro-American literary 'tradition'. The concept of 'tradition' is crucial here because of its incorporation of a historical framework, which is the preferred way in the black world of presenting 'new' information and ideas. Indeed, the most accessible counter-hegemonic work has often been historical, as Raymond Williams has pointed out in *Marxism and Literature*, but the rigorously selective process that defines 'tradition' (as opposed to a radically inclusive social history, for instance) is always linked to 'explicit contemporary pressures and limits'. So while 'history' may seem recoverable as 'tradition', tradition's hegemonic impulse, according to Williams, is always the most active: 'a deliberately selective and connecting process which offers a historical and cultural ratification of a contemporary order'.[2]

Specifically, the way in which this version of 'tradition' and 'history' works to ratify the contemporary order is to reinforce the critical 'silence' of women of color, even as Gates' version of the 'tradition' struggles to include black women writers – who either published in the nineteenth century or who write fiction – on an 'equal' basis. When I discovered, despite my repeated attempts, and Gates' as well, to include them, that not even the names of the best-known black feminist critics – Hazel Carby, Deborah McDowell, Hortense Spillers, Bell Hooks, Barbara Christian, Valerie Smith and Mary Helen Washington – were going to be mentioned, I realized I was confronting precisely this difficulty with 'tradition' as an exclusionary practice. I also realized that to define a 'tradition' that integrates black female critical voices is to be forced to confront the way in which such voices have been systematically excluded from previous notions of 'tradition'. It is, in other words, a 'tradition' of speaking out of turn. The reasons for this are not inherent in the nature of black women, but are, rather, structural; they derive from the 'outsider' position we tend to occupy in critical discourse. When I recommended that there should be profiles of black feminist critics in *Emerge* as well, my black feminist editor went to great pains to make clear to me that it would be impossible to get such an idea past the black male editor-in-chief, who has never heard of any of these women because they've never written for *The New York Times*.

While I would like to focus on black women writers, the degree to which their writing explores a uniquely black feminist problematic, and the manner in which black women writers and academics seem disproportionately under-represented in the sphere of knowledge production, in which literary criticism is included, my larger concern is with black feminist creativity at large as a problem in Anglo-American culture. In such fields as popular music, opera and modeling, the media visibility of the black woman provides a symbolic substitute for substantive black female economic and political power, the lack of which is a good deal less visible. At the same time, in more potentially politically articulate fields such as film, theatre and TV news commentary, black feminist (or female) creativity is virtually invisible. Further, I would like to propose that the lack of black female power in academic fields of knowledge production like literary criticism (of course, the same is even more true of anthropology, history, linguistics and so on) participates equally in this hegemonic scheme. It is a scheme in which black women, as a class, are systematically denied the most visible forms of discursive and intellectual subjectivity.

In referring to all black female creative production as black feminist creativity, I am making two assumptions. First, by feminism I mean a socialist feminism, not yet fully formulated, whose primary goal is a liberatory and profound (almost necessarily nonviolent) political transformation. Second, I assume as well that black feminist creativity, to the extent that its formal and commercial qualities will allow, is inherently critical of current oppressive and repressive political, economic and social arrangements affecting not just black women but black people as a group.

From the black woman whose face is featured on the cover of *Vogue*, to the recordings of black female rappers, to Sue Simmons interviewing 'Wicked' Wilson Pickett on NBC's *Live at Five*,[3] all black feminist creativity wants to make the world into a place that will be safe for women of color, their men, and their children. Nevertheless, I will refer to black feminist creativity at its most cathartic, coded and advanced – as in the novels and poetry of writers like Toni Morrison, Alice Walker and Ntozake Shange, in the performances of singers like Nina Simone, Miriam Makeba and Betty Carter, and in the work of artists like Faith Ringgold and Bettye Saar – as the Incommensurable, or as Variations on Negation. I am thus attempting to characterize the precarious dialectic of a creative project that is forced to be 'other' to the creativity of white women and black men, who are first 'other' themselves.

In an attempt to analyze the unpopularity of Hurston's *Their Eyes Were Watching God* with black male writers in the 30s, Barbara Johnson proposes a formula for understanding Hurston's relationship to the dominant discourse: white men, approximating the Law of the Father, make statements of universality. White women make statements of 'complementarity', indicating their inevitably ambiguous relationship to the seat of power. Black men make statements of 'the other'. These positions, while still marginal and perhaps antagonistic to the status quo, are also essentially dependent for their meaning on their relationship to the center and to the Law. Black women must make do with what's left.

Johnson proposes that black female discourse be represented by the lower-case 'x' of radical negation. 'The black woman is both invisible and ubiquitous,' Johnson writes of more contemporary efforts by black men, white men and white women to include black women in their progressive political and cultural formulations, 'never seen in her own right but forever appropriated by the other for their own ends.'[4]

Moreover, despite a current concern for 'the other' in cultural politics, this situation continues into the present day because, structurally, black feminist creativity and analysis is forced to straddle, combine or supersede the always prior claims of white female-dominated or black male- or 'Third World'- or 'minority'-dominated cultural strategies. The larger question being posed here is this: is there room beyond the 'other', as it is currently defined, for further oppositional discourse?

An instance of the difficulty of posing this question follows. For Marxist historian Hayden White, the tropological – or the tendency of all written argument to rely upon figurative language to persuade – is a good name for the perpetual gaps in that discourse which ordinarily describes itself as rational, logical and, therefore, universally true.[5] I would only add that these tropes or gaps in the dominant discourse constitute signposts where the bodies – that is, the bodies of those who have been ignored or negated – are buried. 'There is no document of civilization which is not at the same time a document of barbarism,' Walter Benjamin once pointed out.[6] Moreover, 'the myth of dispassionate investigation bolsters the epistemic authority of white men,' as feminist philosopher Alison Jagger has said, describing a procedure that results in their 'emotional hegemony'. Therefore, in a subversive critical process, 'outlaw emotions become a primary motivation for investigation', which is another way of saying that the personal was always political even before the Women's Liberation Movement made this fact generally known.[7]

Yet it is never the relationship to black feminist discourse that such investigators propose to interrogate. In this vein, what interests me is the problem of a black feminist cultural perspective, most of which is not allowed to be written in a society where writing is the primary currency of knowledge and power. How does black feminist creativity finally surface as writing? When it does, given that we invariably read in terms of what we've already read (the way Roland Barthes reads in S/Z[8]), isn't misunderstanding, or a total lack of understanding, inevitable? And, perhaps most important, how does black feminist creativity become critical of itself, since it is almost always forced to focus upon such primary issues as the economic survival, censorship and silencing of its own author-ity?

Hayden White uses the tropological to diagnose the discontinuities in white male cultural hegemony, also called phallocentricism, while nevertheless reconsolidating precisely the same hegemony. This move is habitual in critiques of phallocentricism, which continues to be the problem in using this work to other ends. For example, Afro-American literary critic Houston Baker, in *Blues, Ideology and Afro-American Literature*, borrows the tropological from White not in order to dismantle white male cultural hegemony, but rather to add an ancillary form of black male cultural hegemony to it.

Baker's key trope in describing the literature of Richard Wright is a black hole, an area of space in which gravitation is so intense that no light can escape so that it appears absolutely black. Contrary to everything we've been taught to expect of black holes in general, black holes in space are full, not empty. They are unimaginably dense stars. 'They are surrounded by an "event horizon", a membrane that prevents the unaltered escape of anything which passes through,' Baker writes. 'Light shone into a black hole disappears,' converts energy into mass that is infinitely compressed, and 'all objects are "squeezed" to zero volume.'[9] Under Baker's scrutiny, Wright's *Native Son*, together with his autobiography *Black Boy* and his short stories, becomes a black w/hole, satisfying and complete. Or as Baker put it, 'Richard Wright's translation of the desire of a black blues life into an irresistible *difference* makes him undisputed master of Black Wholeness.'[10] Such mastery in the field of Afro-American cultural studies, while seeming to throw off the mantle of white male cultural hegemony, or phallocentricism, only serves to mask its domination and erasure of black feminist (or female) contributions to that field. In other words, it only serves to mask that which it excludes. Thus, phallocentricism's principal cultural operations remain intact as Richard Wright's *Native Son* and *Black Boy* are added to the list of master narratives that make up the canon of American Literature.

On the other hand, if we accept White's and Baker's notion that the deliberate use of tropes can help to reform the logical in counter-hegemonic ways, then the trope of the black hole in space can be pushed further. In fact, a feminist student at the University of Oklahoma who was majoring in physics told me something else about black holes when I told her what Baker had said. Physicists now believe that black holes may give access to other dimensions. An object or energy enters the black hole, is infinitely compressed to zero volume, as Baker reported, then it passes through to another dimension, whereupon the object or energy reassumes volume, mass, form, direction, velocity, all the properties of visibility and concreteness, but in another, perhaps unimaginable, dimension. The idea of a black hole as a process, as a progression that appears differently, or not at all, from various perspectives, seems to me a useful way of illustrating how I conceive of 'incommensurability' or 'variations on negation' as characteristic of black feminist creativity.

So the analogy of the black hole becomes meaningful not only in sexual terms, nor even in the racial terms that would suggest that all the successful cases of creative black women add up to only a small fraction of black women engaged in creative acts. Rather, the point of the analogy is that even successful creative black women have next to nothing to say about the nature of classification, interpretation and analysis in their respective fields. So to the extent that the arts exist as a by-product of diverse acts of interpretation, classification and analysis, black feminist creativity is virtually nonexistent, in the way that black holes were nonexistent until they were discovered by science.

In other words, the black hole represents the dense accumulation, without explanation or inventory, of black feminist creativity. Prevented from assuming a commensurate role in critical theory and the production of knowledge by a combination of external and internal pressures (economic and psychological), it is confined to the aesthetic and the commercial. In order to compensate for ghettoization, black feminist creativity's concentration in music and now literature has become provocatively intense. And yet it is still difficult, even for those who study the music and the literature, to apprehend black feminist creativity as a continuous and coherent discourse because of the failure to read the gaps – the locations from which black women do not speak – as part of the (w)/hole.

What most people see of the black woman is the void, because to many the dark contents mean no content whatsoever. The outsider sees black feminist creativity as a dark hole from which nothing worthwhile can emerge and in which everything is forced to assume the zero volume of nothingness that results from the intense pressure of being the wrong race, the wrong class and the wrong sex – hence our invisibility.[11] Or as Ntozake Shange put it definitively in *For Colored Girls Who Have Considered Suicide/When the Rainbow is Enuf*, the most crucial forms of black feminist creativity sound like 'half-notes scattered/without rhythm/ no tune'.[12]

When a mainstream media production is passed off as a translation of black feminist creativity – as in Steven Spielberg's movie of *The Color Purple* – it is crucial to speak of its inadequacies and failures. Further, recent developments in the visibility of a bourgeois mainstream black feminism will inevitably have a profound effect upon how literature written by black women expresses black feminist thought. Such developments are most prominently represented by Oprah Winfrey's innovations in television programming and producing, or, more distantly, by the problem of how to cast Whoopi Goldberg in films. Oprah Winfrey produces her own television talk show, and she has purchased the movie rights to Gloria Naylor's *Women of Brewster Place* and Toni Morrison's *Beloved*. Winfrey's commercial success seems to render obscure the question of black female 'progress'. Clearly, when black women are 'qualified', they advance.

Yet Hollywood is having a more difficult time coming up with a credible storyline for a black female comedian with dreadlocks, which will commodify racial 'marginality' but isn't racist enough to produce a boycott of the theatre.

Goldberg's problem is that she is black, female *and* wears her hair in a characteristically African-Caribbean-Afro-American style. In order to succeed, black women must become 'white' (think here of Winfrey's 'Valley Girl' speech, her straightened hair, her elegant couture wardrobe, her much reported weight loss), because mass culture can only reify and reproduce 'white woman' (always under erasure and passed off as 'nature') as commodity. Television's most successfully saleable commodity is the 'white woman', the crucial sign in every commercial representation from a vacation in the Bahamas to the effectiveness of a cold medicine.

While Goldberg, because of her hair, is having a problem conforming to the built-in assumption in our culture that every woman wants to be a 'white woman', it will be interesting to see whether or not Winfrey will be able to fit prominent roles as an actress in movie adaptations of key black feminist texts into the pattern of her other successes.

The purpose of what follows is not only to look at contemporary Afro-American literature by women as a field of aesthetic practice, but to see it also as the key manner available to black women to make known their views on history, sexuality and culture. Because of the way that black female analytical interpretation is routinely circumscribed and discounted by a cultural hegemony that is perfectly comfortable with knowing as little as possible about her, it becomes necessary, as well, to interpret her participation and her lack of participation in culture in order to ferret out her 'meaning'. Personally, I think she dares not make herself plain because the consequences in home and community seem too high. But in any case, since I am as concerned to discover how her presence or absence affects the overall patterns of the dominant discourse in regard to sexuality and 'ethnicity' as I am to discover the story she might have written if racism and sexism had not existed, her intentions as author or performer, while significant, are not the sole consideration here.

Given this scheme, two matters especially draw my attention: first, how the successful commodification of black feminism will be reconciled with black feminist idealism; and second, what challenges are posed by adapting critical theoretical frameworks to black feminist use. While critical theory now ignores black feminism's intellectual potential, it is also creating new and unoccupied spaces for subversive literary and cultural production. I am thinking particularly of Fredric Jameson's speculations on postmodernism, Third World Literature and pleasure, as well as of feminist semiotic and psychoanalytic criticism of film, literature and popular culture.[13]

It is hard for us to accept the idea that races are man-made entities, so indoctrinated have we been by the pseudoscientific distortions of the theories of race. And yet nothing could be plainer than the fact that a race only exists because someone calls it so – or that inflation of the informal idea of race into the massive category, Race, is already a product of white racism.

Joel Kovel, *White Racism: A Psychohistory*, 1984

Difference in such an insituable context is *that which undermines the very idea of identity*, deferring to infinity the layers whose totality forms 'I'. It subverts the foundations of any affirmation or vindication of value, and cannot, thereby, ever bear in itself an absolute value. The difference (within) between *difference* and *identity* has so often been ignored, and the use of the two terms so readily confused, that claiming a female/ethnic identity/difference is commonly tantamount to reviving a kind of naive 'male-tinted' romanticism. If feminism is set forth as a demystifying force, then it will have to question thoroughly the belief in its own identity.

Trinh T. Minh-ha, 'Difference: "A Special Third World Women Issue"',
1986–87

The frontiers of a book are never clear-cut: beyond the title, the first lines, and the last full stop, beyond its internal configuration and its autonomous form, it is caught up in a system of references to other books, other texts, other sentences: it is a node within a network.

Michel Foucault, *The Archaeology of Knowledge*, 1972[14]

My reasons for being drawn to the subject of black female 'silence' in the sphere of literary criticism and knowledge production are neither objective nor disinterested. In 1979, I was the author of a highly controversial book of essays called *Black Macho and the Myth of the Superwoman* about the role of racial/sexual myths in Afro-American political self-conception especially during the Civil Rights Movement and the Black Power Movement. Blacks in particular were critical of my motives in 'blaming the victim', and of my qualifications as a black woman writer.

My age, then twenty-seven, my 'middle-class' background, which was not so middle class as I then thought, my lack of first-hand experience in the Civil Rights Movement in the South, and the unscholarly, auto-biographical format of my text were all frequently mentioned as strikes against my project. I was accused not only of getting my facts confused, but of having been naively beguiled by the specious arguments of a mainstream white feminism insensitive to the problems of poor, working-class black women, and also, in general, of trivializing and ridiculing the hard work and courage that had gone into the black struggle for liberation over the years.[15]

As a young black woman writer attempting to think critically and analytically about Afro-American culture, who then encountered extraordinary and almost insurmountable opposition – an opposition that no prior training had even remotely prepared me to anticipate – I've always been my own favorite case study for considering the systematic obstacles to black feminist articulation. While I now recognize that *Black Macho and the Myth of the Superwoman* was annoyingly and provocatively innaccurate in a variety of ways, I'm also inclined to suspect that the dismissive way in which my work was criticized was not intended to correct me, but to prevent my ever being given the opportunity to write critically again. Moreover, the underlying problem was neither my particular approach to black feminism, nor even that it was a black feminism that sexualized the history of the Civil Rights Movement or criticized black men, although both of these caused most of the initial ruckus. Rather, it seems to me now that the problem was an ongoing structural one having to do with the relationship of black female discourse to the production of knowledge and to critical discourses in general. The problem, as I've said, is that this relationship is effectively nonexistent.[16]

Black women barely engage in critical discourses in print, whether scholarly or journalistic. But when and if they do, they are required to do so symbolically either as a white male in the discourse of 'universality', or as a white female in the discourse of 'complementarity', or as a black male in the discourse of 'the other'. For the most part, black women writers choose none of these. There exists no critical discourse – aside from black female contributions to literature and music, which are always coded in their cultural views – no language specifically calibrated to reflect and describe analytically the location of women of color in US culture. When I wrote *Black Macho*, I did not realize what I was up against.

By suggesting that resistance to me as a writer of criticism was socially constructed, I do not mean to denigrate in any way the crucial importance of the arguments I made in the book, nor the fact that there were critics who disagreed with my thesis as well. In particular, many black women found the half entitled 'The Myth of the Superwoman' difficult to swallow. In it, I tried to subsume innumerable smaller, historically specific cultural myths about the strength of the black woman – such stereotypes as 'mammy', 'Sapphire', 'matriarch', 'Aunt Jemima' – under the rubric of one large, all-purpose myth. In the process, of course, I was defeating the very purpose of myth, which is to obscure contradiction and drown out history and the dialectical in the superficial and marketable binary opposition, but at the time I was far too concerned with exposing the hypocrisy of the culture, shared by both black men and white men, regarding the image versus the reality of black women.

It seemed to me the evidence was everywhere in American culture that precisely because of their political and economic disadvantages, black women were considered to have a peculiar advantage. Not only was this premise basic to representations of black women in the dominant, white discourse; it was also fairly characteristic of Afro-American and Anglo-American feminist discourses that treated the black female as well.

No doubt, as Alice Walker said in an essay called 'To The Black Scholar' published in *In Search of Our Mothers' Gardens*,[17] I thought my ideas were more original than they were. I should admit that while my role models for cultural criticism in 1978 were Tom Wolfe, Norman Mailer, Hunter Thompson, Joan Didion and James Baldwin, an emergent feminist cultural studies approach confronting the interplay of race, sex and class difference, perhaps epitomized by the trajectory of such work as Lillian Robinson's, Hazel Carby's and Gayatri Spivak's,[18] has been instrumental in persuading me that style, or strategies of public address, have profound political implications in dealing with material concerning women of color because of the black woman's limited access to mainstream, academic and 'avant-garde' discourses.

Few black critics understood the rhetorical imperative imposed by the combination of 'white' media, marketplace and 'black' audience that produced *Black Macho*. A black woman writer who wants to write seriously about contemporary cultural issues and how they are socially constructed, as I've already said, is faced with an almost insurmountable communication problem: if she takes a scholarly or academic approach, she will find herself virtually outside of language and without authority; she will find herself unable to say what she means as she assumes one or the other of the rhetorical emphases on 'universality', 'complementarity' or 'otherness', none of which, by itself, can describe the complex terms of the black female relationship to cultural production. On the other hand, if she takes a colloquial 'entertainment' approach – as I did in *Black Macho* – then she will be read widely, but only to be attacked and ostracized. Either way cuts the possibility of constructive commentary – in the work itself, or in the criticism of that work – down to zero.[19] The trick may be to fall somewhere in between the academic and the entertaining, as did Walker's *In Search of Our Mothers' Gardens*. Yet her plain-spoken, 'commonsense' style has its limits as well.

Moreover, when Walker included a critique of *Black Macho* in that book of essays, it was only then that I was forced to apprehend the structural dimensions of the problem, for she had been one of my major supporters in the months leading up to the actual publication of the book. As a Ms magazine editor and as a black feminist, she read the book in galleys, helped edit the excerpt that appeared in Ms along with Susan McHenry and Gloria Steinem, and wrote me two private letters of support and encouragement. But as the controversy mounted, and her friend and contemporary June Jordan grew more and more publicly and vehemently opposed to the book, Walker went silent. When I called her during a trip to California and she refused to see me, I knew that our friendship had ended, that the general reception of the book had somehow changed her view of it. The details did not become available to me until four years later, when *In Search of Our Mothers' Gardens* was published.

Yet Walker does not sigificantly disagree with my general thesis in her essay, which was originally written in 1979 as a letter to *The Black Scholar* for inclusion in a forum devoted to 'The Black Sexism Debate'.[20] This issue of *The Black Scholar* responded to the controversy over the publication of my book and the connection between it and Shange's *For Colored Girls*, then playing on Broadway. Briefly, the controversy had to do with the problem of black images, and whether or not my work and Shange's had helped to perpetuate stereotypical images of the race. In a short prologue to the essay, Walker says that *The Black Scholar* refused to publish it because they considered the tone too 'personal' and 'hysterical', which it obviously is not. In fact, Walker made perhaps one of the more insightful criticisms when she took exception to my assertion that 'the myth of the superwoman' was 'unquestioned even by the occasional black woman writer or politician'.

'It is a lie,' Walker reports having written to my publishers,

I can't speak for politicians but I can certainly speak for myself. I've been hacking away at that stereotype for years, and so have a good many other black women writers. I thought not simply of Meridian, but of Janie Crawford, of Pecola, of Sula and Nell, of Edith Jackson, even of Iola Leroy and Megda, for God's sake. (Characters of black women writers Ms Wallace is unacquainted with; an ignorance that is acceptable only in someone not writing a book about black women.)[21]

I agree. And it wasn't true that I hadn't read Walker's second novel *Meridian*, or Toni Morrison's *Sula*, or Zora Neale Hurston's *Their Eyes Were Watching God*, although Frances Harper's *Iola Leroy* wasn't generally available then (and Megda and Edith Jackson I still scarcely know).[22] Like many other black women of my generation, I eagerly awaited the publication or reissue of black women's books. But as a young black woman who was in search of feminist solidarity and a writing career, I wanted something very specific from the black women writers I read. I had grown up in Harlem, where my family had lived for three generations, not in the rural South. 'The South' I had received as a child was either idealized — rural, and without poverty or racism — as in my grandmother's early recollections of Palatka, Florida, or embattled — as in the graphic terms of the Civil Rights struggle broadcast on the television screen on the evening news. Both forms seemed distant. My mother Faith Ringgold was an artist, my stepfather an assembly-line worker at General Motors, my grandmother Willi Posey was a fashion designer, and I had been the beneficiary of a private school education, purchased with greater difficulty than I was then capable of understanding, an education that had fully acquainted me (although I was unaware of it at the time) with the extent to which black female cultural participation was customarily effaced or denied.

As I began to read black women writers, I felt rebuffed by their unwillingness to write about the problem of being a black woman writer, which seemed to me overwhelming. I wanted them to do so immediately and explicitly, to cease their endless deflecting in their lyrical way about a rural, agrarian Afro-American purity forever lost.

Of course, this view was entirely unfair in that it did not take into account the work of Louise Meriweather, Ann Petry, Toni Cade Bambara and Paule Marshall. I had read the black feminist anthology *The Black Woman*, edited by Bambara, from cover to cover when it was published in 1971, and I had also read *The Street* by Ann Petry, *Daddy Was A Numbers Runner* by Louise Meriweather, and some of Bambara's short stories.[23] None of this work had any particular impact on my misgivings about black women's fiction, because I saw it as fundamentally continuous with the kind of mysticism about the magical power of 'roots', both medicinal and geographic, that characterized their fictions in rural settings.

I read *Mules and Men* and *Their Eyes Were Watching God* by Zora Neale Hurston in 1971 and 1972, while I was a student majoring in English and writing at the City College of New York. Fascinated as much by George Eliot as by Hurston, and already thinking of myself as a 'black feminist' thanks to the encouragement and support of an actively feminist mother, I was in the front row when the first Women's Studies classes began at City College.

I read *The Bluest Eye* while working as a secretary at Random House, where Toni Morrison was then an editor. It was my first job after graduating from CCNY in 1974. That summer Angela Davis often came to see Morrison to work on her autobiography. When it was published in 1975, I read it immediately.[24] In 1975, I also attended the first conference of the National Black Feminist Organization (I was a founding member) in New York, at which Shirley Chisolm, Eleanor Holmes Norton and Florynce Kennedy were keynote speakers. Alice Walker led a workshop discussion together with my mother on black women in the arts.

It was around this time I also read Walker's first book of short stories, *In Love and Trouble*, as well as the essay 'In Search of Our Mothers' Gardens', which immediately became essential reading for black feminists, but which struck me as infected with the same nostalgia for, and valorization of, the rural and the anonymity of the unlettered that I considered so problematic in the work of other black women writers. In particular, the premise of the article, which is that black women writers should speak for previous generations of silenced black women, posed certain conceptual difficulties for me. First, no one can really speak for anybody else. Inevitably, we silence others that we may speak at all. This is particularly true of 'speaking' in print. Second was the implicit denial of the necessity for generational conflict and critical dialectic, which I found totally paralyzing. In my case, my mother was a prominent artist, well educated and active in the Women's Movement. So how did one then pursue Walker's proposal? Moreover, didn't it imply that black women writers would always 'speak' from the platform of a silenced past?

Faith was then (still is) involved, on a daily basis, in making politically engaged black feminist art out of quilts, soft sculpture, sewing, painting, and performance. My interest in visual art and art criticism – which was shaped by Faith's involvement with artists on the left organizing to protest the Vietnam War, and the racism and sexism of establishment museums – was perhaps the largest influence on my notion of what black feminist creativity really meant.

So when I completed the manuscript of my book in 1978, my decision to make the statement that black women writers were reinforcing 'the myth of the superwoman' was no accidental afterthought, nor was it made because I didn't think art was important, or because I didn't know of Pecola, Meridian and Janie Crawford. While I would still maintain that there is a problematic shallowness in terms of the range of black female existence, corroborated by those contemporary black female texts now approaching the canonical, I also now realize that I was reading the works of Hurston, Morrison and Walker too narrowly. By too narrowly I mean without the sense that I've since acquired, in part from my adaptive readings of theoretical texts by Roland Barthes, Julia Kristeva, Fredric Jameson and Barbara Johnson, that the writing of fiction inevitably addresses the material conditions, the cultural context and the psychological terms of its own production.

In particular, feminist reinterpretations of Hurston's *Their Eyes Were Watching God* have led the way in reading Janie's ascension to the position of storyteller, despite the obstacle of a twisted sexism coming from a black community besieged by racism, as an allegorical re-enactment of the difficulties facing the black woman writer.[25] Barbara Johnson's reading of this text makes the point that polar or binary oppositions are crucial to the logic of our culture's rhetoric about race and sex, and therefore fundamental to the organization of Hurston's novel, as well as the reception it received at the time it was published. That Hurston occupied the wrong end of each of these oppositions made inevitable the continuous splitting of the difference that marked Hurston's narrative and expositional style.

When Johnson divides the field of the dominant discourse into the four realms of 'universality', 'complementarity', 'the other' and the lower-case 'x' of radical negation, her thesis, no doubt, is meant to be illuminating and suggestive rather than precisely sociological. Yet there is no question in my mind that the unrelenting logic of dualism or polar oppositions – black and white, good and evil, male and female, to name a few – is basic to the discourse of the dominant culture and tends to enforce the automatic erasure of black female subjectivity. The 'on the one hand, on the other hand' logic of most rational argumentation doesn't work if you don't think of yourself as neatly fitting into either the category of the unified, universalizing subject, which white men usually claim, or the category of the 'Other', usually spoken for by white women or men of color, designated by Johnson as 'complementarity' in order to distinguish white women from men of color. But if you happen to think of yourself as occupying two categories simultaneously – if you are black and a woman, and perhaps lesbian and poor as well – or if you simply wish to write about such issues conjunctively, then you're in danger of not making much sense, because you are attempting to 'speak' from the still radically unspeakable position of the 'other' of the 'other'.

It had been my view that black women writers were verifying 'the myth of the superwoman' by the creation of perverse characterizations displaying inordinate strengths and abilities as the inevitable booby prize of a romanticized marginality. The problem with the myth of the superwoman as I saw it once, and still see it, was that it seemed designed to cover up an inexorable process of black female disenfranchisement, exploitation, oppression and despair. Even more important than whether the black woman believes the myth or whether some black women engage in superlative accomplishments (which they obviously do) is the way the dominant culture perpetuates the myth not in order to celebrate them but as a weapon against them: 'she is already liberated' becomes an excuse for placing her needs last on every shopping list in town.

The 'other' of the 'other', or incommensurability, is another approach to the same problem. Whereas the myth of the superwoman was a concept designed to describe the culture's general misapprehension about black women, the 'other' of the 'other' is an attempt to diagnose the black woman writer's relationship to the dominant discourse. It is more important to talk about the 'other' of the 'other' at this point, not because there is no longer a problem of myths (or stereotypes, which seems to me too flat a term), but because myths are in no way dispelled by revelation. In fact, it is part of the nature of mythical meanings that they are impossible to reveal. Rather, to disclose the hidden meaning of a myth is simply to continue the process of myth, as the reception of *Black Macho* tended to illustrate. I myself became the mythical 'superwoman', completely silenced in actuality, yet made to seem powerful, articulate and invulnerable by my critics.

I am tempted to suggest that all 'famous' black women inevitably occupy this unnaturally inarticulate position in the dominant discourse, as the correlative to the official 'silence' of the masses of black women. Or, as I inferred from Claude Lévi-Strauss' account of Freud's encounter with the Oedipus myth,[26] interpretation of myth, which does not focus upon the politics and the history of who speaks, who doesn't and why (as has happened in subsequent feminist and Marxist discussions of Freud)[27] reconsolidates the viability of the myth in a broader context, just as White and Baker reconsolidated phallocentricism in their descriptions of its process. At the same time, the 'other' of the 'other' is resistant to theoretical articulation – hence a black feminist fear of theory, a black feminist interpretation radically nonexistent, or invisible, in the realm of the dominant discourse, and a black feminist literature that prioritizes variations on negation.

Another way of describing variations on negation would be to call them negative images, although I prefer 'variations on negation' because negation seems indispensable to dialectical critical process. My liking for the term 'variations', on the other hand, is more whimsical. It has to do with the idea of musical performance as a reference point, so that variations become a way of indicating multi-logical and experimental approaches that delay closure almost indefinitely. Another way of putting this: Billie Holiday used to sing a line that went 'The difficult I'll do right now, the impossible will take a little while.' Variations on negation confront 'the impossible', the radical being and not-being of women of color.

It appears to me that Barbara Smith and other black feminist critics such as Deborah McDowell,[28] in their pursuit of programmatic concerns, have minimized the variations on negation of a book like *Sula* by Toni Morrison. The capacity for rendering the negative substantial and dialectical has been the particular strength of fiction by black women writers. The way these variations on negation occur is twofold. On the level of content, the reader can't help but notice that the black community, called 'The Bottom', comes to dislike Sula, even as Sula's best friend rejects her for 'stealing her man'. Neither Sula, nor her mother Hannah, nor her grandmother Eva, fits anybody's notion of positive role models – both Sula and Eva murder black males, Sula as a child. Nel, her mother Helene, and her grandmother are hardly positive images either. Rather, their characterizations seem direct responses to the imbalances of Sula, Hannah and Eva as characters, a feature that bears upon the second way of reading variations on negation.

It is the relationship (and gaps) between items in the text – description, character, plot, dialogue – that gives this book its force. Its power lies in this book's willingness to contradict itself. In particular, the reader of black women's fiction must look for items or moments in the text that directly oppose one another in their construction of 'reality'. The first opposition to appear in *Sula* is between the white town and the black 'Bottom', which may have begun as 'a nigger joke' and which no longer exists. From the outset, it is clear that the black community was defined as that which the white community was not. The result is that neither black community nor white town seems fixed geographically – the book begins by noting that a golf course (black people don't play much golf) now stands where the black community once was.

The second level of opposition problematizes sexual difference. It first appears when Nel watches her mother Helene smile at a racist white conductor on a segregated train going South, thus alienating two black soldiers who are watching. A racial opposition coexists here, as well as an implicit class opposition. While the soldiers are trapped both because they're black, and therefore powerless to intervene, and male, and therefore expected to protect her should the occasion arise, if the train weren't Jim Crow, none of this would be happening. When Helene is first reprimanded by the conductor, the two black soldiers won't meet her eye. Yet in the context of the rest of the novel, Helene's poorly timed smile clearly has much to do with her middle-class aspirations.

But oppositions of race, class and sex only support the paramount opposition, which is between Sula – the epitome of the negative being who will not marry and settle down, and who breaks all the rules of conventional adult behavior by living, unhypocritically, for pain and pleasure – and the 'Bottom', whose sentiments are ultimately personified by Nel, who marries and settles down while Sula goes off to college. The tension between Sula and Nel is the level at which Morrison is problematizing issues of black feminist creativity. Sula's and Nel's individual characterizations are less important than the roles they play in the novel's larger problem of working out how black feminist creativity will be written.

Certainly the undermining of facile dualisms or binary oppositions of class, race and sex is a priority in fiction by black women. I find especially useful in the focus on binary oppositions the idea that there may be a systemic disorder within language (and thus within the deepest recesses of culture and individual taste) itself that helps to explain the perpetual and profound invisibility of women of color to the dominant discourse. Provocative, as well, is the possibility that precisely the same process of radical negation, or doubling and tripling the difference, in which black female fiction is engaged, may also provide a way to reformulate the problem of black female subjectivity and black female participation in culture. My sense of Sula when I first encountered her was that she was a perfect example of 'the myth of the superwoman', yet my feelings about her probably had more to do with the more limited observation that she didn't seem 'real'. Precisely her 'strength', I would say at this point.

Perhaps the most important book we could look at in this regard would be Morrison's *The Bluest Eye*, published in 1972. When I first read this book I was deeply troubled by Pecola's characterization as a victim of incest and by her subsequent loss of the ability to communicate rationally because, as it seemed to me, such a story was hopelessly negative, had no value beyond the dismal and unredemptive case study, was not transformational or transcendent in a manner I then considered essential to creative acts. Now I think, however, that in the relationship between the characters Pecola and Claudia, who serves as narrator for much of the book, we have the problematization of the conditions that plague the nether regions of the discourse of the 'other' of the 'other'.

Pecola illustrates the path of those who will never recover, the ultimate victim who will never be able to speak for herself. Claudia is the survivor who sees color and variety even in the somber, severe circumstances of her childhood. Her narration moves smoothly from childhood reminiscence to the occasional adult, editorial reflection of 'the author', incorporating the pain and victimization of Pecola as a crucial factor in her need to be articulate, to write.

In the end – which is where the book begins – Pecola is living on the edge of town permanently isolated from the black community by her inability to rise above the crimes committed against her, itself a species of crime in this text. Morrison writes:

> This soil is bad for certain kinds of flowers. Certain seeds it will not nurture, certain fruit it will not bear, and when the land kills of its own volition, we acquiesce and say the victim had no right to live. We are wrong, of course, but it doesn't matter. It's too late. At least on the edge of my town, among the garbage and the sunflowers of my town, it's much, much, much too late.[29]

Without Claudia's and Morrison's storytelling, Pecola's marginalization and social death become a distinct possibility for any one of us who challenges the present invisibility of black feminist interpretation by speaking the unspeakable hell of Pecola's real-life counterparts. Yet there is no character in *The Bluest Eye* who doesn't possess more psychological resources than Pecola in combating an internalization of self-hatred that might be considered routine in the black community.

The one person as close to the edge is Cholly, Pecola's father, whose maleness, because he's black and poor, is no advantage over his wife Mrs Breedlove. That he will resort to its misuse in a wanton act of sexuality with his daughter Pecola seems almost inevitable. The larger question here, however, is why important black fiction so frequently incorporates incidents of incest – beginning with Trueblood's incest in Ralph Ellison's

Invisible Man.[30] These texts signal psychoanalytically that a world other than white quotidian 'civilization' or civility is being evoked.

Hortense Spillers' essay on father–daughter incest in Afro-American literature does not discuss *The Bluest Eye*, but she poses a question raised by that text which I consider crucial to the development of an Afro-American cultural criticism: 'Is the Freudian landscape an applicable text ... to social and historical situations that do not replicate moments of its own cultural origins and involvements?'[31] In other words, despite the ways in which the Afro-American experience of the family and of patriarchal authority are inscribed by race, does the Oedipal drama, which presumably takes place in the bosom of 'the family' at an early age, still hold supreme psychological importance? Do language acquisition and sexual differentiation, and the so-called mirror stage in infancy, still maintain the position of the preeminent formative scenario? Moreover, a question that Spillers doesn't pose: is the Freudian drama somehow transformed by 'race' in a way that would render it altered but usable?

The background necessary to the question, which is particularly relevant to a discussion of symbolic representations of incest, is that the domestic arrangements of black slaves in North America ignored then conventional gender differentiation. Black women slaves were not considered too delicate or too weak to do hard physical labor, and black male slaves were not considered intellectually superior. Nuclear family organization, or even the family in which the father was the head, was out of the question, since the status of the child followed that of the mother. The 'father' was 'figuratively banished' so that 'the father's law, the father's name' did not 'pass "down" in concentrated linearity and exclusion'.[32] Even after Emancipation, patriarchy's various economic, political, educational and social arrangements, as they determined the relations between white men and white women, were scarcely suitable for the majority of blacks, although where they were suitable – for instance, among middle-class blacks – they were revised and applied as soon as material conditions allowed.

At issue here is not a moral or spiritual superiority by virtue of a greater oppression, or even a distinct 'cultural' difference, that allowed blacks to avoid the standard exposure to patriarchal power. Rather, material conditions delayed the application of the more sophisticated forms of patriarchy, and then continued to cause certain deviations or variations in their use. These variations now make difficult or obscure a potential feminist psychoanalytic interpretation of Afro-American cultural production. And yet it seems to me that accurate interpretation of our history will never be possible without a feminist psychoanalytic framework precisely because of these deviations, which do, after all, share a white patriarchal norm as a central point of reference. As in all of

Morrison's fiction, 'good' and 'bad', 'black' and 'white' would have no meaning outside of the context of a white Eurocentric patriarchy. The problem of the status of Afro-American culture, and, thus, the status of the Afro-American woman, begins with such questions.

Spillers is concerned to uphold the incest taboo in Afro-American culture, despite its seeming transgression in Afro-American literature, and correctly so. But I would propose that the peculiar way in which the black family is positioned in relationship to a white power structure in the US is only adequately represented in Afro-American literature where the problem is taken up of who and what 'father' is. In a society in which patriarchal dominance and the supremacy of the phallus are considered coterminous, the black man is perpetually denied the authority of the Great White Father. The depiction of father–daughter incest in *The Bluest Eye*, where it completely delimits black family life, focuses intently upon the problem of domestic relations in a community in which patriarchal dominance – as in 'a man's home is his castle' – is always withheld. Moreover, in *The Bluest Eye* the preoccupation is with the obstacles, which are considerable, that this situation then poses to black female articulation and coherence in the novel form.

Spillers describes the situation in this way:

> The father and the daughter of this social configuration are 'missing' historically because the laws and practices of enslavement did not recognize, as a rule, the *vertical* arrangements of their family. From this angle, fathers, daughters, mothers, sons, sisters, brothers, spread across the social terrain in horizontal display, which exactly occurred in the dispersal of the historical African-American domestic unit. In this movement outward from a nuclear centrality, family becomes an extension and inclusion – anyone who preserves life and its callings becomes a member of the family, whose patterns of kinship and resemblance fall into disguise. In other words, the 'romance' of African-American fiction is a tale of origins that brings together once again children lost, stolen, or strayed from their mothers.[33]

It is a mistake, however, to forget that *The Bluest Eye* is about the collective internalization of self-hatred, the collective erasure of a people and their mostly unconscious battle with what Western civilization calls 'madness'. That political, economic and cultural process of negation, which Orlando Patterson calls 'social death', and which we date from slavery, is where *The Bluest Eye* starts. Yet even Patterson doesn't take into account how that process of negation, that social death, which denies the possibility of 'honor', falls doubly hard on women whose potential for 'honor' rests in chastity and the denial of desire. Morrison does, and that she will do so is announced from the outset by her repeated use of the 'Dick and Jane' elementary school primer text:

Here is the House. It is green and white. It has a red door. It is very pretty.
Here is the family. Mother, Father, Dick, and Jane live in the green-and-
white house. They are very happy. See Jane. She has a red dress. She wants
to play. Who will play with Jane?[34]

This is not a text written to make sense to adults. Yet countless
American children have encountered it – a text that lays out the world
as classless, flat, homogenized, lily white, gender stratified and sexless,
timeless and without history – as the single path to learning, to the
achievement of knowledge, to education. Morrison announces that the
meaninglessness of this official text (and perhaps all unitary models) will
be a primary focus by repeating it a second time without punctuation –
the Law of the Father, or of the dominant discourse – and the third time
without space between the words, undercutting the very ability of
language to signify. In the process, Morrison suggests that Pecola's
madness originates not only at the level of social construction, but also at
the level of signification, tempting us to think, once again, about the
applicability of the Freudian drama.

Subsequently, the book details the construction of that 'madness' or
'abjection' in relation to the white world of 'Dick and Jane' by
systematically contrasting houses, families, mothers, fathers, siblings and
play as they occur in Pecola's community. 'Mother', 'Father', 'Family',
'Play': the names are the same but the meaning may be entirely different.
Pecola's family is extremely dysfunctional, self-hating, 'ugly'. Claudia's
family is much better. There are other examples, as well, although all
belie the reification of the Dick and Jane model. And yet, everyone and
everything is powerless to protect Pecola from tragedy. She is defenseless
against the ultimate reification, as she is forced to play the binary
opposition of 'Jane'.

Through Soaphead Church as anti-Christ, Morrison designates the
culprit as a European Judeo-Christian patriarchal context. When
Soaphead Church, who once 'dallied with the priesthood in the
Anglican Church', and who has since become a 'Reader, Adviser, and
Interpreter of Dreams' (Freud as villain?), takes God's place by
pretending to grant Pecola blue eyes – the book's symbol of whiteness,
safety and madness – Morrison seems to be saying that Soaphead
Church is all the God that one can expect in a world arranged according
to binary oppositions.[35] This calls to mind the alternative (positive)
conception of God in The Color Purple. Yet both books pivot on the
problem of incest, thus evoking the deadly threat segregation, poverty,
bigotry and political isolation pose to black female creativity.

No doubt, any and all sexuality except that which is woman-centered
(and therefore narcissistic) is dangerous in its ability to defuse the disruptive

force of feminist creativity in a relatively tranquil (natural) act of procreativity. Thus Pecola's baby cannot live, any more than Claudia's
marigolds can grow. Nature and procreativity are doomed to futility in this
consummate act – the novel itself – of black feminist literary production.

I haven't begun to do justice to the compositional complexity of *The
Bluest Eye* if I've given the impression that this novel explicitly advocates
black feminist creativity as a corrective for what ails the black
community. The richness of its variations on negation precisely lies in its
unwillingness to advocate anything but the circular, polysemous progress
of its own logic. Perhaps the difficulty of identifying the novel's opinion
of feminist engagement becomes clearest in the depiction of Poland,
China, and Marie, the three prostitutes who live over the storefront
occupied by Pecola's family. Poland, who sings the blues, China, always
combing her hair or fixing her makeup, and Marie, the storyteller, are
actively deconstructing the patriarchy through parody, pastiche and
outright hostility: their hatred of men, wives and innocence is palpable.

In distinct contrast to the variety of maternal images in the book,
these women neither nurture nor protect children; neither do they
pretend to. Instead they have 'lifestyles' that combine a series of fairly
rhetorical, or pointless, resistances to local male authority. But they have
no capacity for understanding or preventing Pecola's victimization. Their
appearance in the text seems to question traditional modes of black
female creativity for their nihilism and self-involvement, as well as posing
a general critique of ostensibly 'feminist' strategies of 'man-hating' and
self-love as ways of neutralizing patriarchal authority.

What of that other novel, *Meridian*, I was supposed not to have read?
The titular heroine seems to me now a character designed to respond to
all narrow definitions of strength and individual courage. When I first
read *Meridian*, I saw Walker's attempt to balance Meridian's strength as a
potential martyr of the Civil Rights Movement with a series of physical
weaknesses – she faints a lot, her hair falls out, and she is slightly insane
– as Walker's way of redeeming the myth of the superwoman. She was
admitting the shortcomings of the superwoman only in order to further
consolidate and verify her perennial strength and fortitude.

Yet early in the book, Walker briefly introduces a character called
'Wile Chile', whom I hadn't noticed on the first or even second reading.
She is a black girl of thirteen who has no 'parents, relatives or friends'
and who lives from hand to mouth on the streets around the Saxon
campus where Meridian goes to school. Meridian, who herself has been
rescued by the Civil Rights Movement from a life of pathological
boredom as the mother of a small child, attempts to rescue the now
visibly pregnant Wile Chile, clean her up and make her take her meals at

the Saxon table. Wile Chile, who responds only with farts and curses – she is unable to speak – finally runs away, is hit by a car and killed. Like Pecola, her condition epitomizes the average black woman's condition in relationship to the dominant discourse, but still it is precisely her condition to remain powerless to describe it.[36]

I now see that like many other people who read *The Bluest Eye* and other books by black women writers,[37] I was focusing too much on the extent to which they mirrored certain obvious sociological realities. This, too, is part of invisibility, the peculiar limitations of the 'other' of the 'other'. From the perspective of dominance, a woman of color who insists upon functioning as a speaking (writing) subject threatens the status of Truth itself. The indirection of fiction seems essential to override reader resistance; it is, in fact, the shortest distance between two ideological points. Thus, the Afro-American woman writer's talent for fictional narrative steeped in what Susan Willis has called 'the changes wrought by history'.[38] As she suggests, black women writers show an uncanny ability for rendering a history of migration, poverty, segregation and exploitation comprehensible and readable.

While black women writers make it possible to understand how a convergence of racism, sexism and class antagonism marks the Third World woman's peculiar position in discourse, their work, in the US particularly, also calls into question the truth value of any unitary or dualistic apprehension of the world. Not only is it necessary that we focus on difference rather than sameness or universality in describing black female perception, but at every conceivable juncture we must choose and take responsibility for how we will emphasize difference in ourselves and others. Discourse is never a random operation of either/or. And we must respond to Michel Foucault's question, 'What matter who's speaking?' with the recognition that it matters precisely because variety is currently made to seem impossible.

I was struck by these issues most forcefully when I attended a performance of *A Raisin in The Sun* about two years ago at a theatre in Los Angeles. 'Momma', the paradigmatic superwoman, was played by Esther Rolle, who once played the mother on the highly successful television show *Good Times*, and before that the maid on *Maude*. Rolle's performance on television in an ostensibly stereotypical black female role (a role designed by whites to exemplify black inferiority) was somehow completely consistent with her present role in a play by Lorraine Hansberry, a black woman. The first time I ever saw *A Raisin in The Sun*, indeed ever saw evidence that black women produced literature, was when I saw the movie of the play in 1961. I was nine years old, and I remember it well because my entire family went to see it one night. Even more than *The Color Purple*, it was a historic occasion.

Both Broadway and Hollywood versions of A Raisin in The Sun excluded that portion of the play dealing with Beneatha's hair. In the original text by Hansberry, Beneatha decides to wash the straightening out of her hair and leave it natural in order to go with the African dress given to her by her Nigerian boyfriend Joseph Asagai. I've been told that the pretext for editing this scene out of the play was that Diana Sands 'looked like hell with her hair in an Afro'. Of course, any black woman would have looked like hell with her hair in an Afro in 1961. That was, I would think, precisely Hansberry's point in writing the scene.

Yet every time I've seen A Raisin in The Sun, my attention is drawn to the extent of black female characterization – the mother, Walter Lee's wife and Beneatha – how they represent more thoroughly than most other works of American literature the constellation of archetypal choices (except lesbianism) available to black women in this culture, as well as the nature of those obstacles blocking critical self-expression. Even more interesting is the idea that what critics have considered the inherent shortcomings of Hansberry's attempt to recreate Chicago tenement life realistically had to do with depicting her own complex relation to American intellectual and cultural life. In a conventional family drama, Hansberry explores the myriad tensions of race, class and sex that plague the black community. In the end, Beneatha is going off to be a doctor in the Third World.[39] Yet given Spillers' observations about the meaning of 'family' in Afro-American culture, together with the scarcity of black women playwrights, can the family drama still be considered conventional in this context? In relationship to the Oedipal drama, which becomes a privilege instead of a commonplace, the 'family drama' takes on a different meaning.

Nevertheless, there's no question that conventional form functions ultimately as a handicap in Hansberry's attempt to grapple with who Beneatha is/can be, nor that conventionality, in general, limits black feminist explorations of the territory of the black hole because of the restrictions form invariably poses on content. I am also well aware that I lay myself open to charges of elitism when I proceed as though cultural criticism were as crucial as health, the law, politics, economics and the family to the condition of black women. But I am convinced that the major battle for the 'other' of the 'other' will be to find voice, transforming the construction of dominant discourse in the process. Only with those voices – written, published, televised, taped, filmed, staged, cross-indexed and footnoted – will we approach control over our own lives.

NOTES

1. Marjorie Pryse and Hortense Spiller, eds, *Conjuring: Black Women, Fiction and Literary Tradition*, Bloomington, Wisconsin: Indiana University Press, 1985, p. 250; Trinh T. Minh-ha, 'Difference: "A Special Third World Women Issue"', *Discourse* 8, Fall/Winter 1986–7, p. 12.

2. Raymond Williams, *Marxism and Literature*, London: Oxford University Press, 1977, pp. 116–17; Michele Wallace, 'A Race Man and A Scholar', *Emerge*, New York, February 1989, pp. 56–61.

3. *Live at Five* is a local New York news/talk show that airs every weekday. Sue Simmons, a black woman, is co-host and interviewer.

4. Barbara Johnson, *A World of Difference*, Baltimore, Md: Johns Hopkins University Press, 1987, pp. 166–71.

5. Hayden White, *Tropics of Discourse: Essays in Cultural Criticism*, Baltimore, Md: Johns Hopkins University Press, 1978.

6. Walter Benjamin, *Illuminations*, New York: Schocken Books, 1968, p. 256.

7. Alison Jagger, 'Love & Knowledge: Emotions in Feminist Epistemology', in Alison Jagger and Susan Bordo, eds, *Gender/Body/Knowledge: Feminist Reconstructions of Being and Knowledge*, New Brunswick, N.J.: Rutgers University Press, 1989.

8. Roland Barthes, *S/Z: An Essay*, New York: Hill and Wang, 1974.

9. Houston Baker, *Blues, Ideology and Afro-American Literature*, University of Chicago Press, 1984, pp. 145–50.

10. Ibid., p. 172.

11. See Ralph Ellison, *Invisible Man*, New York: Random House, 1952 for the original definition of 'invisibility' from which all my subsequent uses are drawn. For Ellison, 'invisibility' doesn't merely describe a metaphysical 'absence', but rather the peculiar impact that the denial of an Afro-American 'presence' has on the structure and process of American culture and history. Instead of coming up with one process to describe Afro-American culture and another process to describe Anglo-American culture, he comes up with one rather complex process which then describes the relation between the two as more essential than the distinction. Afro-American culture thus becomes the unconscious of 'American History'.

12. Ntozake Shange, *For Colored Girls Who Have Considered Suicide/When the Rainbow is Enuf*, New York: Bantam, 1976.

13. See Fredric Jameson, 'Pleasure: A Political Issue', *The Ideologies of Theory: Essays 1971–1986*, vol. 2, Minneapolis: University of Minnesota Press, 1988; Anders Stephenson, 'Regarding Postmodernism – A Conversation with Fredric Jameson' in Andrew Ross, ed., *Universal Abandon? The Politics of Postmodernism*, Minneapolis: University of Minnesota Press, 1988; and 'Third World Literature in the Era of Multinational Capitalism', *Social Text* (Fall 1986), pp. 65–88. Also Toril Moi, *Sexual/Textual Politics*, London: Methuen, 1985, and 'Feminism, Postmodernism and Style: Recent Feminist Criticism in the United States'. *Cultural Critique*, vol. 9, Spring 1988, pp. 3–22; Kaja Silverman, *The Subject Of Semiotics*, New York: Oxford University Press, 1983, and 'Fragments Of A

Fashionable Discourse', in ed. Tania Modleski, *Studies in Entertainment: Critical Approaches to Mass Culture*, 1986; Meaghan Morris, *The Pirate's Fiancée: Feminism, Reading, Postmodernism*, London: Verso, 1988; Jacqueline Rose, *Sexuality in the Field of Vision*, London: Verso, 1986; Julia Kristeva, *About Chinese Women*, London: Marion Boyars, 1977; and *Powers of Horror: An Essay on Abjection*, New York: Columbia University Press, 1982; and 'Women's Time' in N. Keohane, M. Rosaldo and B. Gelpi, eds, *Feminist Theory: A Critique of Ideology*, University of Chicago Press, 1982.

14. Michel Foucault, *The Archaeology of Knowledge*, New York: Pantheon Books, 1972, p. 23, and Trinh T. Min-ha, op. cit., p. 29.

15. Marcia Ann Gillespie, 'Macho Myths and Michele Wallace', *Essence*, New York: August 1979, pp. 76, 99–100, 102; June Jordan, 'To Be Black and Female', *New York Times Book Review*, pp. 15, 30–31; Darryl E. Pinckney, 'Black Women and the Myths of Macho', *The Village Voice*, April 2, 1979, pp. 85–7; Bell Hooks, *Ain't I A Woman: Black Women and Feminism*, Boston: Southend, 1981, pp. 11–12, 98, 182–4; Linda C. Powell, 'Black Macho and Black Feminism' in ed. Barbara Smith, *Home Girls: A Black Feminist Anthology*, New York: Kitchen Table Press, 1983, pp. 283–92.

16. Obviously, this is a broad generalization. Black women have, on occasion, engaged in effective critical discourse. Besides the variety of black feminist essays that *The Schomburg Library of Nineteenth Century Black Women Writers* Series, general editor Henry Louis Gates, Jr (New York: Oxford University Press, 1989) has uncovered and republished, and the extensive polemical essay written around the turn-of-the-century by Mary Church Terrell, Ida B. Wells and others, which historian Paula Giddings describes in her excellent study of the black women's club movement, *When and Where I Enter: The Impact of Black Women on Race and Sex in America*, New York: William Morrow, 1984, there are also, today: the essays of June Jordan in *Civil Wars* (Boston: Beacon Press, 1981); Audre Lorde in *Sister Outsider* (Trumansburg, New York: Crossing Press, 1984), Barbara Christian in *Black Feminist Criticism: Perspectives on Black Women Writers* (New York: Pergamon Press, 1985); Angela Davis in *Women, Race and Class* (New York: Random House, 1981); Alice Walker in *In Search of Our Mothers' Gardens* (New York: Harcourt, Brace, 1983); and Bell Hooks in *Ain't I A Woman: Black Women and Feminism* (Boston: Southend, 1981), *Feminist Theory: From Margin to Center* (Boston: Southend, 1984), and *Talking Back: Thinking Feminist, Thinking Black* (Toronto: Between the Lines, 1989). But the mainstream critical response to this work has been very thin, and it remains quite invisible to every academic establishment except Women's Studies, where it is still marginal. In Women's Studies, the logic of this work is more often appropriated than seriously considered as a powerful and influential discourse. Also, it is relevant to note two related facts. First, of the recent crop of black feminist books, all were published after *Black Macho and the Myth of the Superwoman*, although none of them acknowledges that earlier work except to attack it. Second, after Barbara Christian's *Black Women Novelists: The Development of a Tradition, 1892–1976* (Westport, Conn: Greenwood Press, 1980), and despite the currently burgeoning interest in black women writers, there are still very few full-length literary critical studies of black women's

literature (or book-length scholarly texts in history, for that matter) written by black women.

17. Alice Walker, *In Search of Our Mothers' Gardens*, New York: Harcourt, Brace, 1983, p. 322.

18. See Lillian Robinson, *Culture, Society and Sex*, New York: Methuen; Hazel Carby, *Reconstructing Womanhood: the Emergence of the Afro-American Woman Novelist*, New York: Oxford University Press, 1988; Gayatri C. Spivak, *In Other Worlds: Essays in Cultural Politics*, New York: Methuen, 1987.

19. See my 'Being a Black Woman Writer', *The Women's Review of Books*, 1:1, Wellesley: October, 1983, pp. 7–8.

20. See Robert Staples, 'The Myth of Black Macho: A Response to Angry Black Feminists', *The Black Scholar*, Mar/Apr 1979, pp. 24–33; and 'The Black Scholar Reader Forum: Black Male/Female Relationships', *The Black Scholar*, May/June 1979, pp. 14–67.

21. Alice Walker, pp. 324–5.

22. Frances Harper's *Iola Leroy* and Emma Dunham Kelly's *Megda* have both been republished in the Oxford Series edited by Henry Louis Gates.

23. Toni Cade Bambara, ed., *The Black Woman*, New York: Random House, 1971; Bambara, *Gorilla, My Love*, New York: Random House, 1972; Paule Marshall, *Brown Girls, Brownstones*, New York: Random House, 1959; Ann Petry, *The Street*, Boston: Beacon Press, 1985; Louise Meriweather, *Daddy Was A Number Runner*, Englewood: Prentice-Hall, 1970.

24. Angela Davis, *Angela Davis: An Autobiography*, New York: Random House, 1975.

25. See my 'Who Owns Zora Neale Hurston? Critics Carve Up The Legend', above, pp. 172–86.

26. Claude Lévi-Strauss, 'The Structural Study of Myth' in Richard and Fernanded DeGeorge, eds, *The Structuralists from Marx to Lévi-Strauss*, New York: Doubleday Anchor, 1972, p. 181.

27. See Silverman, *The Subject of Semiotics*; Rose, *Sexuality in the Field of Vision*; Spivak, *In Other Worlds*. See also Fredric Jameson, *The Political Unconscious: Narrative as a Socially Symbolic Act*, Ithaca: Cornell University Press, 1981; Hal Foster, *Recodings: Art, Spectacle, Cultural Politics*, Port Townsend, Washington: Bay Press, 1985, and *The Anti-Aesthetic: Essays on Postmodern Culture*, Port Townsend, Washington: Bay Press, 1983; Julia Kristeva, *Desire in Language: A Semiotic Approach to Literature and Art*, New York: Columbia University Press, 1980; and Teresa de Lauretis, *Alice Doesn't: Feminism, Semiotics, Cinema*, Bloomington: Indiana University Press, 1984.

28. Barbara Smith, 'Toward a Black Feminist Criticism', pp. 168–85; and Deborah McDowell, 'New Directions for Black Feminist Criticism', pp. 186–99 in Elaine Showalter, ed., *The New Feminist Criticism: Essays on Women, Literature and Theory*, New York: Pantheon Books, 1985.

29. Toni Morrison, *The Bluest Eye*, New York: Holt, Rinehart & Winston, 1970, p. 164.

30. Ralph Ellison, *Invisible Man*, New York: Random House, 1952, pp. 47–66.

31. Hortense Spillers, ' "The Permanent Obliquity of an In[pha]llibly

Straight": In the time of the Daughters and the Fathers', in Lynda Boose and Betty Flowers, eds, *Daughters and Fathers*, Baltimore: Johns Hopkins University Press, 1989, p. 158.

32. Ibid., pp. 158–9.

33. Ibid., p. 175.

34. Morrison, p. 1.

35. Morrison, pp. 130–45.

36. Alice Walker, *Meridian*, New York: Harcourt, Brace, 1976, pp. 35–7.

37. Sociological misreadings of black women writers are legend. See, for instance, Mel Watkins, 'Sexism, Racism and Black Women Writers', *The New York Times Book Review*, June 15, 1986, pp. 1, 35–6; Darryl Pinckney, 'Black Victims, Black Villains', *The New York Review of Books*, January 29, 1987, pp. 17–20; Marlaine Gicksman, 'Lee's Way', *Film*, October 1986, pp. 46–9; Stanley Crouch, 'Aunt Medea', *The New Republic*, pp. 38–43.

38. Susan Willis, *Specifying: Black Women Writing The American Experience*, University of Wisconsin Press, 1987, p. 3.

39. Lorraine Hansberry, *A Raisin in The Sun*, New York: Samuel French, 1959.

24

Negative Images:

Towards a Black Feminist Cultural

Criticism

American mass media rolled the camera away from Black life and the quantity of print on the subject became too small to read. As a result, the number of books published by and about Black people has been negligible since the beginning of the decade. For this reason alone, Michele Wallace's *Black Macho and the Myth of the Superwoman* is ready-made for commercial exploitation. Its destiny, so far, has been further assured by nearly unprecedented promotion and publicity.

June Jordan, *Black History as Myth*, 1979

Phillis Wheatley has for far too long suffered from the spurious attacks of black and white critics alike for being the original *rara avis* of a school of so-called mockingbird poets, whose use and imitation of received European and American literary conventions has been regarded, simply put, as a corruption itself of a 'purer' black expression, privileged somehow in black artistic forms such as the blues, signifying, the spirituals and the Afro-American dance. Can we, as critics, escape a 'mockingbird' relation to 'theory', one destined to be derivative, often to the point of parody? Can we, moreover, escape the racism of so many critical theorists, from Hume and Kant through the Southern Agrarians and the Frankfurt School?

Henry Louis Gates, 'Authority, (White) Power and the (Black) Critic;
It's All Greek to Me', 1988

It is useless to argue with the point of view that sees every successful and controversial black female publication as a monolithic conspiracy to undo the race. I am even ready to concede that the participation of black women (and black men) in American cultural production and reproduction, from TV to literary criticism, shows signs of some regrettable

241

trends. While I am enjoying the increasing visibility of blacks on TV and in films as much as anybody else, I feel compelled to remember the downside: material conditions are not changing for the masses of blacks. Moreover, it may even be that the economic and political victimization of the urban and rural black poor in the US and worldwide is somehow exacerbated by the deeply flawed and inadequate representations of 'race' currently sponsored by both blacks and nonblacks in both 'high' and 'low' culture.

I think, however, that this dilemma is best confronted in an ongoing critical dialectic, not by censorship and foregone conclusions. The possibility that something I've written, or will write, might be part of the problem makes me interested in the problem in general. Because black feminism all but entirely lacks an analytical or self-critical sphere (such as the complex network of conference-journal-and-book production that generally supports the speculation of white, and often 'minority' or 'Third World' male scholars and intellectuals), I would like to take this opportunity to write about how my view of black feminism has evolved under the pressure of the criticism of *Black Macho* and in the light of black feminism's increasingly public presence within literature, film and television.

It is necessary to realize that the voices of black feminism in the US emerge today from a long tradition of the structural 'silence' of women of color within the sphere of global knowledge production. Rarely addressed by mainstream or radical feminism – or indeed by anyone – this 'silence' has doomed to failure most efforts to change the black woman's status or condition within society. There is presently a further danger that in the proliferation of black female images on TV, in music videos and, to a lesser extent, in film, we are witnessing merely a postmodern variation of this phenomenon of black female 'silence'.

I think it is imperative that we begin to develop a radical black feminist perspective. It may build upon the work of Trinh Min-ha, Gayatri Spivak, Hazel Carby, Bell Hooks and Hortense Spillers by examining the interplay of 'sex', 'race' and 'class' in Anglo-American and Afro-American culture as they may shape the 'production' of knowledge, the structure, content and 'circulation' of the 'text', as well as the 'audience' of consumption.[1]

It is crucial that a diagnostic focus on how 'black' and 'white' culture progresses or regresses on issues of race, class, gender and sexuality should not preclude that much delayed 'close reading' or textual analysis of black feminist creativity, particularly in mass culture where it is most neglected. Such textual analysis might begin in several places, but I am particularly interested in the foregrounding and contrasting of psycho-analytic and ethnographic perspectives on the 'other'. As the two sides of a Western modernist regression/progression on 'race' and 'sexuality', they need to be reunited in discussions of postcolonial 'minority' discourse, which is where I would situate black feminist cultural production at present.

In particular, I would emphasize Claude Lévi-Strauss' notion of 'myth' in his work with 'primitive' people of color, and Roland Barthes' notion of 'myth' in his reading of contemporary mass culture,[2] precisely because they both emerge out of modernism's frustration with 'history' as a linear and ideological narrative. Also, both interpretations still seem influential in determining contemporary 'political' definitions (in postmodernism and cultural studies) of incorrect thinking.

In a recent essay called 'Mythology and History: An Afro-centric Perspective of the World', Amon Saba Saakana talks about the juxtaposition of 'myth' and 'history' in terms of Western science's rationalizing the murder of Native Americans and the enslavement and colonization of Africans and Asians. In Saakana's account, European imperialism in the seventeenth and eighteenth centuries was inevitably accompanied by the development of 'history', a form of narrative discourse considered by the Enlightenment as infinitely superior to 'myth', which then was made to stand in for all other approaches to the past. Although the roots of Greek culture in Egyptian and Ethiopian cultures were once recognized as African, these roots were then denied and effaced, even as 'civilization' became the polite word for 'the ability to define, through the power of conquest, the control of knowledge, and the framing of meanings'.[3]

A priority continues to be given to 'history' over 'myth' in even the most sophisticated cases of cultural critique, forming the basis for a much preferred 'historical consciousness' of the kind conventionally necessary to leftist and/or Marxist intellectual production in the West.

To be more specific, I am less interested in the way that Barthes' and Lévi-Strauss' uses of 'myth' are customarily read as colorblind in a secondary process of signification than I am in the distinctions made by these authors between two different kinds of 'readings' of culture on the part of distinct categories of the population of the world. The 'masses' in Barthes' *Mythologies*, and 'primitive' nonwhite poeples in Lévi-Strauss' *Tristes Tropiques* and *The Savage Mind* (the bulk of the postcolonial, nonwhite populations in Europe and the Americas of today could be seen as a combination of the two), are presumed to be less literate, less 'historical' in their thinking, and, therefore, less knowledgeable than that white, male, educated elite who are always in the know.

Beginning with the work of Zora Neale Hurston as anthropologist under Franz Boas at Columbia, the Afro-American literary tradition acquires its present character as the writing down, or the translation, of a predominantly oral or mythic tradition previously sealed off from mainstream white American culture, not only by economic and political disenfranchisement, but also by its enclosure in a system that Barthes and Lévi-Strauss will later bracket as 'myth', and which Trinh Minh-ha has lately called 'separate development'.[4] This is just how people who lack the broader, more 'universal' knowledge of the scholar and the historian think about, or fail to think about, 'History'.

Even as Hurston, Lévi-Strauss and Afro-American literary critic Henry Louis Gates, Jr insist that the formulations of 'myth' or the 'oral tradition' are just as good, just as complex and rigorous, this focus emphasizes the comparative inadequacy of black culture. For it is always in the terms of the dominant critical discourse that the alternative mythic practice is being described and named, not the other way around. Nor does the reversal of the terms of interpretation, so that 'myth' or the 'oral tradition' reads 'History' (as Toni Morrison attempts to do in *Beloved*, for instance), do anything but further mystify the grossly unequal relation between the two discourses.

Psychoanalytic readings, too, will need to be revised in terms of race in order to interpret the complex priority quite typically given to 'family' or its aberrations, in fictional texts by Afro-American women especially. That the development of the Afro-American family bears a necessarily problematic relationship to the Oedipal myth, and that that relationship might potentially reveal much about issues of orality vs. literacy vs. 'silence' in Afro-American culture, is borne out by the narrative choices of Afro-American writers beginning with Ralph Ellison's *Invisible Man*, where folk artist Trueblood's 'incest' is used to bring together psycho-analytical (familial-sexual) and anthropological (ethnographic-racial) notions of 'taboo'.[5]

If the 'close reading' of Afro-American literature or culture is thus attempted by black feminists, it becomes impossible not to draw upon the relationship of the text to other texts that precede and surround it in a web of signification and 'history', as Barthes reads Balzac in *S/Z* but with 'race', class, gender included this time. Yet the 'close reading' should not be employed as the automatic first move, but rather as the subsequent stage of an institutional, theoretical and political critique that leaves key textual issues unresolved. If after one has demystified issues of production and how and where the audience receives or views the text, there is still a 'text' remaining, then the 'close reading' can and should be employed as a means of further investigation and analysis.

The point, finally, is not only to write such cultural criticism but also to promulgate 'cultural reading' as an act of resistance. Whereas most people concerned with political repression in the US seem to view such an analysis of culture as a low priority, particularly when that analysis asks questions about 'race' and 'sex' as well as 'class', I can't any longer imagine how one manages, as a black woman, to get through a single day of television, film, advertising, magazines and newspapers, without interpretation and analysis. For instance, I can't imagine experiencing the recent presidential election process in the US without employing some mode of interpretation that acknowledges the exclusion of 'black women' or 'women of color' from 'the issues'. Black women never came up, even though they might have been considered the object, along with their children, of some of the most repressive policies in both the Democratic and the Republican Parties. So where and how were we then to read ourselves into events? As blacks who are not men, and women who are not white, it simply wasn't safe to accept any representation of the candidates, in television news, in the televised debates, in the newspapers and magazines, or on the 'left' or the 'right', without thinking for oneself. To do so involves 'interpretation', that is, bringing some other information gathered from elsewhere to bear upon the 'official' information so freely and repetitively given.

By contrast, consider some recent instances in which mass culture addresses the black woman in an attempt to mainstream 'black feminism'. You will remember that most of us became familiar with the name Oprah Winfrey when she appeared in the role of Sofia in the movie The Color Purple, which was adapted from the black feminist novel by Alice Walker, but which became, under the guidance and supervision of Hollywood director Steven Spielberg, a sentimental tale having little to do with 'black feminism' – that is, little to do with changing the status and condition of black women as a group. As the most successful daytime television talk-show host the networks have ever seen, and as the first black female ever to own a prosperous TV and film production company, Oprah Winfrey is buying up TV and film rights to all the 'black feminist' literature she can lay her hands on. Not only does she own rights to Beloved by Toni Morrison, and Their Eyes Were Watching God by Zora Neale Hurston (with Quincy Jones), her production of Gloria Naylor's novel The Women of Brewster Place, starring herself in the lead role, was recently aired on network television.

For the Sunday and Monday that the mini-series played, network viewers could witness the contrast of a bubbly, carefree Oprah on her daytime talk show versus a downtrodden, unhappy Oprah playing 'Mattie Michaels' at night. Fat, old and poor, Mattie demonstrated the murky immutability of black female life 'as it really is', even as she was the exact opposite of the daytime Oprah who has all the answers to such problems as domestic violence, marital strife, mental illness and other forms of social 'immorality' and disorder. Don't worry, be 'rich', the talk-show Oprah seems to say via her 'Valley Girl' speech, her straightened hair in a different style on every other show, her elegant couture wardrobe, her much celebrated weight loss, her meteoric industry success.

By contrast, the television version of *Women of Brewster Place* is about a collection of black women who live on a dead-end urban street. It is their 'choice' of men that dooms them to remain there. For instance, Mattie Michaels, Oprah's character, begins the show by mortgaging her house in order to post bail for her 'no-good' son. Predictably, he runs off to avoid trial. Mattie loses the house and ends up in a slum apartment on Brewster Place. While Mattie's son was not exactly her 'choice' in the way that one might choose a lover, it was her 'choice', the drama leads us to believe, as a teenager to have sex with the 'no-good' boy who got her pregnant, and it was her 'choice' to 'spoil' the son that resulted by allowing him to sleep in bed with her because he was 'afraid of the dark'. Whether or not Mattie has also chosen the racism of whites and the poverty of blacks, without which this television drama would make no sense, is a question rendered irrelevant by this story's ideological presupposition, which is that any black woman may freely choose to follow the example of the daytime or the nighttime Oprah.

When Mattie and her friends start to take down that wall blocking off Brewster Place with their bare hands in the rain one night towards the end of the second and final installment of the mini-series, my attention was not focused on the relationship these women have to the 'real world', which is presumably beyond the wall. My attention was focused on their relationship to the discourse of network nighttime television: the series simply confirmed television's currently deplorable record on black female characterization. Black women play two kinds of parts: tragic chippies and weeping mothers. If a black female actress can't or won't cry, she can forget about working in TV drama. What this means, quite simply, is that black women are turned into an unspeakable, unknowable 'other' by nighttime network television.[6]

Before television can be about the politics of real life, it must confront television's own inner politics. Quite predictably, despite her superficially 'feminist' agenda reported in the pages of *TV Guide* in a story titled 'There's Oprah, Jackee, Robin Givens – and a Break Men May Not Deserve',[7] Winfrey's *Women of Brewster Place* has left that picture unchanged. For this reason, the melodramatic, maudlin portrayal of lesbianism and the flat, stereotypical portrayal of black men, despite the effort to provide in casting and script 'a break men may not deserve', seem to me only symptomatic of this production's larger failure to address the underlying problems of television's discourse.[8]

In 1986, in response to the controversy in the 'black community' over 'negative images' of black men in the movie *The Color Purple*, I was asked by an organization of Third World women graduate students at the University of California in Berkeley to speak on the issue of black feminist intellectual responsibility. The organizer of this conference, Carrie Mae Weems (now a well-known artist in New York City), asked me because she saw parallels in the promotion of my book *Black Macho and the Myth of the Superwoman* as a *Ms* magazine cover in 1979, and the translation of Alice Walker's novel *The Color Purple* into a successful movie. Both Alice Walker and I had somehow been used by the white power structure to hurt the image of blacks, or as she put it in a letter to me:

> You experienced a backlash after the publication of your *Black Macho and the Myth of the Superwoman*. Some folks felt that your analysis seemed to validate, for whites, the negative and stereotypic views of Black men held by whites; you were thus 'used' by the media, and the White Feminist Movement. Does a book like *The Color Purple* operate in a similar way?

In 1979, a large number of black critics in *The Black Scholar*, among them a few black feminists, had linked *Black Macho* with Ntozake Shange's *For Colored Girls Who Have Considered Suicide/When the Rainbow is Enuf*, which became a successful Broadway show, in order to make the same kind of argument.[9] The commercially profitable Broadway show, Hollywood movie or 'bestselling' book[10] issuing from mostly lily-white theatre, film and book industries, which rarely provide a hospitable environment for 'black talent', was and is as much the rub as the idea of black women criticizing black men in permanent and public ways. The problem reached critical mass in regard to *Black Macho*, also in 1979, when the book was reviewed in *The Sunday New York Times* by black feminist poet and essayist June Jordan, who characterized its production as part of a massive media conspiracy to deny the historical significance of the Civil Rights Movement.[11]

At Berkeley in 1986, in my first concerted effort to respond to such criticisms, I did not try to defend my version of 'history' against such attacks, especially since the views of people who actually participated in the Civil Rights Movement in the South were clearly more reliable and authoritative than my own. Instead, I made a blanket defense of black feminist creativity as inherently subversive of a racist and exclusionary status quo. The point was to go beyond an argument about 'facts' to a general observation about how rarely black women participate in the production of 'fact' and 'history'. When they make *any* move to do so, it is potentially subversive of a repressive status quo.

I used a black w/hole as a metaphor – a hole in space which appears empty but is actually intensely full – to portray a black feminist creativity that appeared to authorize a 'negative' view of the black community but was, in fact, engaged in reformulating black female subjectivity as the product of a complex structure of American (US) inequality. By black feminist creativity, I meant all public creative acts inaugurated by black women, primarily because I never questioned until recently the intrinsic 'feminism' or progressive politics of black female expression, or, moreover, the power of feminist thought to transform society in a way beneficial to all.

In the process, I advocated a more dialectical and less paranoid interpretation of cultural hegemony which, somewhat randomly, drew upon the insights of Hegel, Gramsci, Raymond Williams, Kenneth Burke and Fredric Jameson. In particular, hegemony as Raymond Williams defined and employed it, together with Jameson's notion of a 'political unconscious', helped to explain how cultural production represents a complex process that is not fundamentally altered by any single cultural event. The individual act of writing a book, regardless of whether Shange or Walker or I was the author, was less significant than the absence of published black female critical voices, the void we wrote into and could never hope to fill.

Since then, I've become more concerned about incorporating the method (not necessarily exhaustively) of Marxist cultural criticism, structuralism, psychoanalysis, deconstruction and postmodernism in the development of a critical practice designed to grapple with the complexities of racial/sexual politics as a constellation of increasingly global issues. I am firmly convinced that if black feminism, or the feminism of women of color, is going to thrive on any level as a cultural analysis, it cannot continue to ignore the way that Freud, Marx, Saussure, Nietzsche, Lévi-Strauss, Lacan, Derrida and Foucault have forever altered the credibility of obvious truth, 'common sense' or any unitary conception of reality. Moreover, there are many feminists who are practicing cultural studies, postmodernist, deconstructive and psychoanalytic criticism who can contribute to our formulations if we read them against the grain. Since the concerns and issues of women of color are so often not included in prevailing definitions of 'reality', any analysis suggesting that 'reality', or 'knowledge', is not simply given but rather produced, seems to me particularly welcome.

Yet this theoretically engaged stance of black feminist cultural theory I advocate challenges some more cautious and skeptical tendencies within Afro-American literary theory. Such theorists emphasize that the canonical texts of the West have never included anything but the most derogatory perception of 'blackness'. As the preeminent Afro-American literary critic, Henry Louis Gates, puts it, the question is whether we as theorists can 'escape a "mockingbird" relation to "theory"'. Is our use of theory 'destined to be derivative, often to the point of parody', as he worries? Can we 'escape the racism of so many critical theorists, from Hume and Kant through the Southern Agrarians and the Frankfurt School?'[12]

Gates' critical work is preoccupied with the idea that a black person will appear ridiculous in the act of adopting the white man's critical discourses. In his introduction to the anthology 'Race', Writing and Difference, while he argues that racial categories are essentially mythological and pernicious, he makes it just as clear that the Afro-American writer and critic is in the uncomfortable position of claiming an intellectual heritage designed to make it impossible for him (never mind her) to write a single word.[13] In Figures in Black, his first book-length study, Gates invokes the Afro-American folk figure of the Signifying Monkey in order to describe the modern black critic's necessarily subversive and problematic relationship to Western critical approaches. Just as blacks have 'imitated' white Western languages, literatures, religions, music, dance, dress and family life, but with a critical, 'signifyin'' difference, so shall Afro-American literary criticism steal the meat from the sandwich but leave the white bread untouched.[14]

Yet for some black critics of deconstructive and postmodern approaches, it's as though white people had come up with critical theory precisely in order to avoid the question that the persistence of racial inequality poses to the epoch. From an 'Afro-centric' perspective, current trends in critical theory look mighty like an exercise in self-absorption designed to reconsolidate the canon of Western Masters (not just Milton and Shakespeare but Hegel, Marx and Freud, too!), thus trivializing the analysis of any aspect of Afro-American or African diasporic cultural development.

But, more to the point, Gates' primary concern is the consolidation of an Afro-American literary tradition. I appreciate this work since it is a fairly futile exercise to try to critique the need for an Afro-American canon when it remains completely questionable, within the dominant discourse, whether such a thing could possibly exist. On the other hand, as Raymond Williams has pointed out, 'canon' and 'tradition' invariably involve highly selective and exclusionary processes which tend to reinforce the status quo. In Gates' case in particular, he often fails to portray Afro-American writing as a 'minority' literature engaged in a contemporary dialogue with a majority 'white' culture for the specific purpose of transcending and/or transforming it.[15] This failure becomes particularly unfortunate in regard to contemporary Afro-American literature by women. Having encountered considerable commercial success and publicity, this literature calls into question, even more than women's books or black books in general, conventional academic

notions of a canonical literary tradition, as well as art-world concepts of
an elite 'avant-garde', as inconsistent with mass appeal.

Any 'close reading' of these texts disassociated from their cultural and
political context is only adequate to the task of a superficial and
temporary canonization. However 'close' that reading may be, it won't
provide much information about how literature by black women alternately conspires with and rebels against our present cultural and political
arrangements. In feminist terms, it is just as important to have a way of
talking about *The Color Purple*'s impact on how racism or sexism is
perceived in contemporary culture, as it is to talk about *The Color Purple*
as a symbolic (literary) resolution of racism's concrete irresolvability.

Gates began to venture into the field of such a cultural problematic
when he wrote recently,

> And, if only for the record, let me state clearly here that only a black person
> alienated from black language-use could fail to understand that we have been
> deconstructing white people's languages and discourse since that dreadful day
> in 1619 when we were marched off the boat in Virginia. Derrida did not
> invent deconstruction, *we* did! That is what the blues and signifying are all
> about. Ours must be a signifying, vernacular criticism, related to other critical
> theories, yet indelibly black, a critical theory of our own.[16]

But a continuation of his own discussion here of the social and political
roots of what might be called a nascent Afro-American 'deconstruction'
and 'postmodernism' only becomes viable in the context of a broader
reading of culture as a complex network of patterns and processes which
coordinate the influence of 'high' and 'low' art, vernacular expression,
and mass culture in a newly variegated field of contemporary mainstream
cultural hegemony. Yet the problem here may be that such an analysis
would require the freedom to say less than glowingly complimentary
things about black women writers on all occasions and as dean of Afro-
American Studies, he is not free to do so. Instead, Gates' primary
intention, which seems to be to establish an Afro-American literary
tradition on firm ground, may have a most unfortunate side effect in
regard to black women writers of repressing those black women writers
who wish to engage in political/critical discourse and favoring those black
women writers who want to ride the bonanza of mainstream popularity
for all it's worth.

Raymond Williams' discussion of a hegemonic impulse towards an
exclusionary elitism embedded in the concept of literary 'traditions'
remains relevant here. But the process bears particular watching in this
case because of the potential danger of metamorphosing contemporary
political texts into dead, historical monuments in order to enshrine
them. That is to say, to pre-select, praise and revere a subset of Afro-

American literature (to be designated the canon) is a process totally antithetical to that of becoming critically engaged by the inevitable political and cultural questions raised by an Afro-American Literature (either inside or outside of the canon).

So what is a black feminist to say about the fact that Gates is not only the editor of the first *Norton Anthology of Afro-American Literature*, but also the editor of an extensive Oxford series of republications of black women writers? He is singlehandedly reshaping, codifying and consolidating the entire field of Afro-American Studies, including black feminist studies.

While Gates is, no doubt, well-intentioned in his efforts to recognize and acknowledge the contributions of black women writers, *The New York Times Book Review* presentation of his recent essay 'Whose Canon Is It, Anyway?' seems to me to alter the stakes, as he demonstrates an ability to define black feminist inquiry for the dominant discourse in a manner as yet unavailable to black female critics. The results, so far, are inevitably patriarchal. Having established himself as the father of Afro-American Literary Studies, with the help of *The New York Times Book Review*, he now proposes to become the phallic mother of a newly depoliticized, mainstreamed and commodified black feminist literary criticism.

There's a clue to this agenda in the anecdote that introduces this essay's black feminist catharsis: at age four, Gates was supposed to perform in church the speech 'Jesus was a boy like me/And like him I want to be', but he couldn't remember it to save his life so his mother, from the back of the church, stood up and said it for him in 'her strong compelling cadences'. Everybody in the church laughed. While Gates presents this anecdote as an example of his symbiotic relationship with his mother, it seems on the contrary a story that justifies, as revenge for this humiliating incident, his appropriation of black female subjectivity or 'voice'. The hostile twist is embedded in the lines themselves, for there was never any question of his mother being a 'boy' anything like 'Jesus'.

Whereas she is powerless to appropriate his 'voice' in any meaningful sense, he is perfectly free to speak for her – and for the rest of us besides: 'learning to speak in the voice of the black mother', Gates ends his article ominously, 'is perhaps the ultimate challenge of producing a discourse of the Other'.[17] Not only is it impossible for anybody to speak in anybody else's voice, such a project tends to further consolidate the lethal global presupposition (which is unconscious) in the dominant discourse that women of color are incapable of describing, much less analyzing, reality, themselves, or their place within the world.

In every case, public statements of black feminism have been controversial in their relationship to an idealized and utopian black feminism, which, nevertheless, remains almost entirely unarticulated and untheorized. It is almost as if black feminism were only called upon to deny all attempts to attach its name to an agenda. Yet I have not abandoned the notion that black feminist creativity is inherently (potentially) subversive of a patriarchal hegemony, as well as of a racist and exclusionary white cultural hegemony.

Let me focus briefly upon the external limitations placed upon a black feminist vision by a society that feeds upon and subsumes all resistance and critique, even as it is broadcasting its open-mindedness via the massive proliferation of the 'mechanical reproduction' of representation, interpretation and analysis in the form of TV, film and print journalism. Again and again, when the negative space of the woman of color meets the Age of Mechanical Reproduction or, worse yet, Baudrillard's 'simulations', the resulting effect is a 'strong black woman' floating above our heads like one of the cartoon characters in Macy's Christmas Parade, a form larger than life, and yet a deformation powerless to speak. This is not so because any black woman anywhere ever meant to come before the American public without a message, but because the culture routinely and automatically denies her the opportunity of producing autonomous or productive meanings.

The genesis of *The Color Purple* as bestselling novel, then blockbuster movie, seems to me to provide an excellent example of a text initially proposing a complex rereading of Afro-American history and Afro-American literature becoming something else entirely in the process of its own success. Finally, the overwhelming urgency of form associated with mass appeal – a Spielberg movie as compelling as *E.T.*, and for all the same reasons – seemed to supersede all other considerations. None of this means that I do not endorse the black feminist voice in such a production, nor does it mean I didn't 'enjoy' *The Color Purple* on some level. It only means that I now better understand how the feminist project, which is actually part of the same scheme as that production of knowledge that trivialized the 'silence' of women of color in the first place, needs profound and multiple acts of revision. It is not enough merely to address the dilemma posed by the black female condition in the US or the world as an object of misery and pathos. Black feminism must insist upon a critical oppositional representation of the black female subject.

While black feminism remains largely undeveloped in terms of its program, it can no longer be regarded as the same mystery that it was in 1976 when *For Colored Girls* was first produced. Although I may be disappointed about its public progress, I can no longer deny that some manifestations of black feminism have entered the public arena. In retrospect, the movie *The Color Purple* seems to have initiated this second stage in the process of black feminism's public articulation.

In 1987, Toni Morrison published *Beloved* to a very warm critical reception by the mass media and book industry. While there were no commensurate changes in the status or condition of black women in general, there was nothing remotely 'marginal' about Morrison's success. Our enemies thus take some pleasure in pointing out that black women writers are now enjoying a certain vogue as publishable authors and as topics of literary critical speculation.

The key event may be the Oxford series of reissues of books by black women writers, the key figure Gates, and the key idea that every book black women have ever written should be in print. As for the status of black feminist interpretation, all of which now springs from the largesse of the 'mother' of them all, Gates himself, the fortunes of a small number of black female academic literary critics are rising.

While I am not suggesting that this movement to canonize black women writers is reactionary, it does seem as though the participants take for granted that the revision of a once all-white, all-male canon is as progressive as anybody needs to get. Perhaps they are right, for this task is far from safely accomplished. But it seems to me that one must also consider whether relations of power in higher education or relations of representation in the production of knowledge are significantly altered by any of this. When I see 'black feminism' being touted by the safest of all possible 'spokesmen' on the cover of the safest of all cultural venues – *The New York Times Book Review* – I say the time has arrived to start asking such questions.

Gates' academic feminist ventriloquism may be just the sideshow. Mass media promise to offer the main attraction, that always seems to determine our image, our absence of critical voice: as in a silent movie, we are always pictures without words, or music without lyrics.

Two names tell the story thus far: Whoopi Goldberg and Oprah Winfrey, both of whom first became widely known as actors in *The Color Purple*. The reputation of each in its own way unsettles previous conceptions of black feminism as inherently a process of collective black female empowerment. This realization is on the same terms as the realization that various landmarks in white female success or black male success have not essentially transformed the brutal overall inequality of the status quo in regard to 'women and blacks'. A black feminist critique must now provide us with a means of investigating and articulating the multiple dimensions of ideological space that define the relationship of a Whoopi Goldberg or an Oprah Winfrey to *The Color Purple*, and a black feminist 'ideal' now hopelessly compromised by concrete substantiation (i.e. Winfrey, Goldberg, *The Color Purple*). Nor can we continue to fail to forge a way to comment upon the successes of Grace Jones, Aretha Franklin, Tina Turner, Diahann Carroll, Diana Ross or any black female artist or performer whose image functions as cultural icon, and thus as battering ram to all our other cultural and political aspirations.

In line with a frustratingly general notion of 'black liberation' presented in mass culture ('the revolution will not be televised'), we still credit and discredit black feminist creativity according to a mechanical concept of 'negative' versus 'positive' images, on the theory that such an evaluation will indicate who is doing more or less for the race, or for the 'cause', as it is sometimes vaguely but appropriately called.

But three years since my trip to Berkeley and the movie release of *The Color Purple*, I am beginning to wonder whether the binary opposition of negative and positive images has any relationship at all to what Jesse Jackson called 'the real world' at the National Democratic Convention this summer, the world of poverty and despair in this country and the 'Third World', which is black and brown and 'homeless', which cannot 'speak for itself', and which one delegate to the convention, a farmer from Kansas, called a 'constituency of pain'.

What I am calling into question is the idea that black feminism (or any program) should assume, uncritically, its ability to speak *for* black women, most of whom are poor and 'silenced' by inadequate education, health care, housing and lack of public access. Not because I think that black feminism should have nothing to do with representing the black woman who cannot speak for herself, but because the problem of silence, and the shortcomings inherent in any representation of the silenced, need to be acknowledged as a central problematic in an oppositional black feminist process.

NOTES

1. Richard Johnson, 'What is Cultural Studies Anyway?', *Social Text 16*, Winter 1986–87, pp. 38–80.

2. Claude Lévi-Strauss, 'A Writing Lesson', *Tristes Tropiques*, Washington Sq. Press, 1977, pp. 331–3; and Roland Barthes, 'Myth Today', *Mythologies*, trans. Annette Lavers, Hill and Wang, New York, pp. 109–59.

3. Amon Saba Saakana, 'Mythology and History: An Afrocentric Perspective of the World', *Third Text 3/4*, Spring/Summer 1988, London, pp. 143–50.

4. Trinh T. Minh-ha, *Women, Native, Other: Writing, Post-coloniality and Feminism*, Indiana University Press, 1989.

5. Ralph Ellison, *Invisible Man*, New York: Random House, 1952, pp. 50–66; I am also borrowing here, in part, from Houston Baker's reading of Trueblood in *Blues, Ideology, and Afro-American Literature*, University of Chicago, 1989, pp. 172–88.

6. This situation is changing as a middle-class black woman, usually as 'wife of' a black male lead, as on *The Cosby Show*, *In The Heat of The Night* or the new show *Men*, becomes more visible. Yet there is little connection between these bourgeois simulations of the 'white woman' and the signifier 'black woman' as it is understood by the rest of television, particularly news shows and documentaries.

7. *TV Guide*, March 18–29, cover and pp. 4–8.

8. These matters have been thoroughly addressed elsewhere, for instance in M. Gurevitch, T. Bennett, J. Curran, J. Woollacott, eds, *Culture, Society and The Media*, London: Methuen, 1982; Donald Lazere, ed., *American Media and Mass Culture*, University of California, 1987; Mark Crispin Miller, *Boxed In*, Northwestern University Press, 1988; Brian Wallis and Cynthia Schneider, eds, *Global Television*, MIT and Wedge, 1989.

9. See Robert Staples, 'The Myth of Black Macho: A Response to Angry Black Feminists', *The Black Scholar*, Mar/Apr 1979, pp. 24–33; and 'The Black Scholar Reader Forum: Black Male/Female Relationships', *The Black Scholar*, May/June 1979, pp. 14–67.

10. The only bestseller list *Black Macho* made it onto was *The Washington Post*'s, but it was widely perceived as a 'bestseller'.

11. June Jordan, 'Black History as Myth' in *Civil Wars*, Boston: Beacon Press, 1981, pp. 163–8.

12. Henry Louis Gates, Jr, 'Authority, (White) Power and the (Black) Critic; It's All Greek To Me', *Cultural Critique* 7, Fall 1987, p. 35.

13. Henry Louis Gates, Introduction to *'Race', Writing, and Difference*, University of Chicago Press, 1986, pp. 2–13.

14. Henry Louis Gates, *Figures in Black: Words, Signs, and the 'Racial' Self*, New York: Oxford University Press, 1987, pp. xxx–xxxi, 235–6.

15. Henry Louis Gates, *The Signifying Monkey: A Theory of Afro-American Literary Criticism*. New York: Oxford University Press, 1988.

16. Henry Louis Gates, *Cultural Critique* 7, Fall 1987, p. 38.

17. Henry Louis Gates, 'Whose Canon Is It, Anyway?', *The New York Times Book Review*, February 26, 1989, p. 45.

Index

Seuss, Dr 200
Seven Days 108
sexual offences 147
Shange, Ntozake 7, 69, 70, 132–6,
    170, 181, 190, 216, 219
    For Colored Girls Who Have
        Considered Suicide 4, 74,
        129–32, 134, 135–6, 219, 247,
        252
Shannon, Susie 26
Sharpton, Al 112, 191
She's Gotta Have It 100–103
Sheena, Queen of the Jungle 74–5
Sheftall, Guy 183
Shelley, Mary 185
Signifying Monkey 172–3, 249
Silver, Ron 121
Simmons, Sue 216
Simone, Nina 28, 54, 124, 188, 216
single-parent families 61, 72
Skelton, Red 62
slavery 9, 137–45, 160–61
    women slaves 137–45, 231
Slewa, Curtis 117
Smith, Barbara 146–7, 181, 184, 228
Smith, Bessie 72, 169, 171
Smith, Doris Ruby 170
Smith, Roger Guenveur 108
Smith, Valerie 215
Smith, Vincent 198
SNCC 167, 169–70
Soap, Charlie 156
SoHo Weekly News 132
A Soldier's Story 75
Solidarity 81
South Africa
    coverage in motion pictures 94,
        103–4
    segregation in 163
    unrest in 81
South Bronx Academy of Fine Art 202
Southerland, Ellease 183
space shuttle explosion 71
Speed-the-Plow (Mamet) 121
Spielberg, Steven 67, 72, 74, 219,
    245, 252
Spillers, Hortense 10, 162, 182–3,

188, 213, 215, 231, 232, 235, 242
Spiro, Nancy 198
Spivak, Gayatri 10, 205, 223, 242
Spivey, Victoria 72
Star Wars 75
Star, The 79
Stein, Gertrude 205
Steinberg case 62
Steinem, Gloria 149
Stevens, May 198
Stewart, Michael 110
Stowe, Harriet Beecher
    Uncle Tom's Cabin 141
Streep, Meryl 62
student unrest
    murder of students (1970) 195
Studio Museum 197, 198
Sun Ra 203
SUNY–Buffalo 95, 97, 99
Swimmer, Ross 155
Szasz, Thomas 63

Tahlequah, Oklahoma 155
Tate, Greg 10, 79, 100–01
Taxi Driver 4
Taylor, Elizabeth 166
television
    and Afro-American women 219,
        242
    and Afro-Americans 91–4, 113,
        147
    see also music videos; Grammy
        Awards
Temptation of Saint Anthony series
    (KOS) 209
theatre 120–22, 129
Thompson, Hunter 223
Thoreau, Henry David 200
Tompkins Square Park, closure of 115,
    120
Tony Brown's Journal 146
Toomer, Jean 103, 174–5, 178, 185,
    206
Tosh, Jon 198
Townsend, Robert 101
Trading Places 75
tramps and hobos 61–2

THE HAYMARKET SERIES

THE RISE AND FALL OF THE WHITE REPUBLIC: Class Politics and Mass Culture in Nineteenth-Century America *by Alexander Saxton*

Forthcoming

BLACK AMERICAN POLITICS: From the Washington Marches to Jesse Jackson (Second Edition) *by Manning Marable*

THE POLITICS OF SOLIDARITY: Central America and the US Left *by Van Gosse*

THE MERCURY THEATER: Orson Welles and the Popular Front *by Michael Denning*

THE SOCIALIST REVIEW READER